Women in Management:
An Annotated Bibliography and Sourcelist

Compiled by Judith A. Leavitt

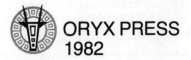

ORYX PRESS
1982

The rare Arabian Oryx is believed to have inspired the myth of the unicorn. This desert antelope became virtually extinct in the early 1960s. At that time several groups of international conservationists arranged to have 9 animals sent to the Phoenix Zoo to be the nucleus of a captive breeding herd. Today the Oryx population is nearing 300 and herds have been returned to reserves in Israel, Jordan, and Oman.

Library of Congress Cataloging in Publication Data

Leavitt, Judith A.
    Women in management.

    Updated ed. of: Women in management, 1970-1979. 1980.
    Includes index.
    1. Women executives—United States—Bibliography.
I. Title.
Z7963.E7L43   1982   016.658'0088042   82-2190
[HF5500.3.U54]   AACR2
ISBN 0-89774-026-2

For
MOM AND POP
who first taught me to love and to work

And for
DAVID, JOE, AND JOHN
whose love makes my work worthwhile

Table of Contents

Acknowledgements   vii

Foreword   ix

Introduction   xi

Progress of Women in Management   **1**
Salaries   **10**
Mentors and Networking   **14**
Management Training for Women   **22**
Sex-Role Stereotypes   **36**
Discrimination and Minorities   **46**
Education   **57**
Profiles of Women Managers   **66**
Career and Family   **79**
Women as Directors   **85**
Women Bosses   **90**
Recruiting Women into Management   **94**
Obstacles   **104**
Comparisons of Men and Women Managers   **112**
Advice Literature   **121**
Psychology of Women in Management   **132**
Women Managers in Various Fields   **148**
Women Managers in Other Countries   **157**
Dress and Travel   **161**
General   **164**

Appendices   **175**
Appendix 1. Films and Filmstrips   **177**
Appendix 2. Pamphlets   **179**
Appendix 3. Other Resources   **180**
Appendix 4. Organizations   **181**
Appendix 5. Network Directories   **182**
Appendix 6. Periodicals   **183**
Appendix 7. Bibliographies   **185**

Author Index   **189**

Acknowledgements

I want to express my sincere appreciation to Sister M. Michele Ransil, head, Division of Processing; Dr. Ray R. Suput, university librarian; and Tom Moore, Dave Tambo, and Don Siefker, members of the Library Service Faculty Research Committee, all of Ball State University, Muncie, IN, for recommending and granting release time for research during Spring Quarter 1981.

Also a special thanks to the librarians and staff of Bracken Library, Ball State University, Muncie, IN; Stewart Memorial Library, Coe College, Cedar Rapids, IA; the Cedar Rapids Public Library; and the University of Iowa Libraries, Iowa City, for assistance in locating materials.

Finally I want to thank my editor, Sandra Liberman, for her support, suggestions, and editorial expertise.

Foreword

This book will play an important role in establishing the topic of women in management as a field of study with the necessary underpinning of theory and empirical research. When developing any new course, an appropriate question would be "Is there a common body of knowledge?" Without this common body of knowledge, consisting of theory and empirical research, a new course will become suspect and doomed to derision. Therefore this book will be a valuable resource for courses which deal wholly or in part with women in management.

Students and faculty who lack either the time during the constraints of a semester or the resources to do a computer search and follow-up will find this book a valuable tool. The annotations are written in a highly readable style. Students who are unfamiliar with research methodology will find that the annotations are valuable interpretive tools for the original research articles.

For the serious researcher who plans a computer search, this book will also be valuable as a source of "key words" that can be determined from both the arrangement of subject categories and the publication titles. Appropriate key words must be determined before any computer search can be successful.

And for the average reader who may be interested in a general overview of the topic women in management, or a specific area such as "career and family," this book can provide a most comprehensive introduction.

Bette Ann Stead
Professor, College of Business Administration
University of Houston

Men always try to keep women out of business so they won't find out how much fun it really is.

Vivien Kellems (1896–1975)

Introduction

A weekly business magazine predicted in 1969 that by 1980 or 1985 women would occupy a substantial number of top executive posts. But in spite of affirmative action and equal employment opportunity legislation, social changes resulting from the women's movement, growing numbers of women MBA graduates, and the fact that women comprise 40 percent of the nation's labor force, the percentage of women in managerial/administrative positions changed hardly at all—from 5 percent in 1947 to 6 percent in 1978. Three years later in 1981 another weekly magazine noted that women still constituted only 6 percent of those in management—5 percent in lower and middle management and one percent in upper-level management.

A September 14, 1981 *Newsweek* article entitled "Women and the Executive Suite" charts the growth in the number of women MBA candidates from 1971 to 1981. In 1971 women accounted for 3.5 percent of the 21,417 MBA candidates compared to 22.3 percent or 12,332 of the 55,325 MBA students in 1980. The National Center for Educational Statistics and the Association of MBA Executives Inc. estimated that women would constitute almost 26 percent of the total MBA population in 1981.[1] With the astounding rise in the number of women MBAs in the last decade, one might expect the percent of women in management to be a great deal higher.

What, then, accounts for the fact that the percentage of women in managerial positions has increased a mere one percent in 34 years? Some believe it can be explained by the fact that women are most frequently hired into staff positions or dead-end jobs, not line positions with real responsibility for profit and loss statements and real opportunity for advancement.

Studies show that upper management tends to help aspiring young male managers with mentors and informal socializing without extending the same opportunities to female managers. While women acquire the technical skills to master their jobs, they still lack the political savvy necessary for success in the corporate world. Others claim that women's self-imposed limitations and lack of long-range career planning often hinder their management progress. In conclusion a recent study of the treatment of women managers indicates that sexist attitudes and behaviors are still a very serious problem in most large corporations.[2]

Many observers believe, however, that, with the influx of women MBAs of the 1970s and 80s into the workforce, the situation is likely to change. One educator predicts a one-to-one male-female enrollment ratio in business schools within the decade.[3] Young female business students themselves are optimistic about management opportunities. Entering the work force more than a decade after affirmative action and equal employment opportunity legislation, they expect to advance in their chosen careers. More women now combine the MBA with an undergraduate technical degree, a combination more likely to guarantee advancement in industry and high technology fields. A futurist predicts that as many as 50 women may be chief executive officers (CEOs) of *Fortune* 500 corporations by the year 2000.[4]

There are now more than 500 networks designed to help women advance in their careers. The author of *Networking,* Mary Scott Welch, estimates that in 1981 one-quarter of the working women in this country will belong to some kind of supportive job network. Finally Helen J. McLane, vice-president of the executive search firm Heidrick & Struggles, lists greater opportunity, higher motivation, greater educational attainment, more useful curriculum, later marriage, pregnancy by choice, rising divorce rates, rising acceptance of the working woman, desire for a higher living standard, and the increase in household technology as 10 reasons why the number of women in executive positions will increase.[5]

SCOPE OF THE BIBLIOGRAPHY

This annotated bibliography covers the literature on women in management written between 1970 and 1980 and includes over 700 citations to books, papers, newspaper and journal articles, and dissertations. Approximately 70 citations to literature published in 1981 are also given. It is arranged in 20 subject categories: progress of women in management, salaries, mentors and networking, management training for women, sex-role stereotypes, discrimination and minorities, education, profiles of women in management, career and family, women as directors of corporations, women "bosses," recruiting women into management, obstacles to women in management, comparisons of men and women managers, "advice" to women in management, women and the psychology of management, women managers in various fields, women managers in other countries, dress and travel, and general.

Appendices list films, periodicals, professional organizations, pamphlets, women's network directories, and other bibliographies. This sourcelist on women in management should be useful to librarians, career counselors, students and business educators, researchers, business organizations, and women managers.

EMPHASIS IN THE LITERATURE

Seven of the 20 subject categories (advice literature, discrimination, sex-role stereotypes, psychology, management training, profiles, and progress of women in management) account for over half of the 700+ citations found in the literature for 1970–80. The majority of the items in these 7 categories were written after 1975, making coverage for these topics fairly recent.

The "advice" books start with Letty Cottin Pogrebin's *How to Make It in a Man's World* (1970) and include *The Woman's Guide to Management Success* by Joan Cannie (1979). Most advice books and articles comment on topics such as time management, decision making, behavior, office politics, career planning, salary, and the use of basic management skills. Much of the recent "advice" literature covers practical aspects of travel and dress for the woman manager.

In his article Donald Stacy (1976) examines in detail affirmative action legislation and the Equal Employment Opportunity Commission's *Guidelines on Sex Discrimination,* and Margery Mitnick (1977) writes on 7 basic EEO and affirmative action areas with which personnel officers should be familiar. Many articles written on discrimination emphasize the advantages and disadvantages of the manager who is both female and Black. Two articles in *Black Enterprise* (September 1980) focus on the competition between Black men and women and White women for management positions.

Writing on the myths of women in management begins with Rosalyn Willett's essay on the women executive in *Woman in Sexist Society* (1971), includes John Athanassiades' "Myths of Women in Management" (1975) and George Biles' 1978 article on "Myths, Management, and Women," and concludes with "How Management Myths Hurt Women" by Julia Kagan (1980). Virginia E. Schein makes 4 important contributions to the literature on sex-role stereotypes as she researches the relationship between sex-role stereotypes, management characteristics, and performance and, in a *Wall Street Journal* article Priscilla Meyer tells male executives 10 ways to avoid sex stereotyping of women managers.

From 1970–80 more appeared on the psychology of women in management (over 75 papers, articles, and dissertations) than any other aspect of the topic. Researchers developed 2 instruments, the Women as Managers Scale (WAMS) and the Managerial Attitudes toward Women Executives Scale (MATWES) to measure attitudes toward women managers; Pereira, Herbert, Garland, and Terborg conducted research to test the validity of the WAMS. Eleanor Brantley Schwartz wrote in 1976 on the self-concept of women managers and the characteristics of female entrepreneurs, and John B. Miner used his Miner Sentence Completion Scale to determine women's motivation to manage. Most recently Harish C. Tewari published *Understanding Personality and Motives of Women Managers* (1980), originally presented as his thesis at the University of Cincinnati in 1977.

Management development seminars and workshops for women proliferated in the 1970s; articles described numerous management development programs for women from the first all-day conference on women in management held in New York in 1970 to university, government, and company-sponsored programs in career counseling, assertiveness, and basic management skills. Most management training workshops lasted from one to 3 days and cost anywhere from $5 to $500. In the late 1970s and in 1980 the debate waxed between those who preferred coed training and those who favored management development programs for women only.

Bolton (1977) argues for selecting only those women already qualified for management, thus eliminating the need for further management development, while Larwood (1978) and the *Small Business Report* (December 1979) list the advantages and disadvantages of single-sex training. Baron, Hartnett, Moore, and Nicholson claim management development for women only is necessary and desirable until women occupy a greater percentage of the available management positions.

In the profiles category the *Wall Street Journal* and *New York Times* comment on the views of Anne Jardim and Margaret Hennig, business professors at Simmons College and authors of *The Managerial Woman* (1977). Numerous articles profile and quote the nation's top female corporate officers, executives, and millionaires, while others describe successful British, French, and German women managers. Mary E. Cunningham makes headlines in 10 articles (late 1980) that chronicle how speculation of a romantic involvement with Bendix chairman William Agee caused the 29-year-old Harvard Business School graduate to resign her position as vice-president of strategic planning at Bendix.

Writers of articles on the progress of women in management concur that federal legislation and the women's movement spurred the advance of more women into the management ranks. They identify personnel, public relations, publishing, advertising, cosmetics, retailing, insurance, communications, and other "female intensive" industries as areas where women have made the most progress in management to date. In a 1975 *Business Week* article women executives who have made it to the top one percent of management comment on the lack of role models, marriage vs job, and the advantages of networks, and in "Women at the Top" (1980) Christine Doudna reviews the last 10 years of women's progress in management.

FURTHER RESEARCH

The Winter 1979 issue of *Signs* includes a lengthy review essay by Linda Keller Brown, social scientist and director of the Cross National Project on Women as Corporate Managers at the Center for Social Sciences at Columbia University, on "Women and Business Management." In the essay she calls for: further research on the new women MBA students; comparative studies of businesswomen in different cultures; sex-role stereotyping research conducted in the real world rather than in the educational milieu; research into the long-range impact of single-sex management development programs and coed training; analysis of the personalities, social backgrounds, performance, and career pathways of women executives; research into the generational differences in the 3 age groups of female managers (senior executives, middle managers 35–45 years of age, and managers under 35); less emphasis on getting women into the managerial pool and more on retention by redesigning jobs; and research on dual-career families.

Hopefully researchers studying any of the topics enumerated by Brown will find this annotated sourcelist useful.

NOTES

1. Lynn Langway et al., "Women and the Executive Suite," *Newsweek* 98 (14 September 1981): 66.

2. John Fernandez, *Racism and Sexism in Corporate Life: Changing Values in American Business* (Lexington, MA: D.C. Heath, 1981), p. 98.

3. Eugene H. Fox, ''Female Enrollment Outpacing Male Enrollment among Accredited AACSB Members,'' *AACSB Bulletin* 13 (Spring 1977): 27–31.

4. Langway, p. 68.

5. Helen J. McLane, *Selecting, Developing and Retaining Women Executives: A Corporate Strategy for the Eighties* (New York: Van Nostrand Reinhold, 1980).

Women in Management:

An Annotated Bibliography and Sourcelist

Progress of Women in Management

1. Adams, Jane. "Fallen Idols." *Working Woman* 6 (February 1981): 63–65+.

Questions whether 1980 was a bad year for women executives since Jane Cahill Pfeiffer was fired from NBC and Mary Cunningham resigned from Bendix after rumors of a romance with chairperson William Agee. Philosophizes that, if some changes in the corporate world come about as a result of the attention these stories brought to the problems of women executives, 1980 will have been a good year.

2. ———. "Life at the Top: Excerpt from *Women on Top.*" *Working Woman* 4 (December 1979): 43–44+.

Sixty women were interviewed about their professional success and personal fulfillment. A psychiatrist believes that women managers cope with job-related stress better than men, but stress-related illness is increasing among women. Rosabeth Moss Kanter describes stress as related to high corporate visibility. Sarah Weddington, Marlene Sanders, Gerry Stutz, and others tell how they deal with stress. Includes portraits and career chronologies of 9 well-known women.

3. Baron, Alma S. "New Data on Women Managers." *Training and Development Journal* 32 (November 1978): 12–13.

Results of a questionnaire sent to 6,300 women managers in the U.S. show that time management is the biggest problem for most women managers. Eighty-three percent of the women polled want to advance.

4. ———. "Women in Management: A New Look." *Personnel Administrator* 23 (December 1978): 52–54.

Reports data from a survey of 1,700 women in management positions. The 4-part questionnaire records demographic information, management information, continuing education data, and responses to an interpersonal checklist.

5. Bates, Mercedes. "Moving Up the Corporate Ladder." *Journal of Home Economics* 66 (March 1974): 26–27.

A vice-president of General Mills, Inc., outlines the steps in her career from home economics major in college to management in a large corporation. She stresses good communication, reading (especially the *Wall Street Journal*), visibility, and hard work as essential elements for management success.

6. Burns, Cherie. "Young Turks Are Coming." *Working Woman* 6 (March 1981): 67–69+.

A program director for a consulting firm divides management women into 3 categories: "women who made it in spite of everything; women who were part of the consciousness-raising era of the past decade; and new, young females." Women in the first 2 groups are experiencing some difficulty with those in the latter group who are often better educated, ambitious, assertive, and expect to get to the top quickly.

7. Doudna, Christine. "Women at the Top." *New York Times Magazine* (November 30, 1980): 54–55+.

A review of the last 10 years of women's progress to the executive suite, with comments on Jane Evans at Butterick, Mary Cunningham's resignation from Bendix, and the appointment of Sherry Lansing, president of Twentieth Century-Fox. Discusses sexual harassment, clothes for the office, travel for businesswomen, the corporate spouse, and changing attitudes toward working women.

8. Ekberg-Jordan, Sandra. "Women in Management—Some Today, Many More Tomorrow." *Atlanta Economic Review* 26 (March/April 1976): 6–8.

Author defines 3 groups of women who will be seeking management positions: young women graduating from business school; women in their late 20s to late 40s who have been married and at home with children; and women already employed by business organizations. Concludes with 3 myths regarding working women and the problems women moving into management will face.

9. "Execs See Bright Future for Women." *Industry Week* 201 (April 30, 1979): 28.

The findings from a survey of 300 business leaders on "Employer Attitudes toward Affirmative Action" by an equal opportunity employment consulting firm show that women have a better chance to succeed in the corporate world than other minorities. Managers still feel there's a lack of minority candidates and 90 percent of the executives polled do not believe women will become chief executive officers of their corporations within the next 10 to 15 years.

10. "Female Executives Become a Target for Ads." *Business Week* (August 22, 1977): 66.

Records the rise in the number of banking, insurance, motel, and airline ads aimed at women executives. One motel chain estimates that one in 6 travelers is a woman, and a major airline notes that in 1971 women comprised 3 percent of their business travel market, compared with 23 percent in 1977. Insurance companies believe their sales will increase as more women move into higher salary brackets.

11. Fowler, Elizabeth M. "A Shortage of Middle Managers Opens Job Opportunities for Working Wives." *New York Times,* 25 October 1971, p. 53+.

The J.K. Lasser Tax Report estimates that, while the number of male employees in the middle management age group will decline by 2 million, the number of middle management jobs will increase and women are expected to fill the vacancies. Outlines tax advantages, investment opportunities, and pension plans for 2-career couples.

12. French, Phyllis V. L. "Women in Management: Success at the First Level." *Supervisory Management* 20 (March 1975): 14–17.

The author, an engineering technician at Motorola, Inc., quotes 5 successful forewomen at Motorola and tells how they develop people for profit, improve attitudes and morale, look for leaders, and disprove stereotypes.

13. Gehret, Kenneth G. "Women Moving Up the Corporate Ladder." *Christian Science Monitor*, 7 July 1973, p. 14.

Dr. Esther Westervelt of Simmons College describes the female college student of today who anticipates combining marriage and career. She says sex discrimination is still widespread in corporations but predicts companies will become more creative about part-time employment.

14. "It's Slow, but Woman Are Moving into the Executive Suite." *U.S. News and World Reports* 77 (September 30, 1974): 43–45.

An optimistic look at the progress women have made in management, partly due to the federal government and the courts. Discusses salaries and business school enrollments. Ten women managers give advice on preparation for management in careers such as public relations, engineering, banking, journalism, economics, and advertising.

15. Lemmon, Melody Kay. "The Unchanging Role of Women." Paper presented at the Annual Meeting of the Midwest Sociological Society, Omaha, NE, 3–6 April 1974.

Abstracted in *Sociological Abstracts,* April 1974, Supplement 40, #SO1373.

16. "Major Banks Have Quadrupled the Number of Women and Minorities in Official and Managerial Positions over the Past Decade." *Wall Street Journal,* 17 July 1979, p. 1.

The results of a survey by the American Banking Association shows that, from 1970 to 1979, the percentage of women in bank managerial positions has increased from 15 to 33 percent. During the same period there was an increase from 5 to 12 percent in minority representation.

17. "Marketers Woo the Executive Woman." *Industry Week* 202 (August 6, 1979): 77–78.

Explores the developing trend in advertising to appeal to the executive woman. Insurance companies and banks are among the first to tap this lucrative market. Statistics given are: earnings of working women have risen 100 percent since 1970; women constitute more than 50 percent of America's millionaires; in 1975 more than 50 percent of all adult stockholders were women.

18. Moneyhun, George. "Women Succeeding in Business." *Christian Science Monitor,* 13 May 1977, p. 2.

Cites statistics on the increasing number of working women and on women in management. It is estimated that women hold 2 percent of top management positions and 6 percent of middle-level management positions. States that 2 women have received Cyanimid's "Golden Oval" award, the highest award given annually to the top salesperson.

19. "More White-Collar Woman." *Christian Science Monitor,* 7 March 1979, p. 10.

A Conference Board study shows that women have made progress in managerial, professional, and white-collar jobs, with the greatest gains in "female intensive" industries like banking, insurance, retailing, and communications.

20. "More Women Executives." *Christian Science Monitor,* 2 May 1979, p. 11.

A survey by a Los Angeles-based executive search firm indicates a significant increase in the hiring of women and minority managers.

Almost 75 percent of the survey respondents noted a 10 to 25 percent increase since 1976.

21. "More Women in Management." *Christian Science Monitor,* 22 February 1979, p. 11.

A Chicago management consulting firm says the number of women in top management positions in the 1,300 largest U.S. corporations increased 30 percent in 1978. They typically earn $30,000 a year and are 50 years old; 65 percent began in clerical positions.

22. Morris, Roger. "Women at the Top." *Training and Development Journal* 31 (May 1977): 39–42.

Statistics show that the situation of women in management is both encouraging and discouraging. The number of women in professional, technical, and administrative positions has increased over the past decade, but women are still paid less than their male counterparts. Female executives from business and industry who were interviewed by *DuPont Context* are quoted regarding changing attitudes, barriers that still exist, and the need for successful examples.

23. Mouckley, Florence. "Women Executives Gain, but Men Still Set the Pace." *Christian Science Monitor,* 24 July 1974, p. 1.

The owner of an executive women search firm reports business is good. Although there are more women executives in business and industry, they still have to play the game by men's rules. Business practices will have to accommodate the needs of women, wives, and mothers before many women will make it to the top in the business world.

24. "New York Telephone Agrees to Increase Management Women." *Wall Street Journal,* 24 April 1973, p. 13.

New York Telephone agrees to a settlement that will promote women to 57 percent of all vacancies in first-level management jobs, 46 percent of intermediate-level vacancies, and 20 percent of top-level management positions. Over 50 percent of New York Telephone's 93,307 workers are women.

25. Patrick, Patricia Ann. "An Investigation of the Progress and Problems of Women in Managerial Positions in Businesses and Other Institutions in the New Orleans Area." PhD dissertation, University of Mississippi, 1979.

Abstracted in *Dissertation Abstracts International,* v. 40, May 1980, #5930-A.

26. Roe, Anne. "Womanpower: How Is It Different?" In *Human Resources and Economic Welfare: Essays in Honor of Eli Ginzberg,* edited by Ivar Berg. New York: Columbia University Press, 1972.

Reviews some of the ways sex has affected working life in the U.S. Covers issues such as how many women work and when they work, marriage and work, the kinds of work women do, work histories, and women and creativity. Includes tables on the percentage of women in the labor force, the effect of marriage on professional careers of men and women, occupations in which women were three-fourths or more of total employed, comparisons of men and women's median wage or salary income, and participation of women in union activities.

27. Rosenthal, Glenn. "Move Over, Jack—Here Comes Jill." *Journal of College Placement* 34 (Spring 1974): 58–62.

The director of placement at Ball State University believes mores are changing which will make the idea of growing numbers of women in upper and middle management positions more acceptable. The graduating class of 1972 at Ball State is proof, however, that women are still filling typically female occupations. Results of a survey conducted by BSU Placement and the College of Business to learn the attitudes of businessmen toward the employment of women show that most employers feel there is an inadequate supply of qualified women for available positions. Lists the 16 academic majors most in demand.

28. Salamon, Julie. "Few Women Get Top Business Jobs Despite Progress of Past Decade." *Wall Street Journal,* 25 July 1980, p. 15.

Although more women earn MBAs and enter management, there are still only 400 women earning $40,000 or more in the nation's top 50 industrial corporations—only 5 percent. Women managers can enter banking, retailing, and advertising more easily than "hard" industries like the steel, construction, and automotive industries.

29. Shatto, Gloria. "Women in Management." *AAUW Journal* 68 (April 1975): 21–23.

The author, associate dean and professor of Economics at Georgia Tech's College of Industrial Management, claims that gains made by women in management are due primarily to militant feminism and government pressure. Discusses opportunities for women's advancement in education and cites stereotypical attitudes that persist regarding women's abilities. Concludes with implications for the future.

30. Smith, Lee. "What's It Like for Women Executives?" *Dun's Review* 106 (December 1975): 58–61.

Women executives at AT&T, First Women's Bank of New York, Exxon, Macy's, Celanese Corporation, and others tell the daily problems of dealing with male colleagues and subordinates: exclusion from the male executive's social world, absence of experienced women to serve as guides, and hostility from older men.

31. "Study Says Women Make Gains into Management." *Wall Street Journal*, 22 May 1978, p. 8.

There was a 24 percent increase in the number of women in professional and technical jobs from 1970 to 1975. Statistics indicate women gained more in large than in small companies, but the Conference Board predicts it will be decades before women enter top decision-making positions in high technology fields.

32. Thackray, John. "The Feminist Manager." *Management Today* (April 1979): 90–92+.

Although the women's movement in the U.S. may appear to be losing ground, American women continue to make progress in the area of management. Two classes of female executives seem to be developing.

33. "Things Are Looking Up for White Collar Women—So They Say." *Management Review* 67 (July 1978): 55.

Eighty-two percent of women managers (subscribers to *Modern Office Procedures*) polled about the progress of women in office hierarchies did not feel they were token women in their organizations. Only 8 percent experienced a "great deal" of animosity from male co-workers; 14 percent earned over $25,000.

34. "Up the Ladder, Finally." *Business Week* (November 24, 1975): 58–68.

Interviews women executives in the one percent of top management. Topics include: success, sex consciousness, where women start, marriage vs job, how to get along, differences in socialization of men and women, the lack of role models, and the advantages of networks.

35. "We've Got a Foot in the Management Door." *Do It NOW* 10 (September/October 1977): 15.

The U.S. Bureau of Labor Statistics for 1975 shows that 19 percent of the nation's 8.9 million managers are female, a 3 percent increase since

1970. However women hold only 6 percent of middle management jobs and one percent of top management jobs.

36. "Where Women Work." *Wall Street Journal,* 1 November 1977, p. 1.
A survey by the National Personnel Association indicates that women in management are most often found in personnel departments. Sales, accounting, data processing, and engineering are also employing more women.

37. "Why Women's Stock Is Rising on Wall Street." *Business Week* (November 10, 1975): 114+.
Brokerage firms are trying to attract women investors: the fiftyish woman with inherited wealth, young women earning at least $20,000 a year, and divorcees with money to manage. Firms are hiring female account executives to handle the "women's market."

38. "Women as a Management Presence." *Management Review* 68 (October 1979): 4.
The president of a consulting firm that specializes in executive outplacement is concerned that women represent 25 percent of his clientele. He feels firings of women are due partly to lack of political seasoning. Another writer feels that a failing economy and the national mood of conservatism will adversely affect the progress of women in management.

39. "Women Executives Edging Up." *Christian Science Monitor,* 28 October 1977, p. 21.
The president of MBA Resources, Inc., an executive search firm, says qualified women are still hard to find. He claims more women are leaving the female ghetto fields of advertising, cosmetics, publishing, personnel, and public relations to enter the banking, financial planning, and legal fields.

40. "Women Gain Job Status, but Slowly, Study Says." *New York Times,* 23 May 1978, sec. 4, p. 16.
A study by Conference Board, a nonprofit business research organization, determined that the number of women managers increased 22 percent from 1972 to 1975. The data, from the Census Bureau, the Equal Employment Opportunity Commission, and a survey of 111 large corporations, indicates that women are still found in traditionally female occupations, with most gains made in banking and insurance. The study credits women's progress in management to federal antidis-

crimination laws and the 1973 AT&T settlement which pledged to increase opportunities for women in management.

41. ''Women-in-Business Week Events Expected to Draw 10,000 in City.'' *New York Times,* 15 October 1979, sec. 2, p. 2.
Announcement of Women-in-Business Week, planned by the New York Association of Women Business Owners and sponsored by New York City companies. Seminars, workshops, luncheons, and presentations cover hiring, getting a loan, coping with stress, estate planning, office politics, the 2-career family, assertiveness training, and reentering the job market.

42. ''Women on Wall Street.'' *Christian Science Monitor,* 13 June 1979, p. 11.
The president of a finance and investment executive search firm estimates the number of women executives on Wall Street has increased fourfold in the last 10 years. Cites statistics on the number of women on the New York Stock Exchange and the American Stock Exchange.

43. ''Women Win More Jobs in Corporate Executive Suites.'' *Wall Street Journal,* 28 July 1970, p. 1.
Cites the increasing numbers of women moving into management positions in companies such as IBM, Proctor and Gamble, General Foods, and New York Telephone. Colorado University's business school places its woman graduates with the help of 200 female ''contacts'' in large corporations.

44. ''Women's Banks Get National Charters to Start Operation.'' *Wall Street Journal,* 7 July 1977, p. 8.
The Comptroller of the Currency grants national bank charters to the Women's Bank N.A. in Denver and the Women's National Bank in Washington, new banks to be managed and directed primarily by women. Within a year the new banks should raise capital and file incorporation papers. Some state-chartered women's banks are already in operation.

Salaries

45. "Administrators' Salaries Climb, Bonuses Soar." *Administrative Management* 33 (June 1972): 26–29.

Tables show the results of a random national sample of *Administrative Management* subscribers regarding salary and benefits. Shows administrators' salaries are expanding at the annual rate of 7 percent, but women in management have trouble breaking the $15,000 barrier.

46. Allen, Frank. "Women Managers Get Paid Less than Males, Despite Career Gains." *Wall Street Journal,* 7 October 1980, p. 35+.

The number of women corporate vice-presidents increases, but their salaries still don't equal those of their male counterparts. Most of the women see an MBA as the quickest route to success; older executive women are more satisfied with their level of achievement than their younger female colleagues.

47. Arrington, Christine Rigby. "The Pampered Princesses." *Savvy* 2 (July 1981): 32–37.

Although their salaries look good, many women in management find that the necessary expenses of their executive life-style keep them perpetually "broke." Part of the difficulty is the "psychology of entitlement" of many baby-boom women who have expectations raised by feminism and by the life-style of the 1960s.

48. Bird, Caroline. *Everything a Woman Needs to Know to Get Paid What She's Worth.* New York: David McKay, 1973.

Gives general information on advancement tactics, availability of qualified women, recruiting, women bosses, titles, training, interviews, discrimination checklists, and meetings and conventions. Includes detailed information on salaries and wages, including bargaining, Civil Service, commissions, education, equalization and back pay, Equal Pay Act, median incomes, managerial salaries, moonlighting, overtime, part-time jobs, seniority, and unions. The book was developed from a course entitled "The Female Job Ghetto" taught by the author at the Center for New York City Affairs of the New School for Social Research in the fall of 1972.

49. Chastain, Sherry. "How to Negotiate Your Way Up." *Working Woman* 6 (June 1981): 81–83.

Ten hints on how to negotiate a raise by the author of *Winning the Salary Game: Salary Negotiation for Women* (Wiley, 1980). Advice includes keeping a running diary of work-related matters and understanding how a performance review can be beneficial for you.

50. "A Double Standard for Women Managers' Pay." *Business Week* (November 28, 1977): 61+.

Results of a *Business Week* survey that asked "Do Women Managers Still Earn Less than Men?" Findings show that there are 2 classes of women managers—new business school graduates who receive pay equal to their male counterparts and women executives of 7 to 10 years' experience whose salaries are about 20 percent below those of men in comparable jobs. When some female executives have uncovered pay inequities, job titles have been "juggled" to eliminate the grounds for comparison.

51. Edmonds, Mim Randolph. "Can Women Really Get Big Jobs?" *McCalls* 100 (March 1973): 20.

Optimistic article about the movement of women into management positions which cites the case of IBM, where, in the first 6 months of 1972, the number of women managers increased by 18 percent. Author admits, however, that companies are having trouble locating enough qualified women; some backlash occurs when unqualified women are appointed to management positions.

52. Flanagan, William. "High Salaries Now Open to Women in Top Management Posts." *Vogue* 169 (August 1979): 91.

Reviews fields that currently provide the greatest management opportunities for women. Women are more likely to get staff, rather than line positions, in fields such as advertising, promotion, marketing, and research. Open areas for women include wage and salary administration, college recruiting, financial analysis, sales, banking, data processing, merchandising, real estate, customer relations, personnel, and executive recruiting.

53. Halcomb, Ruth. "Think Big about Money." *Working Woman* 5 (January 1980): 31–34.

The author of *Women Making It* advises women on financial security and independence. Offers suggestions about investments, landing a job with a 5-figure salary, and learning how to determine the salary for a particular position.

54. Kihss, Peter. "Study Finds New York 'Favorable' for Women Seeking Career Gains." *New York Times,* 20 January 1978, sec. 2, p. 3.

Reports on a study entitled "The Impact of Women on the Economy of New York City" by Women United for New York which shows that New York offers women more management opportunities and better pay than the national average. Women working full-time in New York earn 75 percent as much as men, compared to 57 percent nationally.

55. Klebanoff, Susan. "The Going Rate: A Salary Guide." *New York* (April 4, 1977): 74–75.

A salary ladder published by *Business Week* estimated that only 35,775 women (compared to 1,190,000 men) earn between $20,000 and $100,000. Only 15 women (compared to 2,500 men) earn over $100,000. Figures on specific executive women's salaries, available from professional and businesswomen's associations, show that female doctors earn half as much as male doctors, the situation is better for female lawyers, and women have made gains in business. Identifies areas where women have made progress and areas where there is still room for improvement.

56. Meisner, Dwayne. "Management Compensation: Rising Slower than the Cost of Living." *Administrative Management* 35 (June 1974): 22–25.

Biennial salary and benefits survey of *Administrative Management* subscribers shows that increases were greatest in the specialized administrative management sector; the average bonus dropped from $5,444 in 1972 to $4,895. Eight percent of the survey respondents were women as opposed to 5 percent in the 1972 survey. The average woman administrator's salary is over 40 percent lower than the average administrator's salary.

57. "Pay Lag." *Wall Street Journal,* 20 March 1979, p. 1.

In a study of personnel managers Dartnell Institute of Chicago found that entry-level women managers earned an average $15,507, 4 percent less than entry-level male managers. After 3 years work the pay differential increases to 5 percent, with men earning an average $19,968 and women $18,883.

58. Priestland, Sue. "How Salaries Compare for Men and Women." *Association Management* 29 (March 1977): 32–34.

Latest salary and compensation survey by the American Society of Association Executives reports that women have significantly lower salaries than their male counterparts. Differences range from $5,800 for membership directors to $11,800 for directors of consumer affairs. A profile of women executives in associations is drawn from the information in the survey: most women work for smaller budget associations in the Southeast or Midwest. Approximately 17 percent of the 2,500 association executives surveyed were women.

59. Ronan, W. W., and Organt, G. J. "Determinants of Pay and Pay Satisfaction." *Personnel Psychology* 26 (Winter 1973): 503–20.

Analysis of the responses from 3 work groups (management and supervisory, salaried nonsupervisory, hourly) to questions about pay satisfaction. Results seem to show that both salaried and hourly female employees receive significantly less pay than males, but they are more satisfied with their earnings than their male co-workers.

60. Ulbrich, Holley H. "Women and Wages." *Atlanta Economic Review* 26 (March/April 1976): 44–46.

Notes gains made by women in professional, technical, managerial, and administrative areas. In the managerial category the biggest gains were made by local public administrators, bank officers, purchasing agents and buyers, sales managers, and retail managers. Identifies a definite upgrading of educational levels of the female labor force, especially among younger women. Predicts that, as newly educated women enter traditionally male occupations, salaries in those fields will become depressed.

61. "Women Prodded to Big-Pay Jobs." *Christian Science Monitor,* 5 June 1974, p. 3F.

The president of Women in Communications tells women that management women often don't seek higher-paying jobs because they fear failure. She says that not taking the risk has limited many well-educated women.

Mentors and Networking

62. Bennett, Amanda. "Protege Pitfalls." *Wall Street Journal,* 13 October 1980, p. 18.

Discusses the perils of the male-female, mentor-protege relationship for young women. Offers advice to males who serve as mentors to females: take time to prove her, make her work visible, pay attention to the rank and file, and minimize intimacy.

63. Bolton, Elizabeth B. "Have It Your Way: Mid-Career Women and Their Options." *Vital Speeches* 44 (July 1, 1978): 571–73.

A speech given to the graduating class of Focus on Choice at Virginia Commonwealth University, Richmond, VA, April 13, 1978. Argues the need for peer group support, the development of an "old girl" system for women, and the importance of mentors and role models in fighting the "queen bee" syndrome.

64. Budd, Elaine. "Variation on a Classic Theme: 'Old Boy' Networks for Women." *New York Times,* 11 May 1980, sec. 23, p. 1.

Describes the growth of "networking"—groups of women who meet to help each other professionally—and profiles several Connecticut women's networks.

65. "Businesswomen Want an 'Old Girl' Network." *New York Times,* 5 November 1977, p. 22.

Speakers at a workshop, sponsored by the Federal Trade Commission, that was attended by more than 60 New York and Washington women lawyers, lobbyists, and businesswomen promote the idea of having their own information network similar to the "old boy" network.

66. Cook, Judith A. "Bridging the Gap: Relationships among Business and Professional Women." Paper presented at the Annual Meeting of the North Central Sociological Association, 1–3 May, Dayton, Ohio.

Abstracted in *Sociological Abstracts,* April 1980, Supplement 101, #S11894.

67. Cook, Mary F. "Is the Mentor Relationship Primarily a Male Experience?" *Personnel Administrator* 24 (November 1979): 82–84+.

The manager of employee relations in a Colorado energy firm says that, in the past, mentoring was primarily for males which may be part of the reason why females constitute less than one percent of the country's total number of executives. She claims that mentors, executive sponsors, and development teams are more common today and acknowledges the risk of relying on only one mentor.

68. Daniels, Arlene Kaplan. *Development of Feminist Networks in the Professions*. Evanston, IL: Northwestern University, 1979.

A 16-page monograph on feminist networks in various professions and businesses, including a discussion of professional conventions and job information networks. Tells how informal socialization and pooling of resources help women to form internal reference systems. Includes bibliography. Available from: The Program on Women, Northwestern University, 1902 Sheridan Road, Evanston, IL 60201.

69. Dullea, Georgia. "On Ladder to the Top, Mentor Is Key Step." *New York Times,* 26 January 1981, sec. 2, p. 6.

A mentor (teacher, adviser, supporter) is one of the things a young woman needs to be successful in the corporate world. Profiles 3 women and their mentor relationships. Includes photographs.

70. Fenn, Margaret. "Sponsorship: Finding and Working with a Mentor." In *In the Spotlight* by Margaret Fenn. Englewood Cliffs, NJ: Prentice-Hall, 1980.

Chapter 2, pp. 23–42, of *In the Spotlight* defines and describes the process of mentoring and includes lengthy discussions of what the mentor provides, what the junior provides, and bonding. Tells what to look for in a mentor, whom to look for, and how to attract a sponsor. The chapter concludes with a brief look at 4 disadvantages of the mentor-junior relationship.

71. Fischer, Mary A. "The Problem with Networks." *Savvy* 2 (March 1981): 82.

Although she doesn't question the concept of networks as a communication and resource link among professional women, the author questions the idea of excluding men from active networking. How, she asks, can women move to the top if they don't have access to those in positions of power?

72. Fitt, Lawton Wehle, and Newton, Derek A. "When the Mentor Is a Man and the Protege a Woman." *Harvard Business Review* 59 (March/April 1981): 56+.

Interviews with 30 female managers and 13 male mentors show that mentors offer women legitimacy in the organization, help in advancing careers, career counseling, and personal support. The relationship involves risks for both mentor and protege, especially the risk of sexual involvement, whether real or perceived by others.

73. Fury, Kathleen. "Mentor Mania." *Savvy* 1 (January 1980): 42–47.

Daniel Levinson defines the "true" mentor relationship as having 3 characteristics: intensity, duration, and age difference. According to Levinson, a mentor serves as teacher, sponsor, host and guide, exemplar, and counsel. Article asks and answers the question "Do you have to have a mentor to succeed?" and identifies some dangers in the mentor-protege relationship.

74. Halcomb, Ruth. "Mentors and the Successful Woman." *Across the Board* 17 (February 1980): 13–18.

In an excerpt from *Women Making It: Patterns and Profiles of Success* (New York: Atheneum, 1979), Halcomb claims that women need mentors to succeed in business, especially in times of crisis or indecision. Most mentors are men, since they are in positions that enable them to be helpful, but female mentors can serve as valuable role models.

75. Harris, T. George. "Godfathers and Gossips." *Industry Week* 207 (October 27, 1980): 32+.

Discusses the mentor-protege relationship and comments on the William Agee-Mary Cunningham fiasco at Bendix. Men and women in management share business risks; research shows that risk stimulates romance.

76. Hennig, Margaret, and Jardim, Anne. "Women Executives in the Old Boy Network." *Psychology Today* 10 (January 1977): 76–81.

Interviews with over 100 female senior executives in business and industry point up some informal rules of business behavior that women have not yet learned: the difference between a job and a career, the advantages of taking risks, team play, and the necessity of adjusting to different management styles. Includes an 11-point plan on "How to Make Room at the Top."

77. Hymowitz, Carol. "Sisterhood, Inc. Business is Booming for Those Who Help Women in Business. Workshops in Assertiveness and 'Networking' Grow, but Many Are Skeptical." *Wall Street Journal,* 31 August 1979, p. 1.

Chronicles the rise of workshops and seminars designed to teach women how to succeed in business. Many such seminars are expensive and women are warned to beware of "gimmickry"—amateurs teaching popular or trendy methods for succeeding in the corporate world.

78. Jacobs, Rita. "Corporate Women: Working Together to Get Ahead." *Working Woman* 4 (December 1979): 19+.

Women's networks, devised as alternatives to the "old boy" system, are growing in such corporations as CBS, Equitable Life Assurance, Metropolitan Life Insurance, General Electric, and Atlantic Richfield. The networks serve to help women share resources and support each other in their careers. Includes tips on how to start a network in your company.

79. Johnson, Mary C. "Mentors—The Key to Development and Growth." *Training and Development Journal* 34 (July 1980): 55–57.

The training manager for an insurance company defines mentor, explains how to acquire a mentor, and describes what mentors can do for you. A survey of 1,200 recently promoted business people shows that most have had at least one mentor.

80. Kleiman, Carol. *Women's Networks: The Complete Guide to Getting a Better Job, Advancing Your Career, and Feeling Great as a Woman through Networking.* New York: Lippincott & Crowell, 1980.

Defines networking and describes business and professional networks, support networks, health and sports networks, political and labor networks, artistic networks, and informal networks. Chapter 9 provides a list of 10 checkpoints to follow when setting up your own network. Concludes with a discussion of the direction networks are taking and the national impact of networks. Chapter 10 lists more than 1,400 national, state, and local women's networks in the U.S.

81. "Mary Scott Welch: Networking is 'Beating the System that Isolates Women'." *Media Report to Women* 8 (March 1980): 8–9.

Excerpts from Mary Scott Welch's book *Networking*. Includes information on tour dates and how to schedule Ms. Welch for interviews.

82. "Mentors for Women: Like It or Not, It's a Two-Way Street." *Management Review* 69 (June 1980): 6.

A female vice-president of New York Telephone Company relates the importance of having, early in her career, a boss who also served as her mentor. As is typically the case, her mentors have been men with enough prestige and power of their own to be able to help a protege. Cites the advantages to the mentor of a mentor-protege relationship.

83. Nemec, Margaret M. "Networking: Here's How at Equitable." *Personnel Administrator* 25 (April 1980): 63–64.

The editor of *Personnel Administrator* interviewed Women in Networks, a group at Equitable that emerged from a women's discussion group. Management at Equitable gives the group psychological as well as financial support.

84. "Networks: Women Get Together to Get Ahead." *Christian Science Monitor,* 17 April 1980, p. 17.

More than 500 networks exist to help women workers advance in their careers and earn more money. Mary Scott Welch, the author of *Networking,* estimates that, by 1981, 10 million women, or one-quarter of the total number of women in the workforce, will be part of some kind of supportive job network.

85. "New Newsletters Keep Cropping Up." *Wall Street Journal,* 26 July 1973, p. 1.

Announces *Executive Woman,* the new newsletter for female entrepreneurs.

86. "An 'Old Girl Network' is Born." *Business Week* (November 20, 1978): 154+.

Describes the growth of various women's business networks in the U.S., and shows their value to members. Many exclusive, expensive networks have formed during the past 2 to 3 years, as women moved into middle-level management.

87. Phillips, Linda Lee. "Mentors and Proteges: A Study of the Career Development of Women Managers and Executives in Business and Industry." PhD dissertation, University of California, Los Angeles, 1977.

Abstracted in *Dissertation Abstracts International,* v. 38, May 1978, #6414-A.

88. Roche, Gerard R. "Much Ado about Mentors." *Harvard Business Review* 57 (January/February 1979): 14+.

The president of Heidrick and Struggles, a management consulting and executive search firm, reports the results of a 1977 survey of 3,976 executive men and 28 women executives on the relationships between mentors and proteges. All of the women respondents had mentors; 7 of 10 of their mentors were male. Includes exhibits and bibliographical references.

89. Shah, Diane K., et al. "New Girls' Network." *Newsweek* 92 (December 4, 1978): 114+.

Women are learning the politics of career advancement by joining "new girls' " networks, support systems for female executives. Members of Washington, Houston, San Francisco, Los Angeles, Detroit, and Boston networks have learned the value of having personal contacts in addition to having technical knowledge.

90. Shapiro, Eileen C.; Haseltine, Florence P.; and Rowe, Mary P. "Moving Up: Role Models, Mentors, and the 'Patron System'." *Sloan Management Review* 19 (1978): 51–58.

Discusses the recent emphasis on the necessity for young professional women to have mentors and role models in order to succeed. Authors suggest role models are of limited effectiveness and advisory/support people can be found on a spectrum ranging from mentors at one end through sponsors and guides to "peer pals" on the other end. They relate advisory/support relationship to women's upward mobility. Includes references.

91. Sheehy, Gail. "The Mentor Connection: The Secret Link in the Successful Woman's Life." *New York* 9 (April 1976): 33.

Describes the typical mentor-apprentice relationship of older men-younger men, the lack of mentors for women, and the difficulties in the male mentor-female apprentice relationship. Reviews the doctoral research of Margaret Hennig about 25 high-level women executives, the importance of mentors to these women, and the relinquishing of their mentors upon reaching age 35. Profiles a contemporary woman mentor experience and includes pictures of famous mentor-apprentice pairs.

92. Stern, Barbara S. *Is Networking for You? A Working Woman's Alternative to the Old Boy System.* Englewood Cliffs, NJ: Prentice-Hall, 1980.

A primer on networking, or the "new girl" system, this book defines networks and networking; tells how to organize a network and what to expect in the first 6 months; discusses the difficulties and advantages of publishing a membership directory; investigates the motivation for forming a lunch club; answers questions of membership such as sexual segregation and elitism; tells when, where, and whether to seek publicity; and addresses the question of networking as a technique developed by women to take advantage of other women.

93. Thompson, Jacqueline. "Patrons, Rabbis, Mentors—Whatever You Call Them, Women Need Them, Too." *MBA: Master in Business Administration* 10 (February 1976): 26–27+.

Women's mentors are usually men who are secure in their jobs and have the political knowledge to help advance their proteges. Advice on how to find a mentor includes publicize your goals, seek high visibility, take risks, and read the signals correctly.

94. Warihay, Philomena D. "Climb to the Top: Is the Network the Route for Women?" *Personnel Administrator* 25 (April 1980): 55–60.

The author applauds women supporting other women up the corporate ladder, but she is concerned that there are few women in top management to serve as role models or mentors. Reports the results of a survey of 2,000 women to determine the extent and effectiveness of networking. Includes graphs, charts, and references.

95. Weber, C. Edward. "Mentoring." *Directors & Boards* 5 (Fall 1980): 17–24.

Describes the mentoring process and its rewards and risks. Most mentor-protege relationships last an average of 2 to 3 years, but the friendships may last a lifetime. After age 40, the need for a mentor is less acute.

96. Welch, Mary S. *Networking: The Great New Way for Women to Get Ahead*. New York: Harcourt Brace Jovanovich, Inc., 1980.

Defines networking and relates 25 network success stories. Includes a discussion of 14 questions a group should answer before organizing a network and gives advice on 32 networking *do's* and *don'ts*. Appendices are: "How to Start a Network Group"; "How Other Networks Started"; a network directory (arranged by state); and a reading list. Includes index.

97. ———. "Networking 1981." *Working Woman* 6 (March 1981): 92+.

One-page update on issues in networking by the author of *Networking*. Answers the questions "Should you network with men?" and "Why are some women's networks so exclusive?" and concludes with a list of state and national networks.

98. Wilson, Jane. "Networks." *Savvy* 1 (January 1980): 18–23.

Describes the beginning of formal career networks for women, the requirements for network membership, the primary purpose of a network, advantages of professional networks, information about workshops on networking, and the structure of various networks. Mentions several national networks.

99. ———. "The 'New Girls' Network: A Power System for the Future." *New York* 10 (April 1977): 47.

Points out that the chief benefit of the "old boy networks"—access to information—is also the main reason for the establishment of "new girl" networks (NGNs) such as Women in Business and the Organization of Women Executives in Los Angeles. In addition to career help and advice, networks provide emotional support, role models, sponsors, and mentors.

100. "Women Finally Get Mentors of Their Own." *Business Week* (October 23, 1978): 74+.

Testimony by top women executives about their efforts to aid young women in management concerns the benefits of mentoring to both the executive woman and the subordinates. Role modeling is identified as one of the best ways to do mentoring; women executives may do better with women mentors.

101. "Women Network into Higher Management Jobs." *Christian Science Monitor,* 6 August 1979, p. 19.

Describes the development of a new network for women involved in business education. For information on joining the network, contact: Suzanne Attwood, 107 Vance Hall, University of Pennsylvania, Philadelphia, PA 19104.

Management Training for Women

102. Adams, Velma A. "Management Training for the 'New Woman'."
Training 11 (August 1974): 24–29.

An update on college courses available to women interested in management: the new graduate business program at Simmons College, a program for female bank executives sponsored by the National Association of Bank Women (NABW), and a BA program sponsored jointly by Simmons and the NABW. Includes information on 8 management development programs for women.

103. Alpander, Guvenc C., and Gutmann, Jean E. "Contents and Techniques of Management Development Programs for Women." *Personnel Journal* 55 (February 1976): 76–79.

Discussion and comparison of training and development needs of male and female managers. A "Supervisory Development" questionnaire was used to determine an individual's managerial style, perceived training needs, major job functions, behavioral characteristics, and specific development needs of women managers. Includes tables.

104. Anundsen, Kristin. "Building Teamwork and Avoiding Backlash: Keys to Developing Managerial Women." *Management Review* 68 (February 1979): 55–58.

Describes the Women-in-Management Program for state employees developed by the director of training for the state of California. The year-long program, preceded by a 2-day orientation, includes a comprehensive series of workshops and assignments designed to educate the participant in the operations of the organization and the development of management skills. The program requires a commitment of 145 hours from the individual.

105. Baron, Alma S. "Communication Skills for the Woman Manager—Practice Seminar." *Personnel Journal* 59 (January 1980): 55–58+.

Describes a seminar given by Management Institute at the University of Wisconsin to teach women managers how to communicate on the job. Seminar sessions were on exploring cultural and societal norms, sharing recent research, learning the use of parliamentary procedure, practice in networking, and role-playing. Includes 5 role-play situations: The Ball Game, The Hostess Role, Have Friend—Won't Travel, Sisterhood Is Lousy, and The Big Meeting.

106. ———. "Special Training Course for Women: Desirable or Not?" *Training and Development Journal* 30 (December 1976): 30–33.

Author believes that special programs designed for women entering management are desirable because women were not given the special educational advantages as men in similar positions. The author concludes, however, 'that once women have achieved a degree of competence in the new role of greater responsibility and authority, the training sessions are not valid.

107. Bender, Marilyn. " 'Alice in Corporationland' Is the Game." *New York Times,* 25 June 1976, sec. 4, p. 7.

"Alice in Corporationland" is a strategy simulation game used at AT&T in management development training programs for women. Women choose teams for the game and learn to win, to negotiate, and to form coalitions, according to management consultant Martha C. McKay. Negative social conditioning frequently prevents women from employing political and strategy skills useful in the corporate world.

108. ———. "Behavioral Differences Stressed in Women's Management Training." *New York Times,* 11 February 1974, p. 53+.

Associate professors of management at Simmons, Margaret Hennig and Anne Jardim, have developed a masters program in management and an academic program for female bank executives. The 2 programs focus on behavioral differences between the sexes; the case method is used in the courses. The masters degree program includes courses in organizational structure, management behavior, middle management problems, and management leadership.

109. ———. "Women in Management: Session Looks Ahead." *New York Times,* 10 November 1970, p. 67.

Over 350 women participated in the first all-day conference on women in management held at the New York Hilton. Eli Ginzberg, professor at the Columbia School of Business, spoke on the future for women in management at the conference organized by Charles D. Orth, III, president of Career Development International. Aileen Hernandez, national president of the National Organization for Women (NOW), said the organization had filed discrimination complaints against most of the companies participating in the conference.

110. Bolton, Elizabeth B., and Humphreys, Luther Wade. "A Training Approach for Women—An Androgynous Approach." *Personnel Journal* 56 (March 1977): 230–34.

The feminist movement, legislation, and the shortage of managerial talent led to increasing numbers of women in the work force. Defines the 5 types of training and development for professional advancement identified by Theodora Wells (on-the-job, formal, employer-supported outside study programs, informal sponsor, and participation in conferences) and examines current training practices. Concludes that special training programs for women are not needed; women already qualified for managerial development should be selected and hired.

111. Brenner, Marshall. "Management Development for Women." *Personnel Journal* 51 (March 1972): 165–69.

Author makes 11 recommendations designed to aid organizations in preparing women for management positions. Recommendations fall into categories of recruiting, selection, and support systems.

112. Burkhead, Marie. "Underrepresentation of Women in University-Sponsored Management Development Programs." *Journal of Business Education* 48 (December 1972): 109–10.

In 1971, 92 institutions, members of the American Association of Collegiate Schools of Business, returned questionnaires designed to determine to the extent to which women were participating in university-sponsored management programs. Fifty-six had management development programs, but only 6.4 percent of those attending were women. Author concludes that lack of women participants indicates a subtle, yet effective, discrimination against women in management.

113. Burrow, Martha G. *Developing Women Managers: What Needs to Be Done?* New York: AMACOM, 1978.

Results of a survey of 2,000 respondents shows that self-confidence, education, experience, and opportunity are the most important development needs of women managers. Includes exhibits and bibliography.

114. ———. *Women: A Worldwide View of Their Management Development Needs.* New York: AMACOM, 1976.

Comprises the first part of a longitudinal study of management needs of women. Based on survey and interview data. Includes figures and references.

115. Diamond, Helen, "Management Training for Women, by Women." *Community College Frontiers* 7 (Fall 1978): 9–11.

Describes management training classes for women in a community college. Cites results of a 1977 survey of women in management conducted by Women in Management, a nonprofit educational society.

116. Dorling, Jenny. "Making a Start on Training for Women." *Personnel Management* 7 (December 1975): 18–21.

Eighty percent of women still take commercial and clerical courses in college according to the British publicly-financed Training Opportunities Scheme (TOPS). The Training Services Agency (TSA) proposes change in 4 areas: training for traditional women's occupations, training for other occupations, special training to enable women to compete with men, and cooperation from groups outside the training system.

117. Dubin, Samuel Sanford. *Training Women in Management: A Continuing Education Workshop Approach*. University Park, PA: Pennsylvania State University, Planning Studies in Continuing Education, 1978.

Abstracted in *Resources in Education,* ED 167 750.

118. Fanning, Patricia. "Managerial Women." *Wall Street Journal,* 3 April 1978, p. 20.

Report of a seminar in Washington, conducted by Margaret Hennig and Anne Jardim, which was attended by more than 500 women. Exercises demonstrated behavioral differences in men and women which help to explain why men succeed in management: viewing a career as a series of jobs, long-range goal setting, and risk taking. *The Managerial Woman,* authored by Hennig and Jardim, is based on a study of 25 top management women; some of the authors' suggestions from the book were incorporated into the seminar.

119. Field, Anne. "Seminars on Company Time." *Working Woman* 6 (July 1981): 20.

Tax laws allow employers and employees to take advantage of a myriad of seminars given each year which offer information and self-development. Large firms are more likely than smaller firms to pay the seminar fee for the employee. Employees are advised to do their homework before trying to convince the company to pay for the seminar.

120. Goldstein, Paul J., and Sorensen, Jane. "Becoming the Executive You'd Like to Be: A Program for Female Middle Managers." *SAM Advanced Management Journal* 42 (Fall 1977): 41–49.

The behavior of 5 female middle managers changed as a result of a series of 12 behavioral science-oriented meetings. The women report achieving confidence in their personal strengths and learning about power and authority, styles of communication, and the politics of organizations.

121. Graham, Ellen, "Many Seminars Are Held to Aid Women in Firms; Then What Happens?" *Wall Street Journal*, 26 April 1973, p. 1+.

Management development training programs for women proliferate as a result of business complying with the Department of Labor's "Revised Order 4" regarding affirmative action programs in companies with government contracts.

122. Grina, Aldona Aida Malcanas. "The Effect of Group Experience on Women in a Management Development Course." PhD dissertation, University of Pittsburgh, 1978.

Abstracted in *Dissertation Abstracts International,* August 1979, v. 40, no. 2, #1106-A.

123. Harley, Jan, and Koff, Lois Ann. "Prepare Women Now for Tomorrow's Managerial Challenges." *Personnel Administrator* 25 (April 1980): 41–42.

Authors argue for proactive management training for women as opposed to the reactive training of the 1970s which attempted to help women "catch up." Gives examples of proactive training and what it can do for women managers.

124. Hartnett, Oonagh, and Novarra, Virginia. "Single Sex Management Training and a Woman's Touch." *Personnel Management* (London) 12 (March 1980): 32–35.

Reviews the debate over whether management training courses for women only are desirable or necessary. The authors believe there is a need for revising the curricula of management courses and argue that, during this transitional period when conventional courses are still male-dominated, there is validity in single-sex management training for women.

125. Heinen, J. Stephen; Legeros, Constance; McGlauchlin, Dorothy; and Freeman, Jean. "Developing the Woman Manager." *Personnel Journal* 54 (May 1975): 282–86+.

Based on 5 assumptions about management training for women, a 3-day training seminar, conducted under the auspices of the University of Minnesota College of Business Administration, Continuing Education, stressed the development of self-concept and managerial skills.

126. Hennig, Margaret Marie. "Career Development for Women Executives." PhD dissertation, Harvard University, 1971.
Listed in *American Doctoral Dissertations,* 1971, p. 42.

127. Hoffman, Marilyn. "Move Over Men In High Places . . . " *Christian Science Monitor,* 17 November 1970, p. 18.
Career Development International, Inc., sponsored a one-day conference in New York on "Women in Management: A Look Ahead" which was attended by 374 women and 51 men. Speakers included Aileen Hernandez, president of NOW; social critic Marya Mannes; and Eli Ginzberg, professor at Columbia Business School.

128. "How Volunteers Are Cracking the Job Market." *Business Week* (May 21, 1979): 159–60.
Describes the growing trend of mature women returning to work after several years out of the job market. Most women transfer volunteer skills into salaried jobs in the nonprofit sector, using administrative skills learned in volunteer experiences to land management positions.

129. Commission on the Status of Women. *Women Advancing in Business: The Role of Management Seminars.* Des Moines, IA: The Commission, 1978.
Six management training seminars were conducted to determine what effect training seminars have on the advancement of women into management and supervisory positions. Although participants in the study acquired skills useful in their professional and personal lives, the variables of increase in pay, authority, and number of promotions did not differ significantly between seminar participants and the control group. Includes description of each seminar, conclusions and suggestions for further research, lengthy bibliography, participant questionnaires, and seminar evaluations.

130. "Is HRD A Hoax or a Necessity: Answers from an Organizational Psychologist and a No-Nonsense Chief Executive." *Training* 15 (October 1978): 52–54.
A dialog between psychologist Harry Levinson and chief executive officer (CEO) Richard Sloma, author of *No-Nonsense Management.*

They discuss the CEO's responsibility for facilitating the upward mobility of women and minorities.

131. Jelinek, Mariann. "Career Management and Women." Paper presented at the 27th Annual Conference of the International Communication Association, Berlin, Germany, 3 June 1977.

Abstracted in *Resources in Education,* ED 150 272.

132. Koff, Lois Ann. "Developing Women Managers." *Training in Business and Industry* 10 (February 1973): 54–55.

A survey of women in lower and middle management indicates that half are over 36 years of age and two-thirds have had 7 or more years job experience before becoming a supervisor. Some women advance by completing additional college course work. One business offers a 12-month "internship" where college graduates' management skills are evaluated before they are given supervisory responsibility.

133. Kozoll, Charles E. "The Relevant, the Honest, the Possible: Management Development for Women." *Training and Development Journal* 27 (February 1973): 3–6.

Describes a 3-hour exercise sponsored by the Civil Service Commission and designed for women in supervisory and professional positions. The intent is to encourage women to become more analytical and to teach the development of strategies to solve common problems faced by women managers.

134. Krane, John Charles. "Experiences for Women Leading to Successful Entry into the Post-Secondary Cooperative Work Experience Management Program." EdD dissertation, University of Northern Colorado, 1980.

Abstracted in *Dissertation Abstracts International,* v. 41, November 1980, #2080-A.

135. Larwood, Laurie; Wood, Marion M.; and Inderlied, Sheila Davis. "Training Women for Management: New Problems, New Solutions." *Academy of Management Review* 3 (July 1978): 584–93.

Discusses external and internal barriers to management training for women and identifies ending stereotyping, the provision of models, and emphasis on preemployment socialization as means of overcoming these barriers. Includes an analysis of the values and problems of the segregated classroom in management training.

136. Management Training Programs of Women and Minorities. Survey. *Increasing Participation of Women and Minorities in Education R&D.* Philadelphia, PA: Research for Better Schools, 1978.

Abstracted in *Resources in Education,* ED 156 913.

137. Masters, Robert J., II. "Management Training for Women: University Business Office Program." *Training and Development Journal* 28 (June 1974): 29.

Describes the Management Training Program (MTP) developed by the business office at Purdue University. This 5-week training program is for male and female applicants with bachelors degrees in business; trainees spend time in the Personnel Department, Budget Office, Office of Contract Administration, Accounting Office, Purchasing Department, and with academic business administrators.

138. McCord, Bird. "Identifying and Developing Women for Management Positions." *Training and Development Journal* 25 (November 1971): 2–5.

Identifies sex-role stereotypes, personality and temperament differences, and career and college training as reasons why there are so few women managers. Puts responsibility for change at the organizational level and lists 3 areas where organizations can affect change: selection and identification of women with management potential; management training programs for women; and changes in the promotion and reward system for women.

139. Miranda (L.) and Associates. *Business and Management Development Training for Hispanic Women. Final Report.* Washington, DC: L. Miranda and Associates, 1976.

Abstracted in *Resources in Education,* ED 170 489.

140. Moore, Ronald E. "Management Seminars for Women: Valuable or Not?" *Woman CPA* 40 (April 1978): 22–24.

Lists 5 major reasons for the use of management seminars for women and discusses the role of business and the university in providing such seminars. Notes the shortcomings of some seminars, including evaluation of the special training program. Several reasons are given for the continuation of special seminars for women in management: women need to catch up; women need to become a part of the organization; women need to feel pride in their job environment; and they need to share experiences.

141. Moses, Joseph L. ''The Development of an Assessment Center for the Early Identification of Supervisory Potential.'' *Personnel Psychology* 26 (1973): 569–80.

Describes the Early Identification Assessment (EIA) program designed to evaluate the managerial potential of large numbers of employees. Techniques include: a leaderless group exercise, an in-basket, a personal interview, a written exercise, and a general mental ability test. The author believes a strong relationship exists between performance in the early identification and an expanded assessment center process and sees the value of EIA to identify supervisory potential in women and minority groups.

142. Munson, Mary Lou. ''Less Complaining, More Training.'' *Industry Week* 184 (February 17, 1975): 56+.

Brief hints to male managers on integrating new women managers into the organization: give her a good manager, enroll her in available management training programs, and make her feel part of the team.

143. Murray-Hicks, Margo, and O'Mara, Julie. ''Women in Management Performance and Instruction: Exploring the Role of the Management Trainer in Expanding this Elite Society.'' *NSPI Journal* 19 (September 1980): 7–8, 13.

Advice to manager trainers on upgrading the skills and participation of women in management. Women and men are compared for 16 characteristics of successful managers. Includes tables and references.

144. Nicholson, Delaine R. ''Management Training for Women: A Status Report.'' *Training* 13 (September 1976): 20–32.

Discusses management training workshops and seminars available to women only, men only, and both men and women. Argues for special training for women until women are 50 percent of management. Includes *Training*'s 1976 catalog of women's programs and services for management training (pp. 23–32).

145. Olds, Sally Wendkos. ''Women in Management.'' *Christian Science Monitor* 9 July 1973, p. 8.

Reports on a 3-day workshop for 35 women managers and secretaries sponsored by the Westinghouse Learning Corporation. The workshops, also given at Aetna, Pfizer, Levi Strauss, CBS, Johnson & Johnson, and Warner-Lambert, are designed to change women's basic attitudes regarding their abilities and options.

146. "A Path Up for Women Bankers." *Business Week* (June 13, 1977): 105.

Describes a 3-year program designed by Simmons College in Boston for the National Association of Bank Women (NABW). Participants take courses close to home in order to continue working; often their banks pay all or part of their tuition.

147. Pilla, Barbara A. "Women in Business." *Training and Development Journal* 31 (November 1977): 22–25.

An exploration of Prudential Insurance Company's management development program for women in the Governmental Health Programs Office. Results of the program were impressive: women set career goals, enrolled in other company-sponsored courses, improved communication with their supervisors, gained insight into business theories and practices, and increased their self-confidence.

148. Price, Martha, and Arneaud, Susan. "Administrative Internships: Approaching the Job Market Creatively." *Vocational Guidance Quarterly* 27 (March 1979): 264–69.

An assessment of the 2-month, part-time managerial/administrative internship program designed by the University of Michigan Center for Continuing Education of Women (CCEW) and the Ann Arbor Branch of the Environmental Protection Agency to help mature women with liberal arts degrees reenter the job market. Three of the 4 women chosen completed the internship and all were offered temporary jobs at the EPA.

149. Quint, Barbara Gilder. "Career Courses and Seminars: Management Development Programs." *Glamour* 77 (June 1979): 195–96.

Offers 4 guidelines for evaluating a management development program for women: choose a well-defined program, find a program that has been given before, look for experienced teachers, and check who will attend the course. Gives advice on how to get your company to pay and give time off for participation in the program.

150. Rader, Martha H. "Evaluating a Management Development Program for Women." *Public Personnel Management* 8 (May/June 1979): 138–45.

Discusses the results of a project to fund a series of management training seminars for women employees of the City of Phoenix and its implications for management development programs for women. Includes tables and footnotes.

151. Rhea, Jeanine N. "Status, Training and Future of Women in Business: Critical Questions for Research in the 1980s." *Journal of Business Education* 55 (April 1980): 312–14.

Reviews the recent research on women managers and the reasons why there are still so few women in top management positions. Calls for further research and for management training programs for women and men to educate them in the special needs and problems of women in management.

152. Riccardi, Toni et al. "Careers and Management: Strategies for Women Professionals." Association of College Unions-International, Pre-Conference Seminar, Cincinnati, OH, 24–25 March 1979.

Abstracted in *Resources in Education,* ED 177 311.

153. Robertson, Nan. "Training for Women on the Way Up." *New York Times,* 19 August 1980, sec. 3, p. 14.

Twenty-three middle management women from large corporations completed a 3-week intensive management training program at Smith College. The women found the corporate finance and marketing courses most useful.

154. Schockley, Pamela S., and Staley, Constance M. "Women in Management Training Programs: What They Think about Key Issues." *Public Personnel Management* 9 (1980): 214–24.

Analyzes responses from 400 women who have participated in a seminar series to develop women's management potential offered at the University of Colorado since 1976. Seventy percent felt that women were not promoted as frequently as men, 67 percent had a mentor relationship, and most of the women wanted to be powerful. Includes seminar outline, methodology, findings, footnotes, and bibliography.

155. "Seminar Is Scheduled for Female Aides." *New York Times,* 23 November 1975, p. 100.

Advertises a one-week seminar on business-managerial skills for women scheduled by the Rutgers University Extension Division. The seminar is for women being considered for management positions, newly appointed women managers, and women who already hold management or supervisory positions and will cover communication, philosophy of management, leadership styles, problem solving, and decision making.

156. Stull, Richard Allen. "New Answers to an Old Question: Woman's Place Is in the What?" *Personnel Journal* 52 (January 1973): 31–35.

Cites statistics on working women and reviews the historical perspective and the changing roles of women in the labor force. Describes some management development programs for women and notes available literature.

157. "Teaching Women How to Manage Their Careers." *Business Week* (May 28, 1979): 148+.

Role playing, group exercises and simulated games and videotapes are used in management development workshops and seminars for women. Some corporations encourage and subsidize the workshops which range in price from $5 to $500 and give instruction in career counseling, assertiveness, and corporate politics.

158. Terborg, James R. "Women in Management: A Research Review." *Journal of Applied Psychology* 62 (December 1977): 647–64.

Reviews research on socialization of women, role management, and stereotypes as an explanation for job entry discrimination. Recommends additional research in career choice, vocational counseling, vocational development, the assessment of sex-role stereotypes and sex-characteristic stereotypes, longitudinal field research on the entire socialization process, and conflicts arising from dual-career families. Includes lengthy bibliography.

159. Toyne, Marguerite C. "Women's Career Path to Management through Effective Communication." *Journal of Business Communication* 15 (Fall 1977): 19–27.

A speech delivered at the 40th Annual and First International convention of the American Business Communication Association at Toronto, December 1975. The author believes women entering the world of business must do some goal clarification and learn more about decision making and communication, and she notes the pitfalls that women trainees will encounter in a male-oriented work world.

160. Underwood, June. "Step Up to Management." *Burroughs Clearing House* 6 (November 1977): 22+.

Associate professor of business administration says continuing education or training programs and acceptance and support by men in power positions are necessary ingredients to women's success in management. She cites the advantages and disadvantages of coeducational and women-only management training programs.

161. Vance, Carmen Lee. "Comparison of the Career Development of Women Executives in Institutions of Higher Education with Corporate Women Executives." EdD dissertation, Indiana University, 1978.

Abstracted in *Dissertation Abstracts International,* August 1978, v. 39, no. 2, #717-A.

162. Waling, Ann Marie Britt. "An Analysis of Labor Force Experience and Market Work Commitment of Women Interested in Management Training." PhD dissertation, Purdue University, 1979.

Abstracted in *Dissertation Abstracts International,* v. 41, July 1980, #328-A.

163. Wells, Theodora. "Women's Self-Concept: Implications for Management Development." In *Optimizing Human Resources,* edited by Gordon L. Lippitt, Leslie E. This, and Robert G. Birdwell, Jr. Reading, MA: Addison-Wesley, 1971.

Lists pressures for more women in management training, including the need for more qualified managers, the recognition that women are a major underutilized resource, legal compliance with laws prohibiting sex discrimination in employment, and the women's rights movement. Reviews research over the last 20 years in sex-role stereotypes and self-concepts, sex-role stereotypes and mental health, and women's motive to avoid success. Identifies sources of potential women managers and aspects of management training programs for women.

164. "Women Executives Grow Bolder about Mapping Broadened Careers." *Wall Street Journal,* 9 October 1973, p. 1.

Executive search firm Handy Associates reports a big jump in the number of resumes they're getting from women executives—from only a few to over 100 in the third quarter.

165. "Women Get to Sharpen Their Managerial Skills." *Christian Science Monitor,* 14 March 1975, p. 3E.

The American Management Association sponsors a series of nationwide seminars for women executives; one of the main topics is sexist prejudice. A seminar leader, DeAnne Rosenberg, says women must learn to be visible.

166. Women: The Untapped Management Source." *Small Business Report* 4 (December 1979): 24–27.

Businesses will be competing for good managers in the 1980s. In order to make good use of women's management talents, companies will have to discard the myths that women are too emotional, men won't work for a woman manager, women are undereducated, turnover rates are higher for women, women are often sick, and women managers are radical feminists. Debates the advantages and disadvantages of women only and coed management development programs and calls for companies to support women managers in the informal management structure.

167. "*Working Woman* Seminars." *Working Woman* 6 (August 1981): 92. Information is given about 3 seminars for women sponsored by *Working Woman* to be held in New York, Los Angeles, Chicago, and Houston. Course fees range from $495–575 for the 2- and 3-day seminars. See the September 1981 issue of *Working Woman* for further details.

Sex-Role Stereotypes

168. Alpert, Dee Estelle. "The Struggle for Status: Accepting the Aggressive Female Executive." *MBA: Master in Business Administration* 10 (February 1976): 25–28.

Discussion of the difficulties some men have adjusting to female executives due to the image they have of women as mothers, wives, and lovers. Difficulties are often compounded when aggressive female managers ask for a raise, promotion, or transfer. Author's solution is simple—get more women into management.

169. Athanassiades, John C. "Myths of Women in Management: What Every Businessman Ought to Know about Women but May Be Afraid to Ask." *Atlanta Economic Review* 25 (May/June 1975): 4–9.

Reviews past, present, and future myths regarding sex discrimination and mentions 4 institutions—the church, the military, government, and business—as major institutions that exclude women from upper levels. Author draws some "tentative but pessimistic conclusions" about the nature of new myths. Includes bibliography.

170. Baron, Alma S., and Witte, Robert L. "New Work Dynamic: Men and Women in the Work Force." *Business Horizons* 23 (August 1980): 56–60.

Role, organizational problems and inequities, and personal issues emerged as concerns from a seminar on men and women in the work force. The participants, 11 men and 13 women, were divided by sex; then they identified the behavior by the opposite sex that they found most annoying.

171. Biles, George E., and Pryatel, Holly A. "Myths, Management and Women." *Personnel Journal* 57 (October 1978): 572+.

Reviews and discusses common myths and barriers to women in management, such as low commitment to the world of work, lack of motivation to achieve, and lack of education and experience. Outlines steps personnel managers can take to aid women entering and advancing in management.

172. Cohen, Stephen L., and Leavengood, Sally. "The Utility of the WAMS: Shouldn't It Relate to Discriminatory Behavior?" *Academy of Management Journal* 21 (December 1978): 742–48.

A study conducted with 78 male students in upper-level management courses used the Women as Managers Scale (WAMS) to attempt to validate the idea that sex-role stereotypical attitudes and discriminatory behavior are different. Researchers question the utility of the WAMS to predict personnel decisions made in the business world. Includes tables and references.

173. Costello, John. "The Best Way to Deal with Women Co-workers." *Nation's Business* 65 (February 1977): 8.

The Research Institute of America, Inc., in a survey of men and women managers, found that the "old boy" network, women's lib rhetoric, and the male ego are the biggest difficulties in establishing a normal business relationship between men and women. Researchers say the best way for businessmen to deal with their female colleagues is to "treat them as people."

174. Davidson, M.J., and Cooper, Cary L. "Executive Stress in Women." *Accountant* 183 (August 21, 1980): 297–99.

A survey of 135 British women executives identified the strains and stresses unique to female managers: the role of the "token" woman; isolation and lack of role models; career and marriage/family life conflicts; coping with prejudice and stereotyping; and organizational structure and climate. Researchers suggest the higher levels of stress that women managers face may prevent women from entering management or applying for promotions and increase the risk of stress-related illnesses.

175. "Debunking a Myth, Women Managers Don't Leave Jobs More Often than Men." *Wall Street Journal,* 14 November 1978, p. 1.

Data from companies indicates that, contrary to popular belief, women professionals do not have a higher turnover rate than men. Turnover rates for men and women managers are identical in some corporations; one Chicago bank reports a higher turnover rate for men.

176. "Exploding a Myth of Executive Job-Hopping." *Business Week* (June 11, 1979): 127+.

A study of 40 companies shows that, contrary to popular belief, women executives earning more than $30,000 don't leave jobs more frequently than men. Reasons women cite for leaving a good job are challenge of a new position, scope of responsibility, and opportunity for upward mobility.

177. Gackenbach, Jayne I.; Burke, Marian; and Auerbach, Stephen M. ''A 'Women in Business' Seminar: Exploring an Approach to Change in Sex-Role Awareness.'' *Atlanta Economic Review* 26 (March/April 1976): 32–37.

A look at courses and seminars taught by business or academia that are aimed at changing the attitudes that discriminate against women in business. Discusses the procedures used in developing such a course and the attitudinal and personality measures used to evaluate the impact of the course on its participants. In particular, describes the Managerial Attitudes towards Women Executives Scale and the Women as Managers Scale.

178. Geach, Lillian. ''Why Are More Women Not in Management?'' *Times (London) Educational Supplement* 3067 (March 8, 1974): 43.

An educator blames schools for perpetuating the myths about women's lack of management capabilities by directing young women to secretarial skills rather than preparing them to enter industrial training. She calls on government to increase the percentage of women in Civil Service posts.

179. Greisman, Harvey C. ''The Image of the Business Executive on Television.'' *Journal of Contemporary Business* 5 (Autumn 1976): 71589.

Reviews the characters who portrayed business executives in several television shows of the last 2 decades, and notes the absence of female business executives.

180. Griffin, William. ''More than a Tempest in a Coffeepot: How a Manager's Consciousness Was Raised.'' *Across the Board* 15 (January 1978): 4–5.

Describes what happened at a commercial bank when a 53-year-old male officer asked his 25-year-old computer programmer to get coffee. The problem is a psychological one for older men raised to believe in traditional sex roles.

181. Hennig, Margaret, ''What Happens on the Way Up.'' *MBA: Master in Business Administration* 5 (March 1971): 8–10.

Based on Hennig's doctoral dissertation, ''Career Development for Women Executives,'' a study of the personal lives and careers of 25 women executives. Describes 2 stereotypes of businesswomen, ''the general business type'' and the ''style and fashion group'' and analyzes women managers' behavioral style.

182. Johnson, Michael L. "Women: Born to Manage." *Industry Week* 186 (August 4, 1975): 22–26.

A study by the Johnson O'Connor Research Foundation, Inc., shows that there are no sexual differences in 14 of 22 basic aptitudes, and that women excel in 6 of the 8 aptitudes where there are sexual differences. Includes a profile of the typical woman manager compiled by the Psychological Services of Pittsburgh (PSP).

183. Jones-Parker, Janet. "And Women's Jobs." *New York Times,* 19 October 1980, sec. 3, p. 3.

Warns U.S. corporations against sexual prejudice of the kind involved in the Cunningham-Agee situation at Bendix. Author claims the number of talented managers needed in the 1980s will rise sharply, creating a demand for female as well as male managers.

184. Kagan, Julia. "How Management Myths Hurt Women." *Working Woman* 5 (December 1980): 75–76+.

An interview with Linda Keller Brown, director of the Cross-National Project on Women as Corporate Managers at the Center for the Social Sciences at Columbia University. Brown discusses the factors and myths that block women's management progress. Her latest research on women managers will be published by the Business and Professional Women's Foundation in 1981 as *Women Executives: A Commentary and Bibliography*.

185. "Management—Striving for Sexual Detente." *Industry Week* 200 (March 5, 1979): 56–57+.

A discussion of the problems some men experience with the entry of more women into management, particularly their uncertainty and anxiety about saying and doing the right things. Mentions old myths and stresses the need for more sensitivity from both men and women.

186. " 'Masculine' Traits Equal Business Success." *New York Times,* 30 August 1977, p. 25.

A national survey of 110 part-time graduate students with business jobs and 575 undergraduate business students indicates that both men and women who exhibit traditionally masculine traits, such as self-reliance and ambition, are more likely to succeed in top management positions. The University of Connecticut and University of Massachusetts professors who conducted the survey noted that successful post-graduate women felt they had more masculine than feminine character-istics.

187. Meyer, Priscilla S. "A Handy Guide to Everyday Dealings with Women." *Wall Street Journal* 4 January 1973, p. 8.
Lists 10 ways for well-meaning male executives to avoid sex stereotype pitfalls. Discusses language, courtesies, private clubs, proper form of address in letters, who pays for lunch, and patronizing.

188. Michinsky, Paul M., and Harris, Sharon L. "The Effect of Applicant Sex and Scholastic Standing on the Evaluation of Job Applicant Resumes in Sex-Typed Occupations." *Journal of Vocational Behavior* 11 (August 1977): 95–107.
Fifty male and 50 female students in an introductory psychology course took part in a study to examine sex discrimination in 3 occupations. Participants evaluated the suitability for a managerial role of male and female job applicants for a position as a mechanical engineer, a child care center director, and an assistant copy editor for a newspaper. Findings concur with the results of other studies that discrimination on the basis of sex occurs frequently when screening applicants for managerial positions.

189. Morrison, Robert F., and Sebald, Maria-Luise. "Personal Characteristics Differentiating Female Executive from Female Nonexecutive Personnel." *Journal of Applied Psychology* 59 (October 1974): 656–59.
Thirty-nine executive and 39 nonexecutive women were measured for comparisons of early socialization, current environmental factors, and needs. The executive group ranked higher in self-esteem, need for power, and mental ability. Early socialization processes, husband's role behavior, and need for affiliation were not significantly different for female executives and female nonexecutives.

190. O'Leary, Virginia E. "Some Attitudinal Barriers to Occupational Aspirations in Women." *Psychological Bulletin* 81 (November 1974): 809–26.
Reviews in detail the literature on psychological factors which keep women workers from activities which would ensure promotion to managerial status. Factors which are external to the woman but which create barriers to achievement include societal sex-role stereotypes, attitudes toward women in management, attitudes toward female competence, and the "male managerial" model. Internal factors include

fear of failure, low self-esteem, role conflict, fear of success, and perceived consequences of occupational advancement.

191. Osborn, Richard N., and Vicars, William M. "Sex Stereotypes: An Artifact in Leader Behavior and Subordinate Satisfaction Analysis?" *Academy of Management Journal* 19 (September 1976): 439–49.

Employees of 2 mental-health institutions were surveyed using the Leader Behavior Description questionnaire and the Job Descriptive Index to determine if female managers behave differently toward subordinates than male managers and if female managers have a different effect on their subordinates than male managers. Results indicated that leader sex does not appear to have a consistent influence on either leader behavior or subordinate satisfaction.

192. Penley, Larry E., and Hawkins, Brian L. "Organizational Communication, Performance, and Job Satisfaction as a Function of Ethnicity and Sex." *Journal of Vocational Behavior* 16 (June 1980): 368–84.

Employees of a southwestern financial company answered questionnaires about job satisfaction and communication as a result of supervisor's ethnicity, sex, age, and tenure. Results show that these factors significantly affect communication behavior and employee performance.

193. Powell, Gary N., and Butterfield, D. Anthony. "The 'Good Manager': Masculine or Androgynous?" *Academy of Management Journal* 22 (June 1979): 395–403.

Over 680 undergraduate and graduate business students completed the Bem Sex-Role Inventory (BSRI) to test the hypothesis that the "good manager" is seen as androgynous in sex-role identification. Students, both male and female, described the good manager in masculine terms. Includes tables and references.

194. Quinn, Jane Bryant. "When Does a Businesswoman's Word Count?" *New York* (April 4, 1977): 76–77.

Author of a syndicated personal-finance column says *Business Week*'s 16-month-old "Corporate Woman" department has timely stories but that the rest of the magazine is male-oriented. Although a study shows that 25 percent, or some 766,000, of *BW* readers are women, most of the magazine's advertising portrays women in stereotyped roles.

195. Raffel, Dawn. "Workaholics." *Working Woman* 5 (June 1980): 38–42.

Review of the research done by Marilyn M. Machlowitz for her book *Workaholics: Living with Them, Working with Them.* Her findings show that most women workaholics defy the stereotype of the unhappy woman with an ulcer; they simply enjoy working. Offers tips for workaholics.

196. Reif, William E.; Newstrom, John W.; and Monczka, Robert M. "Exploding Some Myths about Women Managers." *California Management Review* 17 (Summer 1975): 72–79.

Reviews research on the question of whether women managers are psychologically and socially different from men managers and gives the results of a study which examined whether women's views of formal and informal organizational concepts differ from men's. Includes tables and references.

197. Rosen, Benson, and Jerdee, Thomas H. "Sex Stereotyping in the Executive Suite." *Harvard Business Review* 52 (March 1974): 45–58.

HBR surveyed 1,400 subscribers in management positions to determine the extent of unintended sex bias in decision making. Participants were asked to solve a series of hypothetical situations involving either male or female employees. The findings indicated greater organizational concern and support for male employees, and the authors concluded that, in matters of career demands and family obligations, personal conduct, and selection, promotion, and career-development decisions, managers are biased in favor of males.

198. Schein, Virginia Ellen. "The Relationship between Sex Role Stereotypes and Requisite Management Characteristics." *Journal of Applied Psychology* 57 (April 1973): 95–100.

Researchers posed the hypothesis that successful middle managers are perceived to possess characteristics, attitudes, and temperaments more commonly attributed to men than women. Results of a survey of 300 male middle managers confirms the hypothesis. Discusses implications for selection and promotion, a woman's self-image, and stereotypical perceptions of men and women among older managers.

199. ———. "Relationships between Sex Role Stereotypes and Requisite Management Characteristics among Female Managers." *Journal of Applied Psychology* 60 (June 1975): 340–44.

In a replication of a 1973 study of male middle managers, 167 female middle managers were surveyed to determine whether successful middle managers are perceived to possess characteristics, attitudes, and temperaments more commonly ascribed to men than women. Results of the survey showed the author's hypothesis to be true, and they suggest that women in the early years of a career in management are especially apt to accept the masculine stereotype as more successful.

200. ———. "Sex Role Stereotyping, Ability and Performance: Prior Research and New Directions." *Personnel Psychology* 31 (1978): 259–68.
Reviews research in sex-role stereotypes and performance perceptions and examines the ways placement, tokenism, supervisory bias, power, and political behaviors actually affect women's management performance. Calls for research to determine what organizational factors limit women's performance in the organization. Includes references.

201. ———. "Think Manager—Think Male." *Atlanta Economic Review* 26 (March/April 1976): 21–24.
Describes a study created to determine if it is true that when we think "manager" we think male—that is, to determine if successful managers are thought to have characteristics usually attributed to men. Identifies sex-typing of the managerial job as a major barrier to the progress of women in management.

202. Schoonover, Jean Way. "Why Corporate America Fears Women: Business and the New Woman." *Vital Speeches* (1974): 414–16.
Discusses 10 reasons why men fear women as peers on the job, including sexual tension, fear of women's superiority, women's ability to concentrate on her career, and dealing with extraordinary women. Author encourages corporate America to profit and grow through the entry of women into business.

203. "Sex-Related Problems Aren't the Biggest Job Woes of Most Women Managers." *Wall Street Journal*, 29 May 1979, p. 1.
Only 10 percent of the 1,400 women managers surveyed by Alma Baron, University of Wisconsin, listed sex-related problems as their greatest job difficulties. Seventy percent believed they had training opportunities equal to those of male managers, but 25 percent felt they received less informal training than young male managers.

204. Silber, M. "Lady Leaders and Management." *Training and Development Journal* 35 (January 1981): 62–65.
The president of an international psychological consulting firm who conducts workshops for "The Newly Appointed Woman Manager" says attitudes and assumptions about women managers are changing.

He calls upon men and women managers to cooperate and to get down to the "P's" of managing—power, people, politics, and pressure.

205. Smudski, Martha Dardarian. "Sex and the Single Stereotype." *Educational Horizons* 54 (Summer 1976): 167–71.

One of 6 women directors or deputy directors in the 76 Housing and Urban Development field offices, the author says being a woman in management is like being an illegitimate child at a family reunion. This personal account of her experiences in HUD since 1969 details her rise in the management ranks. She calls for a college course designed to overcome cultural stereotypes and to give training in neutral interviewing and the use of assessment centers for identifying potential managers.

206. Spain, Jayne B. "Job Stereotyping—A Time for Change." *Vital Speeches* 39 (July 1973): 549–51.

In a speech delivered at the annual meeting of Printing Industries of Cincinnati (PIC), the vice-chairperson of the U.S. Civil Service Commission says only 3 percent of all women in the labor force are managers and administrators. She cites mental attitudes or stereotyping as the greatest obstacle to the elimination of sex discrimination in employment and asks that women be included in training programs and be considered for jobs on the basis of ability, training, and qualifications.

207. Tobias, Sheila. "Male Chauvinism in Employment." *Journal of College Placement* 33 (1973): 51–56.

Examines 2 studies of managers' perceptions of women and working women's perceptions of themselves. A questionnaire testing managers attitudes toward women includes 7 categories: career orientation, supervisory potential, dependability, deference, emotionality, capability, and life-style. Also includes guidelines for interviewing and hiring women candidates.

208. White, Kay S., and Rowberry, Stewart H. "Management Is a Family Affair," *Atlanta Economic Review* 27 (May/June 1977): 40–47.

Men attending 6 management seminars in the southeastern U.S. in 1975 and 1976 identified 9 major concerns about working with women. Authors suggest comparing work to family situations to help deal more effectively with these concerns.

209. Wilhelm, Marion Bell. "Career Woman's Ally." *Christian Science Monitor,* 30 November 1973, p. 16.

An interview with Jayne Raker Spain, vice-chairperson of the U.S. Civil Service Commission. She tells why able men fear able women and what kind of women are most likely to succeed in the male-dominated executive world.

210. Willett, Rosalyn S. "Working in a 'Man's World': The Woman Executive." In *Woman in Sexist Society: Studies in Power and Powerlessness,* edited by Vivian Gornich and Barbara K. Moran. New York: Basic Books, 1971.

Reviews the status of women workers and myths about women in management and discusses the biological and behavioral differences between men and women as related to ability, aptitude, and qualification. Concludes with a discussion of stress and responsibility and calls for more equal work and child care arrangements within families.

211. "Women's Plaint: Executive Suite Out of Reach." *U.S. News and World Report* 84 (December 8, 1980): 54.

Progress report on the number of women executives indicates that, while male and female MBA graduates were hired for similar jobs at nearly equal pay, after 7 years men held better jobs and earned, on the average, $14,000 a year more than women with identical social/academic backgrounds. Female stereotypes make it difficult for women to remain at the top once they get there. Author cites cases of Jane Cahill Pfeiffer at NBC and Mary E. Cunningham at Bendix.

Discrimination and Minorities

212. "Bank Aide Sees Misunderstanding of Women's Role in Work Force." *New York Times*, 18 September 1977, p. 9.

The female vice-president of a Philadelphia bank told the Joint Congressional Economic Committee that there are large numbers of women entering management and the professions, but employers and government don't have the facts and perspective to understand how this is changing social and economic issues. She states that most women work to support themselves and others.

213. "Bank of America Bias against Women Is Seen by Equality Unit Aide." *Wall Street Journal*, 24 December 1971, p. 16.

According to the Equal Employment Opportunity Commission, the nation's biggest commercial bank, Bank of America, discriminates against women employees. Women are not treated fairly in promotion to management positions, particularly in the international division.

214. Baron, Alma S., and Reeves, Elton T. "How Effective Has Affirmative Action Legislation Been?" *Personnel Administrator* 22 (January 1977): 47–49.

Teachers in the Management Institute surveyed over 1,000 management women to determine if there was a difference in their positions in the work force since affirmative action and if affirmative action rulings opened new opportunities for them giving them a reasonable chance for promotions in their companies. Responses led the authors to conclude that affirmative action has changed the job climate.

215. Bartol, Kathryn M.; Anderson, Carl R.; and Schneier, Craig Eric. "Sex and Ethnic Effects on Motivation to Manage among College Business Students." *Journal of Applied Psychology* 66 (February 1981): 40–44.

College business students at 2 state universities—one predominantly White and one predominantly Black—participated in a study to determine possible sex and ethnic differences in the motivation to manage. Significant differences were found, and the authors call for longitudinal studies to find to what extent the differences slow the upward mobility of Black and female business students. Includes tables and references.

216. Beckman, Gail McKnight. "Legal Barriers, What Barriers?" *Atlanta Economic Review* 26 (March/April 1976): 15–20.

Reviews 7 major areas in laws pertaining to business where women have experienced discrimination: (1) common law restrictions on the capacity of married women; (2) prohibitions about sex appropriate employment; (3) wage differential; (4) hours of work; (5) pregnancy and maternity leaves-of-absence; (6) educational opportunity and the law; (7) weight-lifting requirements. Compares aptitudes and attitudes of males and females and outlines problems of married women managers.

217. Bender, Marilyn. "Black and Female: Asset." *New York Times,* 6 June 1971, sec. 3, p. 3.

The first Black women MBAs are entering the job market and finding that it's an advantage to be both Black and female. Women MBAs graduating from the Columbia Graduate School of Business in the past 2 years were all placed with major corporations at salaries of $14,000 plus. Several women executives, including Patricia Roberts Harris, are quoted. Includes photographs.

218. "Black Women Executives Speak Out." *Black Enterprise* 5 (August 1974): 20.

Text of interviews with 6 successful Black businesswomen. They discuss proteges/mentors, personal role models, conflicts between their personal and professional lives, occupational mobility, and the future of Black women in business. Includes photographs.

219. "Black Women Managers." *Management Review* 70 (March 1981): 6.

Only 2 percent, or 107,000 of Black women workers, are managers. However more Black women are earning the technical degrees that qualify them for management positions, and more of them are assertively seeking their own advancement.

220. Blaxall, Martha, and Reagan, Barbara, eds. *Women and the Workplace: The Implications of Occupational Segregation.* Chicago: University of Chicago Press, 1976.

Based on a 1975 conference on occupational segregation sponsored by the Committee on the Status of Women in the Economics Profession, American Economic Association. Includes chapters by Kenneth

Boulding, Harold J. Leavitt, Martha W. Griffiths, Jessie Bernard, Elise Boulding, Rosabeth Moss Kanter, and Myra H. Strober. Covers the social institutions, historical roots, and economic dimensions of occupational segregation and suggests ways of combating it.

221. Burrow, Martha G. "New Wine in Old Goatskins: Creating New Management Settings." *Personnel Administrator* 25 (April 1980): 51–53+.

Author divides male managers into 2 groups—those who have accepted women in management and those who haven't. Although many corporations espouse integration of women managers, the reality is often different.

222. Clarke, Richard V. "Playing to Win." *Essence* 11 (March 1981): 45+.

In an excerpt from his book, *Opportunities for the Minority College Graduate 1980,* the head of a New York executive search firm gives minority women advice on management positions. He says social conditioning, competition, and specialization are obstacles to women's success.

223. Cook, Joan. "Company Aides Ponder Women's Rights." *New York Times,* 21 May 1975, p. 93.

An assistant vice-president of AT&T speaks at the Stevens Institute of Technology's conference on "Women in Management." He discusses AT&T's 1973 settlement of a federal sex-discrimination suit, notes that the time-frame for complying with most mandated changes is difficult, and feels that consciousness raising at all levels of management is necessary for examining attitudes and prejudices against women in management.

224. Đ'Aprix, Roger M. "Blacks, Women, and the Conscience of a Company Man." *Business and Society Review* (Summer 1976): 55–57.

The manager of employee communications for Xerox Corporation chronicles his growth from a "card-carrying, Establishment, White liberal" to a manager who takes responsibility for corrective action in matters of sex and racial discrimination, not because it's the law, but simply because it's the right thing to do. He believes that White males may have to accept some career delays in order to share available management positions with women and minorities.

225. DeWitt, Karen. "Black Women in Business." *Black Enterprise* 5 (August 1974): 14+.

Notes the rise in the number of Black women in banking, the stock market, real estate, and as business owners. Profiles 5 successful Black women and includes photographs and graphs.

226. Eby, Sheila Mary. "One of the Gang—But Not One of the Boys." *Working Woman* 5 (June 1980): 31–35+.

Identifies specific problems involved in being the "token" woman in a male-oriented business world: visibility, undue attention, questions about one's personal life, isolation, and subjective performance evaluations. Includes tips for locating companies that deal fairly with women.

227. Fernandez, John P. *Racism and Sexism in Corporate Life*. Lexington, MA: D.C. Heath, 1981.

Results of a study of the attitudes and opinions of 4,209 Native American, Asian, Black, Hispanic, and White male and female managers. Chapter 4 summarizes the present situation and treatment of female managers and concludes that sexist attitudes and behaviors are still a very real problem in most corporations. Includes numerous tables and figures, index, extensive bibliography, and appendix, "What Are Racism and Sexism?"

228. Flanders, Dwight P., and Anderson, Peggy Engelhardt. "Sex Discrimination in Employment: Theory and Practice," *Industrial and Labor Relations Review* 26 (April 1973): 938–55.

Microeconomic theory is used to test 4 hypotheses regarding male-female labor force mix. A sample of male and female managers from personnel departments in 61 firms were studied to test the hypothesis that annual salaries, educational levels, work experience patterns, and age patterns do not differ significantly between males and females within any industrial group or managerial level.

229. Fretz, C. F., and Hayman, Joanne. "Progress for Women, Men Are Still More Equal." *Harvard Business Review* 51 (September/October 1973): 133–42.

Twenty companies were surveyed regarding their equal opportunity programs. Results of the research survey show that women at all levels represent 36 percent of the 20 companies' total work force, but female officials, managers, and professionals comprise only one percent. The status of management involvement, compensation and benefits, and affirmative action in the 20 companies were reviewed, and 6 recommendations for implementing an EEO policy are included.

230. Gallese, Liz Roman. "30% Women." *Wall Street Journal*, 1 December 1980, p. 26.
Describes CBS' affirmative action program which raised the percentage of women in management positions at CBS from 20 to 30 percent in 7 years. Their policy includes a women's advisory panel, posting of all management positions below the level of vice-president, and management seminars for women.

231. ———. "Up the Ladder Blues: White Males Complain They Are Now Victims of Job Discrimination." *Wall Street Journal*, 28 February 1974, p. 1.
White males claim reverse discrimination as a result of the implementation of EEOC's affirmative action policies in large corporations. The president of a consulting firm specializing in affirmative action problems says males are being treated fairly: it's just that their previous privileged position as White males hasn't prepared them to compete with the other three-quarters of the world.

232. Graves, Earl G. "Battle of Sex and Race." *Black Enterprise* 11 (September 1980): 7.
This editorial provides background for this issue's cover story on how Black men and women and White women are competing for jobs in the executive suite. The editor claims that much of the progress White women have made in the past 15 years is due to affirmative action programs originally developed for Blacks and that Black women face a double jeopardy in their search for success—racism and sexism.

233. Hancock, Wilma Loraine Bergman. "An Analysis of the Impact of Federal Laws and Regulations on Opportunities for Women in Management." DBA dissertation, Mississippi State University, 1973.
Abstracted in *Dissertation Abstracts International*, v. 34, 1973, #2095-A.

234. Hechinger, Grace. "Catty Claws on the Lib Ladder." *Wall Street Journal*, 24 April 1973, p. 24.
Regrets the attitude of many women professionals and executives who exhibit the "queen bee" syndrome, refusing to help other women achieve the same success they worked so hard to achieve. Men are more likely to be pleased with the success of a protege, believing it reflects on their training abilities.

235. Hennig, Margaret, and Jardim, Anne. "Office Tests Women Face—Sexual and Social." *New York Times,* 1 May 1977, sec. 3, p. 4.

A reprint from the 1976 book *The Managerial Woman* by Hennig and Jardim gives advice on strategies and styles for women to adopt in working effectively with men in the office. Topics discussed include social, sexual, and intellectual tests involved with being the only female in the group, techniques for managing emotions, and advice on dealing with career/family conflicts.

236. Horn, Jack. "Being in the Minority: More Comfortable for Women than Men." *Psychology Today* 10 (October 1976): 38–39.

A professor at the Wharton School studied 83 4-person teams of students in management and organizational behavior courses to determine what happens when men are in the minority. Sixty-two teams had 3 men and one woman, and 21 teams had 3 women and one man. Results showed that men still dominated, even in the 3-women teams, but that they were the least satisfied with their experience. Female members of the male majority teams were the most satisfied with their group experience.

237. Huffmire, Donald. "U.S. Business: The Sex Equality Myth." *Industrial Management* (March 1976): 31–32.

A review of the obstacles remaining to women in management in spite of equal opportunity laws. Advice to upper-level managers and to women who want to become managers.

238. Jensen, Beverly. "Black and Female Too: Career Women Find that the Road to the Top May Be Paved with Racism, Sexism, and Sometimes Both." *Black Enterprise* 6 (July 1976): 26–29.

Profiles and quotes several Black women professionals and managers who have achieved success in spite of the double onus of racism and sexism. The women, who include an administrative assistant, a lawyer, a life insurance general agent, and vice-president and general manager of a radio station, agree that sexism is more of a problem.

239. Lambert, Marge. "The Women Executives." *New York Times,* 11 January 1981, sec. 6, p. 86.

A reader comments on Christine Doudna's November 30 article on "Women at the Top." She accuses corporations of relabeling female-dominated clerical positions as "manager" to influence affirmative action.

240. Larwood, Laurie, and Blackmore, John. "Sex Discrimination in Managerial Selection: Testing Predictions of the Vertical Dyad Linkage Model." *Sex Roles* 4 (June 1978): 359–67.

A study of the behavior of 60 male and female business students shows that members of the same sex tend to aid and promote one another in managerial situations.

241. Lear, Frances. "Industry's Abuse of Women." *New York Times,* 13 June 1974, p. 43.

The head of a management search agency believes that, although corporations employ equal opportunity staff and have lost over $100 million in court actions brought by women, discrimination against women in management still exists. Cites examples of paying women less than male applicants for a position, not hiring qualified women, not promoting highly competent women, and paying lower search fees to women's search firms.

242. " 'Love' in the Office." *Management Review* 68 (November 1979): 5.

According to one estimate, 50 to 80 percent of women workers have faced verbal or physical sexual harassment on the job. A woman who has been sexually harassed must prove that, when she refused the advance, her superior retaliated with threats of firing or loss of promotion.

243. Lublin, Joann S. "The Managers: Mrs. Lowe Has to Deal with Stress and Sexism as Bank-Branch Head; She is among Rising Number of Management Women, But Isolation Is a Problem." *Wall Street Journal,* 26 April 1977, p. 1+.

Profiles Challis Lowe, a woman branch bank manager who earns $25,000+ a year and supervises a staff of 26. Lowe, the first Black female officer, describes her rise to the top, an average work day, and the stresses she encounters trying to combine career and family.

244. Martin, Claude R., Jr. "Support for Women's Lib: Management Performance." *Southern Journal of Business* 7 (February 1972): 17–28.

A study of male and female buyers for 21 retail stores shows no significant difference in their self-evaluation or actual performance of buying responsibilities and activities. Author concludes that, although women perform as well as their male colleagues, they are paid less. Includes footnotes and several tables.

245. "The Mary Cunningham Story." *New York Times,* 15 October 1980, p. 30.

An editorial satirizing the blown-out-of-proportion reporting of 29-year-old Mary E. Cunningham's promotion at Bendix. Claims personal favoritism is nothing new to the corporate world and that gender is the real reason for such attention to Cunningham's case.

246. Mitnick, Margery Manesberg. "Equal Employment Opportunity and Affirmative Action: A Managerial Training Guide." *Personnel Journal* 56 (October 1977): 492–97.

Outlines a presentation personnel officers can give to supervisors regarding Equal Employment Opportunity and Affirmative Action Revised Order No. 4. Discussion should encompass the following areas: laws and enforcement agencies, meaning of EEO and affirmative action, content of affirmative action programs, types of discrimination, penalties, employment practices affected, and review of the company's affirmative action program.

247. "Rarest Breed of Women: Black Businesswomen in the Executive Suites." *Time* 98 (November 8, 1971): 102.

More Black women are entering the fields of advertising, stock brokerage, and banking, but they still have a long way to go in large corporations. The women see sexism as more of a problem than racism.

248. Rayburn, Leticia Gayle. "Do Women Discriminate against Each Other?" *National Public Accounts* 16 (October 1971): 16–19.

A survey of women CPAs indicated they had better working relationships with male supervisors. The author exhorts women to give each other more encouragement and support and to prefer women for positions when male and female candidates are equally qualified.

249. Rose, Gerald L., and Andiappan, P. "Sex Effects on Managerial Hiring Decisions." *Academy of Management Journal* 21 (March 1978): 104–12.

Male and female upper-level students evaluated hypothetical applicants for managerial positions to determine what effect sex of applicant and sex of subordinates have on hiring decisions. Findings indicate that females tend to evaluate applicants more favorably than males. Many participants mentioned sex as a factor when female applicants would be supervising predominantly male subordinates. Includes bibliography.

250. ———, and Stone, Thomas H. "Why Good Job Performance May (Not) Be Rewarded: Sex Factors and Career Development." *Journal of Vocational Behavior* 12 (April 1978): 197–205.

Reported findings of a study to test the effects of 3 sex variables on managerial career evaluations. Findings show no differences in evaluations by male and female evaluators.

251. Rosen, Benson, and Jerdee, Thomas H. "On-the-Job Sex Bias: Increasing Managerial Awareness." *Personnel Administrator* 22 (January 1977): 15–18.

The authors of the multimedia "SRA Sex Discrimination Awareness Program" discuss the consequences of sex bias as it affects job assignments, experience, and reward systems. They suggest using in-basket exercises, role-play exercises, and case discussions in workshops on how sex bias affects managerial decisions.

252. Schwartz, Eleanor Brantley, and Rago, James J., Jr. "Beyond Tokenism: Women as True Corporate Peers." *Business Horizons* 16 (December 1973): 69–76.

Discusses male-female role conflicts related to corporate management. Social propaganda, family environment, expectations of family members, and parental deprivation are listed as factors in the socialization process that cause many executives to become deprived-dependent people who have difficulty accepting women in roles traditionally considered male. Advice to corporations on goals, policy, and action for integrating women into management. Includes bibliographical references.

253. Shaeffer, Ruth Gilbert, and Lynton, Edith F. *Corporate Experiences in Improving Women's Job Opportunities.* New York: Conference Board, 1979.

A study of major organizations and changes in the status of working women from 1970–75. Chapter 5, "Some Experiences with Improving Women's Opportunities in Managerial and Professional Jobs," discusses recruiting, hiring, and upgrading women into professional and managerial roles.

254. Sheperd, William G., and Levin, Sharon G. "Managerial Discrimination in Large Firms." *Review of Economics and Statistics* 55 (1973): 412–22.

Results of research on managerial discrimination in 200 U.S. industrial firms show that participation of male Blacks and women in managerial jobs is still token. Most opportunities for women are in traditionally "women's" industries. Includes tables and references.

255. Simmons, Judy. "Struggle for the Executive Suite: Blacks vs White Women." *Black Enterprise* 11 (September 1980): 24–27.

Affirmative action programs aimed at helping Blacks have benefited White women, says the author. Between 1974 and 1978 the percentage of White women in managerial jobs increased from 3.6 to 15.5 percent, but during the same period the percentage of Blacks in management increased only eight-tenths of a percent to 3.7 percent. Personnel officers cite lack of education and experience as the factors that keep Blacks from management ranks.

256. Simpson, Janice C. "Woman Boss." *Black Enterprise* 11 (January 1981): 20–21+.

Only 2 percent of all Black working women are managers; most of them are in personnel and public relations. Middle-aged White men frequently experience difficulty in working for a Black woman boss, says Cecilia Johnson, director of the Human Rights Commission in Des Moines, IA.

257. Smolowe, Constance. "Corporations and Women: A Decade of Near-Ms.'s." *MBA: Master in Business Administration* 8 (February 1974): 32–34.

Reviews the progress or lack of progress in affirmative action in such firms as AT&T, Sears, GE, Ford, Xerox, IBM, and Aetna as they face the possibility of legal suits under Title VII of the Civil Rights Act.

258. Stacy, Donald R. "The Intrepid Executive's Guide to Avoiding Sex Discrimination." *Atlanta Economic Review* 26 (March/April 1976): 9–14.

Focuses on the courts' attempt to deal with the sex discrimination which has impeded the entry of women into management. Gives a detailed look at the Equal Pay Amendment to the Fair Labor Standards Act (1963), Title VII of the Civil Rights Act (1964), and Executive Order 11,246 (1965). A guide to interpreting Title VII is followed by information on portions of the Equal Employment Opportunity Commission's *Guidelines on Sex Discrimination*.

259. Thompson, Jacqueline A. "On Being Black and Female and an Accountant." *MBA: Master in Business Administration* 9 (February 1975): 35–38.

Black professional women encounter 2 forms of discrimination—sexism and racism—but they are making gains in the field of accounting.

Women accountants in private industry and government discuss salary, opportunities for advancement, and being the only woman on an auditing team.

260. Weathers, Diane. "Winning under the Double Whammy." *Savvy* 2 (April 1981): 34–40.

Although being a "two-fer," or Black and female, may be an advantage at the entry level, promotions and positions with real responsibility are still difficult to obtain. So far most Black women managers work in the public sector.

261. "Women Offered Managerial Aid." *Christian Science Monitor,* 9 April 1975, p. 22.

James L. Hayes, president of the American Management Association, says sexist prejudice still exists in business. A major concern of women attending seminars sponsored by AMA is how to get ahead.

Education

262. Abrahms, Sally. "Future Captains of Industry." *Working Woman* 6 (June 1981): 67–70.
Profiles 7 women in the 1981 graduating class at Harvard Business School. The average starting salary for a 1981 Harvard MBA is $34,500. Includes photographs.

263. Baron, Alma Spann. "Management Women Ask: Where Can I Go from Here?" *Business Quarterly* 45 (Summer 1980): 33–36.
Of over 200 women who attended a management development seminar at the University of Wisconsin within the past 5 years, 85 percent said they wished to advance in management. Forty percent perceived their chances as very good to excellent. Some women feel lack of education has hampered their management progress and they are correcting the situation—25 percent of MBA students today are women.

264. Burke, Ronald J., and Weir, Tamara. "Readying the Sexes for Women in Management." *Business Horizons* 20 (June 1977): 30–35.
Describes courses and workshops including the study of women in management offered to MBA candidates at York University, Ontario, Canada. Analyzes some handicaps to women in management.

265. Comer, Nancy Axelrad. "Executive Jobs: How You Can Land Them; Women MBAs." *Mademoiselle* 79 (September 1974): 160–63.
Author says the first step towards landing an executive job is getting an MBA. Article notes the increase in the percentage of women in MBA programs and lists the top 7 graduate business schools. The average salary for a newly-graduated MBA is $14,500 and large corporations afford more opportunity to women business graduates.

266. "Convention Planned by Career Women." *New York Times*, 5 May 1974, p. 119.
Announces a Sears-Roebuck Foundation grant to assist women in graduate business education. Grants will be in the form of revolving loans with repayment beginning after graduation. The intent of the

program is to enable more women to obtain MBAs, and the deans of 110 graduate business schools will be informed that, under the program, students may apply for up to $2,000 worth of loans a year.

267. Cooper, Cary, and Lewis, Barbara. "Femanager Boom."*Management Today* (July 1979): 47–48.
Results of a questionnaire which received responses from 532 female management undergraduates shows that women are now more optimistic about management opportunities.

268. Diamond, Helen. "A New Responsibility for Business Education." *Journal of Business Education* 53 (October 1977): 7–8.
Identifies communication, leadership, accounting, and decision making as skills female students need for management positions. Includes questions and suggestions for business educators who are responsible for educating women in these skills.

269. "Female Enrollment: Explosive Growth." *MBA: Master in Business Administration* 11 (September 1977): 40–41.
From 1971–72 to 1975–76 the number of women taking the Graduate Management Admissions Test increased from 8,234 to 29,741. Data from the Educational Testing Service indicate the number of women working toward PhDs in business administration is also on the rise.

270. Fox, Eugene H. "Female Enrollment Outpacing Male Enrollment among Accredited AACSB Members." *AACSB Bulletin* 13 (Spring 1977): 27–31.
Results of a study of member schools in the American Association of Collegiate Schools of Business to determine answers to questions about female enrollment. Predicts a one-to-one, male-female enrollment ratio in business schools within the next decade, especially in MBA programs and certain majors. Includes tables and appendix.

271. Gordon, Francine E., and Strober, Myra H. "Initial Observations on a Pioneer Cohort: 1974: Women MBAs." *Sloan Management Review* 19 (Winter 1978): 15–23.
A study compared men and women from the 1974 MBA class at Stanford to determine whether female MBAs were more or less likely to succeed than their male peers. Graduates were compared on the basis of background, career planning, career and life-style goals, job search, and starting salaries. Includes references.

272. Guidry, Frederick H. "More Women Managers? Pioneer Graduate Program in Management at Simmons College Draws 600 Applicants." *Christian Science Monitor,* 2 April 1974, p. 5.

Describes the first graduate program in management at a women's college. The program was designed by professors Anne Jardim and Margaret Hennig, authors of *The Managerial Woman.* There were over 600 applicants for the first section of students.

273. Hammel, Lisa, "For Liberal Arts, a Business Touch." *New York Times,* 21 March 1974, p. 48.

Marymount Manhattan College announces a pilot program combining liberal arts study with a 4-year management course for women. In addition the liberal arts faculty will train in management techniques. Management faculty and a planning coordinator will be paid through a $75,000 Mellon Foundation grant.

274. "HBS Management Internships for Women." *MBA: Master in Business Administration* 7 (March 1973): 48.

Four women participate in a deferred admission program at Harvard. The women will gain experience by working for 2 years for employers contacted by Harvard and will then enter the MBA program at Harvard.

275. Jensen, Michael C. "Students Are Bullish about the MBA." *New York Times,* 30 April 1978, sec. 12, p. 8.

Enrollments surge at the more than 500 graduate business schools in the nation. In 1976 5,000 of the 42,728 MBAs were awarded to women whose job prospects upon graduation were good. Starting salaries for Harvard MBAs in 1977 were averaging more than $22,000, and the employment trend demanding MBAs is expected to continue for some time.

276. Johnston, Mary Jean. "A Study of Women MBA Graduates in Management Positions." PhD dissertation, University of Pittsburgh, 1974.

Abstracted in *Dissertation Abstracts International,* September 1974, v. 35, no. 3, #1419-A.

277. ———. "Women MBA Graduates in Management Positions." *Delta Kappa Gamma Bulletin* 41 (Summer 1975): 31–36.

Survey of women MBA graduates of 5 leading MBA programs between 1968–72 provides data on types of positions they hold, starting salaries compared with male MBAs, evaluation of their training, and their perceptions of problems unique to women in management. Predicts gradual increase in the number of women in management. Includes tables and references.

278. Kirmser, Earl. "MBA Program Aids Women." *New York Times,* 18 February 1973, sec. 1, p. 140.

The C. W. Post Center of Long Island University established a scholarship program to help pay tuition for women seeking graduate business degrees. Twenty-three-year-old Margaret Murphy, the first graduate of the program, seeks a marketing management position in a large corporation.

279. Krasny, Robin. "Storming Harvard Business School: Diary of the First Year." *Savvy* 2 (June 1981): 32–38.

The diary of a Princeton *cum laude* graduate's first months at Harvard Business School. Her first semester grades included one Excellent, one Satisfactory, and one "loop" or Low Pass.

280. "Labor Letter." *Wall Street Journal,* 13 May 1980, p. 1.

Chatham College in Pittsburgh and IBM give women liberal arts graduates the opportunity to take a 6-week introductory business administration course.

281. Langway, Lynn; Dentzer, Susan; Malamud, Phyllis; Foote, Donna; and Copeland, Jeff B. "Women and the Executive Suite." *Newsweek* 98 (September 14, 1981): 65+.

Although women now account for 25 percent of all MBA candidates, they still comprise only 6 percent of all managers. Many obstacles still remain for women in management and, as the number of women increases in certain fields, so does evidence of male hostility and sexual harassment. A futurist predicts that 50 women may be chief executive officers (CEOs) of *Fortune* 500 corporations by the year 2000.

282. Maeroff, Gene I. "Tight Job Market Adds to Demand for Admissions to Business Schools." *New York Times,* 3 March 1976, p. 33.

With the exception of the oil, mining, and natural resources industries, promotions aren't coming very readily, thereby leading people to return to school. Many are choosing graduate business school, and the number of candidates for the Educational Testing Service's business school board examination increased 12 percent during the last year. More women and Blacks are seeking admission; 10 percent of this year's freshmen women desire careers in business.

283. "MBAs and Sex." *Wall Street Journal,* 25 February 1980, p. 21.
A 1978 graduate of the Stanford School of Business disputes language in Charles W. Steven's February 11 article on competition for MBAs. The writer claims that 28 percent of the "top men" mentioned in Steven's article were women.

284. Moorhead, John D. "Getting More Women Executives." *Christian Science Monitor,* 1 April 1976, p. 2.
Describes the Simmons College program of management training for women. The 3-semester course has 85 women between the ages of 22 and 51 enrolled and emphasizes the behavioral differences between men and women.

285. O'Toole, Patricia. "The Truth about the Value of an MBA." *Savvy* 2 (July 1981): 14–15+.
Over 650 institutions now offer MBA degrees, and 54,000 students will graduate with MBAs this year, twice as many as in 1970. Women now comprise 30 percent of MBA classes, compared to 4 percent 10 years ago, but their average salaries 5 years after graduation are only $30,000, compared to $38,000 for men. The best combination is an MBA with an undergraduate technical degree.

286. Rankin, Deborah. "Business of Women is Business." *New York Times,* 30 April 1978, sec. 12, p. 8.
A 23-year-old woman who is a member of the Washington staff of Ernst and Ernst, a national accounting firm, joins the growing number of liberal arts students who combine traditional liberal arts courses with business majors. A survey of 67 women's colleges shows that almost one-third of the women undergraduates major in business administration, management, or economics. Describes course offerings at several well-known colleges.

287. Reha, Rose K. "How Colleges of Business Prepare Women for Management Roles." *Delta Kappa Gamma Bulletin* 45 (Fall 1978): 41–46.
Most of the 397 colleges of business in the U.S. and Canada do not offer any course about the special needs and problems of women in management, according to data from a questionnaire on the preparation of women for management roles.

288. ———. "Preparing Women for Management Roles." *Business Horizons* 32 (April 1979): 68–71.
Presents data from a survey of 397 deans or administrators of colleges of business in the U.S. and Canada. The author notes the lack of

courses geared to specific problems of women in management and the lack of female faculty in management schools, despite the fact that 21 percent of the 1976–77 MBA student population was female.

289. Reynolds, Sydney. "Women on the Line." *MBA: Master in Business Administration* 9 (1975): 27–30.

The president of a recruiting firm which places women MBAs says that more women are moving into line positions in corporations. She tells how several women have solved the problem of gaining the respect and cooperation of employees and offers advice to management about supporting their female managers.

290. Robertson, Wyndham. "Women MBAs, Harvard '73—How They're Doing." *Fortune* 98 (August 28, 1978): 50–54+.

Five years later the 34 women (out of a class of 776) who graduated from the Harvard Business School in 1973 were all working or looking for work: 26 of them were full-time salaried employees, half were married, and 6 were mothers. They were all over the world in jobs in banking, consulting, sales, marketing, advertising, accounting, government, college administration, and corporate planning. One also graduated from Harvard Law School and is a member of a law firm; another received a doctorate in business from Harvard. The median salary for those working full-time is $32,250, more than half of the 34 live in New York, Boston, or their suburbs. Individual women in the group are profiled in detail.

291. Rolfes, Rebecca. "Work/Study Programs for Exec MBAs." *Working Woman* 6 (March 1981): 16+.

Describes the "Executive MBA," an 18-month to 2-year program of full-time work and part-time concentrated study. Admission is competitive and many students have already earned MAs or PhDs. Includes a partial list of colleges and universities that offer Executive MBA programs.

292. Sandler, Bernice. "A Feminist Approach to the Women's Colleges." Speech presented to the Southern Association of Colleges for Women, Washington, DC, 30 November 1971.

Abstracted in *Research in Education,* ED 071 561.

293. Schermerhorn, John R.; Snelson, Ann L.; and Leader, Gerald C. "Women in Management: The MBA Student's Perspective." *Academy of Management Proceedings* (1975): 451–53.

Researchers surveyed male and female MBA candidates regarding their views of effective managers and women managers. Results show male and female students view the effective manager similarly, but male students already exhibit tendencies to sex-stereotype their female classmates. Includes table, summary, appendix, and bibliographical references.

294. Schwartz, Eleanor Brantley. "An Evaluation of the Application and Implementation of Title VII as It Applies to Women in Management." PhD dissertation, Georgia State University, 1970.
Abstracted in *Dissertation Abstracts International*, April 1970, v. 30, no. 10, #4080-A.

295. Stead, Bette Ann. "Educating Women for Administration." *Business Horizons* 18 (April 1975): 51–56.
A business administration professor identifies 6 course objectives of the "Woman in Administration" course taught spring 1974 at the University of Houston and gives examples of successful class activities. Reading, class participation, and a major project constitute the 3 requirements for a grade in this senior level course.

296. ———. "Women Management Faculty: An Empirical Look at Their Status." Houston University, TX, 1975.
Abstracted in *Resources in Education*, ED 122 693.

297. Steiger, Jo Ann M., and Szanton, Eleanor S. *Women's Participation in Management and Policy Development in the Education Division*. Washington, DC: National Advisory Council on Women's Educational Programs, 1977.
Abstracted in *Resources in Education*, ED 146 696.

298. Stronk, Mary E. "Women's Job Market: A Paradox of Sorts." *MBA: Master in Business Administration* 7 (March 1973): 11.
Presents the views of women MBA students, corporate recruiters, and business school placement officers regarding the enthusiasm or reluctance to hire women MBAs. Banks are most likely to hire women; investment houses are the most reluctant.

299. Underwood, June. "Leadership Training in the Business Curriculum." *Business Education Forum* 32 (December 1977): 5–6+.
Answers to questionnaires given to management employees of one of Oregon's largest financial institutions were compared to see what men

and women felt women needed to be effective managers. Seventy percent of those responding agreed that women need special training for management. Training needs most frequently checked by respondents include in ranked order: (1) handling career and family responsibilities; (2) working with customers who lack confidence in women managers; (3) building self-confidence as a manager; (4) women supervising men; and (5) obtaining acceptance in a male peer group.

300. Werner, Laurie. "MBA: The Fantasy and the Reality." *Working Woman* 4 (December 1979): 37–41.

Women MBAs say the degree means opportunity, money, credibility, faster promotions, and job mobility. Statistics show that in 1979 20 to 35 percent of all MBA candidates were women with almost 5,000 women earning MBAs in 1976, over 6,500 in 1977 and an estimated 10,000 women graduating with MBAs in 1979. Although the situation looks good the author cautions that an MBA does not guarantee a job or future promotions, nor does it guarantee job or field satisfaction. The dean of Harvard Business School predicts a glut of MBAs by 1983.

301. "What's Needed to Become a Company Superstar." *Business Week* (September 15, 1980): 145–46.

The fastest route to success for women in management is to combine an undergraduate degree in engineering with an MBA, says the owner of a Boston human resources management firm. The dean of the Graduate School of Management at Purdue University claims almost all of the women degree candidates there have technical or engineering backgrounds.

302. Whitcomb, Helen. "Preparing Women Business Students for Executive Positions." *Business Education World* 58 (May/June 1978): 3–4, 19.

Advice to women business students and teachers includes the philosophy of upward job mobility, importance of role models, career planning, and assessing the job market. Stresses the importance of self-knowledge and the evaluation of personal attributes as essential in career planning.

303. "Why Women Need Their Own MBA Programs." *Business Week* (February 23, 1974): 102+.

Professors Jardim and Hennig, authors of *The Managerial Woman*, designed a graduate business program especially for females to be initiated in the fall of 1974 at Simmons College in Boston. The program will stress course work in the behavioral, structural, and psychological aspects of management from a woman's viewpoint. Case studies will be used in the curriculum.

304. "Women MBAs Earn Less than Male Counterparts." *Christian Science Monitor,* 29 April 1981, p. 23.

A survey of 73 female and 50 male MBA graduates shows that 2 to 3 years after graduation, women earn an average of $4,000 less than their male classmates. Men said they would like to earn $42,000 and women said $31,000.

Profiles of Women Managers

305. Ahnen, Pearl. "How Business Editor Broke 'Bill and Mary Saga'." *Editor & Publisher* 113 (October 25, 1980): 10.

Louis Heldman, business editor of the *Detroit Free Press,* relates how reliable sources tipped him off to the announcement William Agee, chairperson of Bendix, made at the September 24 meeting with 600 employees. Agee denied a romantic involvement with 29-year-old Mary Cunningham, vice-president for strategic planning at Bendix, and Heldman's byline appeared on the story nationally.

306. Bekey, Michele. "Overnight Success." *Working Woman* 5 (December 1980): 60–62+.

Describes the "overnight success" of 4 women: a vice-president at 20th Century-Fox, a California congresswoman, a U.S. congress-woman, and a screenwriter. Talent, being in the right place at the right time, the help of mentors, and the willingness to take risks are factors in the quick rise to the top.

307. Bennetts, Leslie. "Many Widows Find a New Life Running Husband's Business." *New York Times,* 24 September 1979, p. 16.

Instead of selling businesses when their husbands die, more and more widows are electing to run the businesses themselves. They experience problems initially with some employees and clients who don't want to work with a woman, but advice from accountants and lawyers and business courses and federal programs for minority business owners help the women succeed. Profiles women who have tripled or qua-drupled sales in their companies.

308. Bernstein, Peter W. "Upheaval at Bendix." *Fortune* 102 (November 3, 1980): 48–50+.

In-depth report on troubles at Bendix Corporation over the appointment of Mary E. Cunningham, 29, as vice-president for strategic planning only 15 months after graduation from Harvard Business School. Some believe her promotions were so rapid because of a romantic involvement with 43-year-old Bendix chairperson William M. Agee. Discusses in detail Agee's plans for expanding the corporation.

309. Bethany, Marilyn. "Woman's Ways with Executive Suites." *New York Times Magazine* (August 10, 1980): 48–51.
Colored photos of the offices of 6 executive women are shown, with descriptions of each decor. Women include Brooke Astor, Diane von Furstenberg, Beverly Sills, Dianne Feinstein, Mary Wells Lawrence, and Barbara Gallagher.

310. Bradley, Tess. "A Roll-Call of Enterprising Women in U.S. Business History." *Christian Science Monitor,* 1 March 1976, p. 11.
A book review of Caroline Bird's *Enterprising Women: Their Contributions to the American Economy, 1776–1976.* The careers of 100 women are reviewed under such headings as "Family Business," "Money Makers," and "The Professionals."

311. Campbell, Bebe Moore. "Diary of a Corporate Misfit." *Essence* 11 (March 1981): 100–01+.
A personal narrative of one woman's entry into the corporate world. After evaluating her year's tenure as assistant editor of an employee newspaper in Washington, DC, she returned to free-lance writing.

312. "Confident Enough to Drop Out." *Business Week* (July 7, 1980): 96–97.
Some women are leaving the corporate world for freedom and personal growth. Most are in their 30s and 40s in middle-level management positions and have exchanged salary and perks for independence.

313. Cook, Joan. "Women in Industry to Be Honored." *New York Times,* 9 April 1976, p. 79.
Announces the second annual Tribute to Women and Industry (TWIN) awards banquet, to be held in Cresskill, NJ, to honor 38 women in middle- and upper-management and their companies. The Ridgewood YWCA sponsors the event to increase awareness of women achievers and encourage young women to plan their careers.

314. Cook, Suzanne Mary Halbrook. "Personnel Value Profile of Selected Women Executives." DBA dissertation, Texas Tech University, 1973.
Abstracted in *Dissertation Abstracts International,* July 1974, v. 35, no. 1, #26-A.

315. Cummings, Judith, and Krebs, Alvin. "Ripples of Bendix Resignation Reach Washington Press." *New York Times*, 15 October 1980, sec. 2, p. 2.

A series by Gail Sheehy on the Mary E. Cunningham-William Agee situation at Bendix precipitates a clash between the *Washington Post* and the *Washington Star*. Both papers claim exclusive story rights.

316. Cunningham, Mary E. "Mary E. Cunningham on: Corporate Ethics and Social Prejudice." *Working Woman* 6 (July 1981): 53.

The 29-year-old MBA who resigned from Bendix in October 1980 after rumors of a romantic involvement with chairperson William Agee says U.S. productivity is affected by 3 factors: the absence of a shared system of values, a less than humane working environment, and prejudice. She advises the corporate world about utilizing women managers to avoid the unseen costs of prejudice.

317. Cunningham, Sheila. "She Bought the Place." *Working Woman* 6 (September 1981): 67–71.

Profiles Geraldine Stutz, head and part-owner of Henri Bendel, the New York women's specialty store. Since becoming president in 1957 at age 33, Stutz has increased annual sales from $3 million to $20 million in 1981.

318. Durie, Elspeth. "McCann & Co. Elects Woman Chairman: Burdus; I'm Really Interested in People." *Advertising Age* 50 (May 14, 1979): sec. 2, S16+.

Ann Burdus becomes head of Britain's second largest advertising agency after a year as executive vice-president with McCann-Erickson International in New York. She compares the advertising business in England and the U.S.

319. "Executive Suite: Interviews with Women Executives." *Harper's Bazaar* 109 (August 1976): 83+.

Ten women achievers agree that hard work is the fastest way to get ahead. Includes photographs and direct quotes from an editor, a publisher, a college president, a corporate president and vice-president, and the secretary of Housing and Urban Development.

320. Faier, Joan. "Three Top Women Discuss Success: C. A. Hills; J. Pauley; P. R. Harris." *Harper's Bazaar* 111 (January 1978): 72–73+.

Jane Pauley, television newscaster; Patricia Roberts Harris, secretary of Housing and Urban Development; and Carla Anderson Hills, former secretary of HUD, discuss political life, supportive families, career planning, and discrimination. Includes quotes.

321. Fischer, Mary A. "Step by Step: The Smart Moves and Big Hurdles of Rollene Saal." *Savvy* 2 (August 1981): 39–42.

Chronicles the rise of 48-year-old Rollene Saal to editor-in-chief of Bantam Books and her resignation in June after the appointment of Jack Romanos as publisher at Bantam. Her forte is finding best-selling popular entertainment books for women, who make up 80 percent of all book buyers.

322. Flanagan, William. "What Are Top Women Earners Like? Some Clues from Corporations." *Vogue* 168 (September 1978): 186.

A management consulting firm conducted a survey of women corporate officers and found that women do not have the highest job titles; their salaries are as much as $10,000 below those of their male peers; they are older, have worked longer for their promotions, and rarely get the same "perks" as their male colleagues. The study reveals most of the women officers refuse transfers and spend less time traveling than male officers.

323. "Four Who Made It." *Time* 99 (March 20, 1972): 82–84.

Profiles 4 entrepreneurial women: the president of a computer time-sharing company, the chief of an ad agency, a savings and loan owner, and a supermarket vice-president. All 4 are over 40 and earn $45,000–$60,000.

324. "The Game's Played that Way, Lady!" *Forbes* 120 (July 15, 1977): 56.

Janice LaRouche, a successful career counselor for women, teaches a 10-week course on corporate politics, the negative aspects of social conditioning, taking responsibility, and being assertive. She earns over $100,000 a year without advertising.

325. Halcomb, Ruth. *Women Making It: Patterns and Profiles of Success.* New York: Atheneum, 1979.

By the author of *Money and the Working Ms.* (1974), *Recession-Proof Jobs* (1976), and *Get Yours* (1976). Chapters 1–9 cover topics of women and success, money, power, networks and mentors, competition, and balancing career and family. Chapters 10–15 profile 6 successful professional women in the public, corporate, and academic spheres.

326. Hayes, Thomas C. "Agee's Design Now Clouded." *New York Times,* 14 October 1980, sec. 4, p. 1.

William Agee, chairperson at Bendix, discusses his plans for large-scale changes in the corporation and the resignation of Mary E. Cunningham, vice-president for strategic planning, after speculation of a romantic involvement with Agee. Agee wants to move Bendix from automobile and housing markets to high technology.

327. ———. "High Bendix Executive Quits Post amid Controversy over Favoritism." *New York Times,* 10 October 1980, p. 1+.

Mary E. Cunningham resigns as vice-president for strategic planning at Bendix Corporation after 2 weeks of controversy over her promotion by chairperson William Agee. Her plans are unclear, but the directors of Bendix indicate there are several opportunities available for her.

328. Hennig, Margaret, and Jardim, Anne. "Superwomen." *Across the Board* 14 (July 1977): 27–33.

Authors Hennig and Jardim, founders and directors of Simmons College Graduate Program in Management, give excerpts from their book *The Managerial Woman.* Twenty-five top management women in business and industry relate stories from their childhood, and Hennig and Jardim draw conclusions about the common experiences which shaped the women's personalities and made them successful.

329. "How to Make the Most of Today's Opportunities." *U.S. News and World Report* 81 (September 27, 1976): 79–82.

In an interview Dr. Barrie Sanford Greiff, psychiatrist at Harvard Business School, tells how a woman can prepare herself for a business-management career and describes a course titled "The Executive Family" which he teaches at Harvard. Dr. Greiff answers questions about career conflicts between husband and wife, the stereotype of the woman boss, the problems involved with combining careers and family, the possibility of a woman president, and the dangers of the dual-career family.

330. Jacoby, Susan. "William and Mary . . . ." *New York Times,* 19 October 1980, sec. 3, p. 3.

A look at the problems inherent in combining personal and professional lives as more women join men in the executive suite. Author criticizes the handling of the Agee-Cunningham situation at Bendix.

331. Jewell, Donald O. "The Female Corporate Jock: What Price Equality?" *Atlanta Economic Review* 26 (March/April 1976): 25–31.

An in-depth interview with Natalie Lang, vice-president of Corporate Social Policy for Booz, Allen & Hamilton, Inc. Lang answers questions about how she decided to seek a career in business, what effect her presence in the organization has had relative to opportunities for other women, what special problems are created by being the visible woman, does she anticipate having the time or energy for marriage, why women have to give 110 percent, and her current role in the organization.

332. ——, and Pollard, Carolyn R. "Women on the Executive Ladder: Performance Is the First Criterion: An Interview with Anne B. Skae." *Atlanta Economic Review* 26 (November 1976): 50–54.

Anne B. Skae, national branch manager of a large corporation, discusses aspects of women in management: training, career plans, opportunity, benefits, visibility, sponsors, education, social life, and advantages of women in management. Stresses career and time commitments.

333. Klemesrud, Judy. "Behind the Best Sellers: Hennig and Jardim." *New York Times,* 23 October 1977, sec. 7, p. 50.

Article in the *New York Times Book Review* tells how Margaret Hennig and Anne Jardim's scholarly book, *The Managerial Woman,* became a best seller. The authors gave free seminars on career planning for women in New York City, Chicago, Washington, Los Angeles, and San Francisco, with copies of the book available at the door. Hennig and Jardim currently direct Simmons College's Graduate Program in Management for Women and will work next on a book about men in the business world.

334. ——. "Women Executives: View from the Top." *New York Times,* 11 March 1979, p. 50.

Catalyst, a nonprofit corporation to help career women, honors 5 women directors at a dinner for 1,000 corporate executives. Those honored are: Barbara Scott Preishel, Carla Anderson Hills, Hanna Holborn Gray, Juliette Moran, and Nancy Hanks. Includes photographs.

335. Koff, Lois Ann. "Age, Experience, and Success among Women Managers." *Management Review* 62 (November 1973): 65–66.

A study of 200 female managers showed that successful managers were more likely to have 4 or more years of experience before assuming a supervisory role and that 50 percent were over 36 years old. One business initiated a 12-month internship for male and female college graduates to ameliorate the need for experience.

336. Larkin, Kathy. "The Homecoming of Helen Galland." *Savvy* 2 (August 1981): 62–66.
Profile of Helen Galland, president and chief executive officer of Bonwit Teller. Includes brief information on 4 other women retail executives.

337. Lipson, Eden Ross. "In the Carter Administration Big Jobs for Young Lawyers." *New York Times,* 1 May 1977, sec. 3, p. 1+.
Statistics reveal that more than one-third of graduating law classes are now female. One in 6 of Carter's cabinet, sub-cabinet, federal agency, and White House staff level appointees are women, one-third of them lawyers who have taught law at least part-time. Several Carter appointees are quoted. Includes photographs.

338. Lohr, Steve. "Bendix Episode Called Isolated by Women in Management Jobs." *New York Times,* 10 October 1980, sec. 4, p. 3.
Management women comment pro and con on William Agee's handling of the Mary E. Cunningham situation at Bendix, claiming that it was an isolated incident. Madelon Talley, Wall Street's first woman stock fund manager, said, "It was probably the worst imaginable handling of a nonissue."

339. Louis, Elaine. "Success Scenes." *Working Woman* 5 (January 1980): 39–42+.
Detailed descriptions of the offices of 4 women executives: Joanne Creveling, fashion publicist; Lynn Salvage, president, First Women's Bank, New York; Barbara Schubeck, advertising art director; and Georgette Muir, Faberge, Inc. Includes colored photographs.

340. Lyman, Ralph. "She Swapped an Opera Career for Success as a Detail-Oriented Production Manager." *American Printer and Lithographer* 184 (November 1979): 76.
Jill Gardner, head production manager of a Seattle printing plant, relates how she entered the printing field and what management style she finds most useful. She discusses acceptance of her by customers and salesmen and tells her plans for advancement.

341. Moorhead, John D. "How Women Fare in Business." *Christian Science Monitor,* 3 May 1977, p. 10.

A review of Margaret Hennig and Anne Jardim's book, *The Managerial Woman,* the result of interviews with over 100 women managers. Moorhead says this book is a must for any woman who is a manager or wants to be and for men who supervise or work with talented women.

342. Neal, Patricia. "Special Women." *Wall Street Journal,* 17 April 1978, p. 21.
In "Letters to the Editor" a reader strongly disagrees with authors' Hennig and Jardim's use of behavioral differences to encourage "special" help for women in management. She views this attitude as insulting to women and expensive to corporations.

343. "The New Breed of Studio Executives Talk about Power." *Ms.* 6 (December 1977): 53.
Women vice-presidents at Filmways, Warner Brothers, United Artists, Columbia Pictures, Universal Pictures, and Paramount Pictures discuss men and women and power in the big studios.

344. "The New Wave at Waterman." *Business Week* (October 25, 1976): 138.
Profile of Francine Gomez, president and board member of Paris-based Waterman since 1969 who turned a $570,000 yearly loss into a $1.8 million profit in 6 years. Gomez' executive team is 40 percent female.

345. "100 Top Corporate Women." *Business Week* (June 21, 1976): 56–60+.
Profiles of 100 women executives in banking, broadcasting, cosmetics and fashion, electrical and electronics, financial services, food, manufacturing, petroleum, public relations and advertising, publishing, retailing, services, and utilities. Includes photographs.

346. "An Organization Woman Remakes the *Post.*" *Business Week* (September 29, 1975): 43–44+.
Profile of Katharine Graham, chairperson of the Washington Post company, who became owner when her husband died in 1963. Discusses the organizational structure of the publishing empire which encompasses 2 newspapers, *Newsweek,* 5 television stations, and 2 radio stations.

347. "Pacesetter: Laura Kaiser; Who Says It's a Man's World?" *Industrial Distributor* 70 (October 1980): 61–62.
Tells how Laura Kaiser earned the title of general manager at Fastener Systems, the Indianapolis branch of Flexalloy, after starting as a

receptionist. She says women have more opportunity to get into management in smaller companies.

348. "Pfeiffer Seems to Be Highest-Paid Female after Move to NBC." *Wall Street Journal,* 7 March 1979, p. 29.

Forty-six year-old Jane Cahill Pfeiffer, director of RCA and chairman of NBC, earns $425,000 annually, making her the highest-paid woman executive in a public corporation. Mrs. Pfeiffer has been an independent consultant and from 1970 to 1976 was vice-president, communications and government relations at IBM, where her husband is a senior vice-president.

349. Piot, Debra K. "Twelve Women Who Earned the Title 'Millionairess'." *Christian Science Monitor,* 7 February 1979, p. 15.

A review of *Millionairess: Self-Made Women of America* by Lois Rich-McCoy, which gives portraits of 12 women millionaires. None of the women inherited wealth; all call themselves opportunists.

350. Pitts, Elaine R. "Managerial Success for Women." *Business Education Forum* 31 (April 1977): 29–30.

The personal experience of a corporate vice-president, with emphasis on the role she plays helping other women.

351. Place, Helen. "A Biographical Profile of Women in Management." *Journal of Occupational Psychology* 52 (December 1979): 267–76.

A biographical study of 130 New Zealand female managers to determine what factors are predictors of managerial effectiveness. Suggests that early identification of factors such as self-confidence, social conformity, competence, and socioeconomic status can help in determining which girls are more likely to do well in management. Includes tables and references.

352. Political and Economic Planning. *Women in Top Jobs: Four Studies in Achievement.* London: Allen & Unwin, 1971.

Gives the results of a study on women and their careers directed by Michael P. Fogarty and Rhona and Robert Rapoport. Covers occupations such as the independent professional practitioner, the head of a business, the free-lance writer or producer, the "entrepreneurial" bureaucrat, and the professional employee or manager below policy-making level. Includes questionnaires, tables, bibliographical references, and index.

353. Reilly, Theresa M. "Women in Key Positions." *Delta Kappa Gamma Bulletin* 43 (Fall 1976): 55–58.

A professor of business profiles several women in business she has met. The women managers include general counsel and vice-president of a large insurance firm, an attorney, a personnel manager, and a college president.

354. Rich, Les. "24 Women: 24 Managers." *Worklife* (U.S. Department of Labor. Employment and Training Administration.) 2 (November 1977): 24–26.

Two dozen women participated in the Women's Career Project, a year-long intensive management training program sponsored by Northeastern University in Boston. With the help of a grant from the Fund for the Improvement of Post Secondary Education, the program provides women with experience (but no credentials) in the organizational skills necessary to get a management job.

355. Rich-McCoy, Lois. *Late Bloomer: Profiles of Women Who Found Their True Calling*. New York: Harper & Row, 1980.

Fourteen biographical profiles of middle-aged women who, after divorce, child raising, or the death of a husband, became successes in new careers. Included are a career counselor, a pediatric cardiologist, chairperson of the National Advisory Committee for Women, a sculptor, the owner of a women's wear shop, a state representative, a radio and television personality, the owner of a reality firm, an Episcopal priest, the owner of an architectural and interior decoration business, the owner of a travel business, a mayor, a goat farmer, and a model and author. Each chapter concludes with a list of "How . . . Did It." Epilogue includes questions to ask yourself when considering a change in life direction.

356. ———. *Millionairess: Self-Made Women of America*. New York: Harper & Row, 1978.

Gives the biographies of 10 women millionaires: the owner of Vera Industries, 2 bikini manufacturers, the founder of a food corporation, a toy manufacturer and distributor, a pattern designer, the president of a medical electronics firm, the president of an airline, an architect, a rancher, and an advertising executive.

357. Robertson, Wyndham. "The Ten Highest-Ranking Women in Big Business." *Fortune* 87 (April 1973): 81–89.

Profiles of the 10 highest paid women corporate officers show that most began careers 30 to 40 years ago and were helped by marriage or a family connection, or they created the corporations they presently manage. Most combined careers with marriage and motherhood.

358. ———. "Top Women in Big Business." *Fortune* 98 (July 1978): 58–62.

Profiles 10 women executives whose salaries range from $55,000 to $300,000 per year. Vice-presidents, presidents, and heads of banking, manufacturing, and publishing concerns, they are the only women of some 6,400 officers and directors of 1,300 major companies. Includes photographs.

359. Rupp, Carla Marie. "Women Settle into Ranks of Management." *Editor and Publisher* 112 (April 14, 1979): 14.

Comments from 9 women in newspaper management who attended a seminar for city editors. Author encourages management to train women reporters to be editors since 53 percent of journalism students are women.

360. Safran, Claire. "Rags-to-Riches Female-Style." *Today's Health* 52 (March 1974): 34–37+.

Chronicles the rise to success of 5 self-made women millionaires. A record company executive, a financial manager, a hair and skin care distributor, a business entrepreneur, and the owner of a toy company tell how ambition and determination got them to the top. Includes photographs.

361. Shapiro, Mildred B. "Split-Level Journalism." *New York Times*, 25 October 1980, p. 22.

A reader comments on the *New York Times* October 15 editorial on the Mary E. Cunningham-William Agee situation at Bendix.

362. Sheils, Merrill; Foote, Donna; Dentzer, Susan; and Marbach, William D. "Three Who Made It to the Top." *Newsweek* 98 (September 14, 1981): 67.

Profiles 3 management women: CEO of IHSS, Inc. (a former division of Jewel Tea); a securities vice-president who never went to college; and a physicist who is the first woman vice-president at GM. Only one of the 3 is married; the marriages of the others ended in divorce due, in part, to the strain of a dual-career family.

363. Shifren, Carole. "Trailblazing In a Man's World." *MBA: Master in Business Administration* 9 (February 1975): 12.

Profiles Barbara Hackman Franklin, one of 2 women members of the Consumer Product Safety Commission who at 34 is the youngest commissioner of a federal agency. Franklin discusses the advantages of an MBA, the positions she held prior to being named a CPSC commissioner, and women's opportunities in government and business.

364. Slappey, Sterling G. "Those Powerful Powder Puff Executives." *Nation's Business* 58 (November 1970): 80–88.

A pictorial essay on 9 top women executives, including an advertising executive, a banker, 2 insurance company executives, a member of the New York Stock Exchange, a publisher, 2 company presidents, and a chairperson of the board. Quotes from each women are included.

365. Stashower, Gloria. *Careers in Management for the New Woman.* New York: F. Watts, 1978.

Vocational guidance for young women. "An introduction to the world of management and some women now involved in that field." (*National Union Catalog,* 1978, v. 14, p. 126.)

366. Stead, Bette Ann. "Women's Contributions to Management Thought." *Business Horizons* 17 (February 1974): 32–36.

A review of the contributions of women to 3 management eras: scientific management (1910–late 1920s); human relations (1920s–1959); behavioral science (1960–present). Lillian Gilbreth is credited with contributing much to the scientific management school of thought; Mary Parker Follett is seen as heralding the human relations era; and the accomplishments of Jane Mouton, Joan Woodward, Riva Poor, and Christel Kammerer are listed under the section on behavioral science.

367. Sullivan, Colleen. "Bendix Ex-Aide a Hit at Lunch." *New York Times,* 20 November 1980, sec. 4, p. 4.

Mary E. Cunningham, who resigned as vice-president of strategic planning at Bendix after rumors of a romance with chairperson William Agee, was inducted into the New York YWCA's Academy of Women Achievers at the Salute to Women in Business Luncheon. She received well wishes and job offers at the luncheon which raised $230,000 for the YWCA.

368. "There's a Girl in My Soup." *Economist* 277 (October 4, 1980): 77.

Update on the scandal at Bendix involving 29-year-old Mary E. Cunningham, vice-president for strategic planning, and chairperson William Agee. Cunningham asked for a temporary leave of absence after speculation that a romance with Agee accounted for her rapid rise to vice-president.

369. Tracy, Eleanor Johnson. "She Has Three Years to Turn Olivetti America Around." *Fortune* 100 (October 22, 1979): 87–88+.

Carlo DeBenedetti, boss of Olivetti, appointed 44-year-old Marisa Bellisario head of Olivetti Corporation of America and gave her 3 years to turn the corporation's $39 million loss into a profit. Bellisario started by announcing Olivetti's new electronic typewriter and a full range of word-processing equipment.

370. Weber, Elizabeth. "Characteristics of Selected Women Managers: Personal, Educational and Career." EdD dissertation, Columbia University Teachers College, 1978.

Abstracted in *Dissertation Abstracts International*, December 1978, v. 39, no. 6, #3317-A.

371. "Why So Few Women Have Made It to the Top." *Business Week* (June 5, 1978): 99–100+.

Of the 43 corporations surveyed by *BW*, only 7 name women in top management posts. Most companies employ women, earning $20,000–$50,000 a year, at the middle management level and cite women's background and training as reasons they are not promotable to higher levels. Most women are specialists; they have professional rather than managerial backgrounds. Women managers in several major U.S. corporations are quoted.

372. Wood, Marcia Donnan, and Candela, Cristine. "A View from the Top." *Working Woman* 6 (March 1981): 40–41+.

An interview with 7 women executives who received the Women's Equity Action League Economic Equity Awards for 1980. They talk about recession and inflation, salary inequities, power, and the impact of the women's movement on women managers.

373. Yelverton, Sandra, ed. "Business Ownership and Management Opportunities for Women." *Business Education Forum* 31 (April 1977): 23–24+.

Introduces several articles containing biographies of successful businesswomen. Advises business educators that training is the key to developing the management skills of women.

Career and Family

374. Bender, Marilyn. "Families Adapting As More Women Take Job Transfers." *New York Times,* 23 July 1974, p. 60.

The growing trend for women to accept job transfers has created problems for many dual-career families. Equal employment opportunity consultants offer management awareness training to help corporations avoid discrimination by assuming that women, particularly married women, will not relocate.

375. ———. "Women Managers and Marriage." *New York Times,* 26 December 1971, sec. 3, p. 3.

Interviews William J. Goode, professor of Sociology at Columbia and president of the American Sociological Association, about his paper "Family Life and Women Managers." Dr. Goode predicts a sharp increase in the next decade in the number of women in management and discusses the impact this will have on women's independence, on families, and on marriage relationships.

376. Botto, Louis. "The Executive Mother." *Look* 35 (January 26, 1971): 73+.

Joan Glynn, advertising executive and mother of 4, is profiled by Mary Wells Lawrence, top woman in U.S. advertising. Includes photographs.

377. "Canadian Firm Merges Management and Motherhood." *Management Review* 68 (July 1979): 41.

The largest personnel firm in western Canada allows women to take up to 18 months maternity leave and return at their previous salary level. The company, owned and operated almost exclusively by women since 1951, sees 3 advantages: trained workers are ready to assume management roles as substitutes, workers continually learn new jobs, and morale is high. The leave policy is the same for male workers.

378. "Company Couples Flourish." *Business Week* (August 2, 1976): 54–55.

Some companies are revising their policy about employing only one member of a family, and, as a result, are seeing a rise in the number of company couples. Advantages are that husband and wife share common interests and understand each other's work problems; one disadvantage is the possibility that spouses will be competing for the same job. The biggest concern for companies and couples is the possibility of transfers to different cities.

379. Coumbe, John W. "Management and Marriage—Push and Shove." *SAM Advanced Management Journal* 43 (Summer 1978): 32–39.
Describes the difficulties in managing work and home life and the effects on personal relationships. As more women enter management, the problems of work vs. family, job relocation, and sharing family responsibilities become even more acute. Suggestions for couples and companies on finding a satisfactory solution.

380. Edmiston, Susan. "They Made It Work Their Way." *New York* (April 4, 1979): 50–54.
Profiles 4 women executives who have established their own values regarding work, career, and family. Tells how an associate publisher at Simon and Schuster, a literary agent, a marketing manager and assistant branch manager in IBM's second-largest branch office, and the president and executive director of the Council on Economic Priorities have learned to overcome the "superwoman" syndrome.

381. Fogarty, Michael Patrick; Rapoport, Rhona; and Rapoport, Robert N. *Sex, Career and Family: Including an International Review of Women's Roles*. London: Allen & Unwin, 1971.
Results of a study on how to get more women into top jobs reviews the problem of women's promotion to top jobs and the situation in East Europe and in western countries. Part 3, "Studies of Family and Work Careers," is a detailed analysis of family patterns and work and the dual-career family. Part 5, "Conclusions," includes suggestions to families, governments, and public policymaking groups for dealing with problems of work and family life. Includes indices, statistical and technical appendices, and bibliographical references.

382. Friedman, Dick. "Where His Career Leads, Would You Follow?" *Working Woman* 6 (June 1981): 74–78.
Some dual-career couples solve the dilemma of relocation with commuter marriages or a take-turns approach, and some end their relationships. Includes quotes from Maryanne Vandervelde, author of *The*

Changing Life of the Corporate Wife and the forthcoming *On the Move: Whether to Go—How to Cope*.

383. Gallese, Liz Roman. "Moving Experience: Women Managers Say Job Transfers Present a Growing Dilemma." *Wall Street Journal*, 4 May 1978, p. 1+.
Women managers face the possibility of transfer to gain promotion, and, as the number of dual-career couples increases, the problems of combining career and family multiply. Estimates show that 100,000 employees were relocated by the 600 largest U.S. corporations in 1976, 5 to 10 percent of them were women. Some companies still consider women "transfer risks," but others are helping to find jobs for the husbands of newly transferred women executives.

384. Greiff, Barrie S., and Munter, Preston K. "Can a Two-Career Family Live Happily Ever After?" *Across the Board* 17 (September 1980): 40–47.
Lists 8 factors responsible for the rise in the number of dual-career families. Includes sections on the health of executive women who are also members of dual-career families and the nature and quality of dual-career family life.

385. Harkinson, Daniel J. " A Mother's Work." *Wall Street Journal*, 15 May 1978, p. 29.
A reader comments that the author's sentence, "She stopped working between 1958 and 1961 to care for her two young daughters," (Liz Gallese, 4 May 1978) is nonsensical, since most mothers work very hard caring for 2 young children. Otherwise, he compliments the *WSJ* and author Liz Gallese on an interesting article.

386. Klemesrud, Judy. "Finding the Right Career-Family Mix." *New York Times*, 20 July 1980, p. 36.
The Career and Family Center in New York, a part of Catalyst, receives over $400,000 from the W. K. Kellogg Foundation and Exxon to do research on the dual-career family. A questionnaire will be sent to 1,300 top corporations, and 2,000 2-career couples will be surveyed about problems and satisfactions of 2-career families.

387. ———. "Success at Work and as a Woman." *New York Times*, 26 January 1981, sec. 2, p. 6.
Four businesswomen lead a seminar on "Women and Power—The Actual and Psychological Struggles" to discuss the fear that, as women

succeed in business, they fail as women. Linda Greenberg, co-director of Workshop for Women in Business, defined the "bright woman's dilemma," and Anne Hyde, president of Boyden/Management Woman, tells women to establish a balance between the perfect career woman and the perfect mother.

388. Larue, Robert. "Helpmate's Role." *Wall Street Journal*, 13 October 1980, p. 19.
A reader takes issue with Maryanne Vandervelde's terminology in her September 29 *WSJ* article on corporate husbands.

389. Martin, Virginia H. "Recruiting Women Managers through Flexible Hours." *SAM Advanced Management Journal* 39 (July 1974): 46–53.
Flexible work hours may be a way for companies to attract women managers and comply with affirmative action guidelines. Article describes patterns and advantages of flex-time.

390. "More and More Women Professionals Accept Career Relocation." *Wall Street Journal*, 13 September 1977, p. 1.
Labor Letter report quotes an Amoco Production Co. official as saying that refusal to move can diminish a woman's career potential by as much as 50 percent, but companies are finding it easier to transfer women as they become more committed to their careers. Some corporations have a policy of searching for jobs for employees' spouses in the new location.

391. "Now Eager to Accept Transfers." *Business Week* (May 26, 1980): 153+.
Corporations find that more women managers are willing to relocate upon promotion. Many single women find relocation increases their self-reliance and the opportunities to meet new people, but for married women the decision to move is often complicated by family considerations.

392. "Pluck—and Partners—Help Mothers Make It as Managers." *Industry Week* 183 (October 14, 1974): 13–14.
Women managers at Lockheed, Resistol, Foseco, and U.S. Civil Service Commission relate how they have combined career and motherhood. One was named "Woman of the Year" in 1973–74 by the American Business Women's Association, and most credit families and "considerate partners" to some degree for their success in combining the 2 roles.

393. Smith, Ralph E., ed. *The Subtle Revolution: Women at Work.* Washington, DC: The Urban Institute, 1979.

Smith claims that, when a wife's employment is viewed as secondary, the wife relocates with the husband's job demands and relocation generally means the husband's wage increases while the wife's declines. He recommends that married couples consider the wife's long-term job prospects when deciding where to live and suggests that married men need more flexibility to relocate due to the fact that 50 percent of married men have working wives.

394. Vandervelde, Maryanne. "Corporate Husbands." *Wall Street Journal,* 29 September 1980, p. 30.

The author of *The Changing Life of the Corporate Wife* and *On the Move: Coping Creatively with Relocation Stress* defines 3 types of executive husband: the nonachiever facilitator, the achiever obstructionist, and the achiever facilitator. The latter makes the best choice as partners for women executives, but they are found in only about 25 percent of dual-career marriages.

395. "What Should a Mother Do about Her Career?" *Wall Street Journal,* 21 March 1980, p. 24.

Joanne Lublin, a member of the *Journal*'s Washington bureau, and Carol Falk, a former member of the *Journal*'s Washington bureau who covered the Supreme Court, take opposite sides in the working mother debate. They write of the sacrifices and satisfactions of both choices.

396. Whelan, Elizabeth M. "Confessions of a Superwoman." *Working Woman* 6 (July 1981): 61.

The personal story of a woman's conflict between career and the family. Starting in high school with 4 goals (education, husband, baby, home), Whelan tells how she finally solved the question "Can you be both a successful wife and a successful career woman?"

397. "When Career Couples Have Conflicts of Interest." *Business Week* (December 13, 1976): 86+.

Describes how companies and couples deal with the issue of conflict of interest when a person's mate is employed by a company's suppliers, competitors, or clients. Some companies have policies that prohibit anyone in their employ whose spouse works for a competitor. Some couples keep business and home life separate, and in some industries, like publishing, spouses working for competitors or clients is a common occurrence.

398. "When Mothers Are Also Managers." *Business Week* (April 18, 1977): 155–56+.

Executive mothers account for 10 percent of the 48 percent of mothers who work. Their problems as working mothers are compounded due to greater commitment to work and home. Child care arrangements and irregular hours are only 2 of the difficulties, but some corporations are helping with shortened work days or flexible scheduling for mothers. Most mothers believe their career progress is slowed somewhat by having children but feel their children are receiving quality time—not quantity time—from both parents.

399. "Women at the Top Are Less Likely to Be Married than Their Male Counterparts." *Wall Street Journal,* 20 February 1979, p. 1.

A survey by Wareham Associates, Inc., New York, reveals that, of 13 women executives of large firms, 23 percent have never been married and 31 percent have been divorced. Male executives are almost always married and few have ever been divorced.

400. "Women Executives Who Were Relocated by Companies Last Year Numbered 20 Times More than They Did 5 Years Ago." *Wall Street Journal,* 27 February 1979, p. 1.

A brief paragraph in *Labor Letter* cites statistics from a survey by Merrill Lynch Relocation Management, Inc. Only 8 percent of the 300,000 U.S. employees transferred in 1978 were women.

Women as Directors

401. Anderson, Ellen. "Why Aren't There More Women in the Board-room?" *Director* 32 (November 1979): 62–63.

Two factors, women's acceptance of their traditional role and the barriers in male-dominated industry, help to account for the fact that there are no women on the boards of medium or large British industrial corporations. The author claims women's main contributions to industry will be in communications and industrial relations.

402. Barmash, Isadore. "Women Recommended as Potential Directors." *New York Times,* 6 March 1979, sec. 4, p. 4.

The 23-year-old Financial Women's Association compiled a list of 10 women qualified to serve as corporate directors to present to 30 corporate chief executives at a breakfast in a business luncheon club in New York. The 10 candidates, who have an average of 16 years in business, are listed with their companies.

403. "Big Jump in the Ranks of Female Directors." *Business Week* (January 10, 1977): 49–50.

Cites the rising number of women serving on boards of directors, an estimated 400 at the time of this article. Profiles Juanita Kreps, Patricia Roberts Harris, Jane Cahill Pfeiffer, and Joan Ganz Cooney. Together they serve on 14 corporate boards. Most women on corporate boards see their role as women's representatives, but one says she represents stockholders and the public, not exclusively the women's point of view.

404. Carlson, Elliot. "A Woman's Place . . . " *Newsweek* 85 (April 21, 1975): 82.

More women are chosen for corporate boards, and the few women with business experience are offered several directorships. Although some women take the opportunity to lobby for more women executives or social responsibility, most are interested primarily in the company's profit and loss statement.

405. Eiseman, Alberta. "For Women Only." *New York Times*, 2 November 1980, sec. 23, p. 6.

A New Haven businessman and the Chamber of Commerce offer women a 10-week course on "How to Become an Effective Board Member." Topics covered include finance and accounting, the role and composition of a board, relations between boards and officers, and differences between profit and nonprofit boards; the course includes speakers and homework.

406. "Good Woman Is Easier to Find: Candidates for Board Membership." *Time* 113 (March 19, 1979): 71.

The Financial Women's Association presents 10 qualified women as potential directors for 30 major corporations. At present only 276 women serve as directors on 1,300 corporate boards.

407. Herrick, Snowden T. "Voting for Women." *New York Times,* 29 April 1981, sec. 3, p. 14.

A reader comments on Enid Nemy's "Women on Boards," April 22. He questions the optimism of her article which notes that only 1.8 percent of total board membership is female.

408. "More Women Elected to Boards of Directors." *Industry Week* 185 (May 19, 1975): 19–20.

More women are chosen for corporate boards of directors, partly because of pressure from stockholders and civil rights groups. Unlike the 65 female directors of 855 companies in a 1972 Conference Board survey, many women are now chosen for outside achievements and not because they hold a large number of shares of stock in the company.

409. "More Women Move into the Boardroom." *Business Week* (March 1, 1976): 26.

There are 202 women directors of 239 major U.S. corporations. There were few women officers before 1972; 80 of the 202 women received their appointments in 1975. Lists some women who hold multiple board memberships.

410. Nemy, Enid. "Commissions for Women's Conference Stresses Economic Issues." *New York Times,* 16 June 1980, sec. 2, p. 6.

Women and corporate life was one of the themes at the 11th Annual Conference of the National Association of Commissions for Women. Workshops covered women on corporate staffs, directorships, wage discrimination, and funding for women's programs.

411. ———. "Women on Boards: A New Perspective." *New York Times,* 22 April 1981, sec. 3, p. 1.

The number of women on corporate boards increased 25 percent in 3 years, but they are still only 1.8 percent of total board membership. Quotes Carla Anderson Hills, former secretary of HUD, who is one of 24 women to serve on 4 or more boards.

412. Orr, Leonard H. "Out of the Typing Pool and onto the Board: A List of Women Directors." *Business and Society Review* 22 (Summer 1977): 27–33.

Eighteen months after *Business and Society Review* published a list of women on corporate boards, 100 corporations have added women to their boards. More than 340 companies now have women directors, with some women serving on more than one board. Includes a revised list (5 p.), listed alphabetically by corporation.

413. Overton, Elizabeth. "What Makes an Executive Woman?" *Working Woman* 5 (January 1980): 35–38.

Charts statistics from the 1979 Heidrick and Struggles *Profile of a Woman Officer,* a study of 485 women corporate officers. Data show one-third of all management women are in government. Hennig and Jardim (*The Managerial Woman*) dispute some of the statistics, claiming the study doesn't include the growing number of women earning MBAs and doesn't give an accurate picture of the salary situation. Followed by the 17-point questionnaire used in the Heidrick and Struggles survey.

414. "Profile of a Woman Officer." *Personnel Administrator* 25 (April 1980): 80–81.

Gives statistics on female corporate officers from the third annual study by Heidrick and Struggles. Compares men and women upper-level executives and lists the fields of greatest opportunity for women.

415. *Profile of a Woman Officer: Findings of a Study of Executives in America's 1300 Largest Companies.* New York: Heidrick & Struggles, 1977.

This report has been published annually by the management consultant/ executive search firm of Heidrick and Struggles since 1977. Gives statistics on the age, education, marital status, salary, career planning, and politics of women officers in the nation's largest corporations. Reports from 1977, 1978, 1979, and 1980 are available from: Heidrick & Struggles, Inc., 245 Park Avenue, New York, NY 10017.

416. Schwartz, Felice N. "Invisible Resource: Women for Boards." *Harvard Business Review* 58 (March/April 1980): 6–8+.

The president and founder of Catalyst, a nonprofit corporation that promotes women in business and the professions, discusses 4 aspects of the problem of how to increase the number of women in corporate boardrooms: the preferences of the chairperson, contracts with women directors, challenges for women directors in the 1980s, and selections of women candidates. Quotes several women serving on boards, and describes Catalyst's Women Director's Program.

417. "Six Businesswomen Receive Catalyst Award." *Christian Science Monitor,* 8 March 1978, p. 2.

Reports on the third annual Catalyst awards dinner, held in New York at the Waldorf-Astoria. Catalyst, a nonprofit women's career advancement organization, honored 6 women who serve on corporate boards.

418. "Sperry Rand Assailed Over Lack of Females among Its Directors." *Wall Street Journal*, 1 August 1973, p. 17.

Female stockholders at the annual shareholder meeting contest board chairperson J. Paul Lyet's assertion that Sperry Rand still hasn't found a qualified woman to serve on its board. One female stockholder claimed that putting a woman on the board would attract more stockholders to Sperry's declining number of shareholders.

419. Stultz, Janice E. "Madam Director." *Directors and Boards* 3 (Winter 1979): 6–20.

A lengthy article on the status of women on corporate boards tells which corporations have elected women to their boards, gives the percentage of companies with woman directors, suggests what types of women are chosen for boards, and profiles 4 top women directors who offer observations, predictions, and advice to aspiring women directors. Describes how the Financial Women's Association of New York and the Corporate Board Resource at Catalyst help corporations find qualified women to serve as directors. Includes footnotes and a bibliography of books, reports, and articles.

420. "Who Are the Women in the Boardrooms?" *Business and Society Review* (Winter 1975/1976): 5–10.

Cites the rise in the number of Blacks and women on corporate boards of directors. Eighty women were appointed to boards in 1975, and approximately 237 boards now have women directors. Includes a 5-page comprehensive list of women board members, listed alphabetically by corporation.

421. "Who Washes Dishes?" *Wall Street Journal,* 23 September 1980, p. 1.
Executive recruiting firm Heidrick and Struggles' study shows that
two-thirds of married women officers in 1,300 major corporations
spend more than 10 hours a week on household chores. Two-thirds of
their husbands spend less than 10 hours weekly at household tasks.

422. "Women Directors Have Had More Diverse Career Backgrounds than
Their Male Counterparts." *Wall Street Journal,* 15 November 1977, p. 1.
A study by the Burson-Marstellar public relations firm says the trend
for more women to be named as directors of corporate boards will
continue "for years if not decades." The styles and experiences of
women directors are similar to those of male directors, according to the
study.

423. "Women Executives Sit on 25% of Corporate Boards of Directors."
Wall Street Journal, 21 March 1978, p. 1.
A survey of 501 companies by Korn-Ferry of New York, an international search firm, says that there are women executives on 25 percent
of corporate boards of directors, a jump of 13 percent in 4 years.

424. "Women on the Board." *Time* 100 (October 16, 1972): 85.
Catherine Cleary of General Motors joins the growing list of women on
corporate boards. Quotes other women directors: Patricia Roberts
Harris, Joan Ganz Cooney, Jane Spain, and Dinah Shore. Includes
photographs.

Women Bosses

425. Bender, Marilyn. "When the Boss Is a Woman." *Esquire* 89 (March 28, 1978): 35–41.

Explores the difficulties some males experience working for a woman boss. Sharon Kirkman of Kirkman Boyle Associates, a management consulting firm that trains women and minorities, offers 5 guidelines for the novice woman boss.

426. Bremer, Roslyn. "When the Supervisor Is a Woman." *Supervisory Management* 18 (July 1973): 16–22.

Advice to women supervisors on dealing with problems encountered with subordinates, peers, and superiors. With subordinates Bremer advises women supervisors not to play "mother." With the boss she advises awareness of the nonverbal message you send and avoidance of behavior that reinforces stereotypical attitudes about women; with peers she recommends that you not be one of the boys and that you give up your own stereotypes about women.

427. Burgen, Michele. "The Problems of Women Bosses." *Ebony* 33 (November 1977): 94+.

An *Ebony* poll of 10 women executives shows support from their staffs but difficulties with male colleagues and superiors. Problems include the necessity to work harder than men to prove qualifications, lack of trust, and affirmative action backlash.

428. Comer, Nancy Axelrad. "Lady Is the Tiger: Woman as Boss." *Mademoiselle* 76 (March 1973): 153+.

Young women bosses describe their styles of management and tell of problems they encounter with resistance to women managers because of their age. Visibility as the only woman in an organization has advantages and disadvantages. Seven young women executives give advice.

429. Ferber, Marianne, and Huber, Joan. "Preference for Men or Women Bosses Or Professionals." Paper presented at the 9th World Congress of the

International Sociological Association, Uppsala University, Uppsala, Sweden, 14–19 August, 1978.

Abstracted in *Sociological Abstracts,* December 1978, Supp. 82-II, # 78S09729.

430. Hammer, Signe. "When Women Have Power over Women." *Ms.* 7 (September 1978): 49–51.

Author of *Daughters and Mothers, Mothers and Daughters* exhorts women to admit the conflicts involved in working for another woman. She identifies 4 types of female bosses: earth mother, egalitarian, manipulator, and workaholic.

431. Harragan, Betty Lehan. "Resenting the Woman Boss." *Savvy* 2 (March 1981): 19+.

Warns that women at varying levels in an organization will inevitably collide. Offers suggestions to the subordinate for obtaining a position as assistant to the woman manager.

432. ———. "When Female Subordinates Undermine Your Authority." *Savvy* 2 (April 1981): 30+.

Advice to a woman manager on dealing effectively with women subordinates and professionals in her department. Suggests explaining how their behavior has implications for the ambitions of all women in the organization.

433. "How Men Adjust to a Female Boss." *Business Week* (September 5, 1977): 90+.

Male executives discuss working with a female boss. Some have been successfully working with female superiors for a number of years, others who have had good experiences with female bosses would still prefer a male boss, and some executive search firms indicate their clients will take young female MBA graduates but are not interested in hiring women at higher levels. Most men think their female bosses should exhibit superior ability, be strong, and have the unqualified endorsement of her superiors.

434. Jacobs, Rita. "That Was No Lady: That Was My Boss." *Working Woman* 4 (March 1979): 51–53+.

Author describes the categories of women bosses: the motherly boss, the sibling boss, the dean-of-women boss, the nit-picker, the buck passer, the boss lady, and the perfect boss. She also offers advice on how to learn from your boss and how to love and leave your boss. Gives a list of rules on how to be/choose a good woman boss.

435. Kanter, Rosabeth Moss. "Why Bosses Turn Bitchy." *Psychology Today* 9 (May 1976): 56–57+.

Author says opportunity, power, and tokenism rather than sex differences explain the lack of women managers. In her book *Men and Women of the Corporation,* Kanter suggests that changing the structure of the organization will provide more equitability for women in management, not merely changing personalities or attitudes.

436. "Picture Called Bleak for Businesswomen." *Christian Science Monitor,* 22 January 1976, p. 2.

A 1972 survey shows only 3 percent of the nation's businesses are owned by women. Most of the women-owned businesses are small operations.

437. Pogrebin, Letty Cottin. "When Men Have Women Bosses." *Ladies Home Journal* 94 (May 1977): 24+.

Interviews with several women executives and their employees confirm some generalizations about women bosses and contradict others. Most women bosses interviewed agreed with Rosabeth Moss Kanter that "power drives out sex."

438. Raphael, Bette-Jane. "Why I'm a Rotten Boss." *Mademoiselle* 85 (January 1979): 96+.

Amusing anecdote about one woman's difficulties hiring secretaries. The problem, she believes, is that women don't learn to use power.

439. Shapiro, Ruth. "Should You Work for a Woman?" *Harper's Bazaar* 110 (August 1977): 85+.

A management consultant discusses the stereotype of the woman boss who can't learn to delegate responsibility, who is devious and emotional, and who refuses to help other women get promoted. Five women executives give advice on how to be a good boss.

440. "This Woman Could Be Your Boss." *Industry Week* 183 (October 14, 1974): 36–39.

A 30-year-old woman who is manager of equal employment opportunity affairs for a division of Union Carbide and president of 2 companies of her own gives advice to women on overcoming emotional responses to many situations, tempering aggressiveness, and learning to delegate responsibility. She believes women have the advantages of intuition and a high degree of sensitivity and that successful women managers retain their femininity.

441. Trahey, Jane. "How's the Air Up There?" *Working Woman* 6 (March 1981): 36.

Six women executives were asked the question, "What do you hate most about your job?" The answers—working with lawyers, firing someone, misuse of expense money by employees, inability to delegate, playing mediator, correcting an employee—indicate women still want the approval and love of their employees.

Recruiting Women into Management

442. Arvis, Paul Frederick. "Factors Affecting the Recruitment and Advancement of Women to Managerial Positions in Federal Agencies." PhD dissertation, The American University, 1973.

Abstracted in *Dissertation Abstracts International,* v. 34, December 1973, #3511-A.

443. "B. F. Goodrich by '79 to Add 260 Women to Its Management." *Wall Street Journal,* 7 June 1974, p. 20.

A former employee of B. F. Goodrich, who was fired from a management training program, is awarded $7,742 in back pay in a sex discrimination suit. The company plans to increase the number of women in management to 338 by 1979. Presently women comprise only 3.9 percent of the total professional staff.

444. Baron, Alma S. "Selection, Development and Socialization of Women into Management." *Business Quarterly* 42 (Winter 1977): 61–67.

Author claims 2 severe problems impede the progress of women in management: selection, development, and training of women for higher positions and the socialization of women into the management structure. She lists the 4 steps for training and developing executives, male or female, as: on-the-job training, formal training programs, outside study programs, and participation in conferences. Includes bibliographical references and a photograph of the author.

445. Bray, Douglas W. "The Assessment Center: Opportunities for Women." *Personnel* 48 (September/October 1971): 30–34.

Author suggests greater use of the assessment center method of evaluating management potential of women employees. Describes how assessment centers work and what they do to identify promotable women and minorities.

446. ———. "Identifying Managerial Talent in Women." *Atlanta Economic Review* 26 (March/April 1976): 38–43.

Describes the assessment center method of evaluating management ability. The method involves the use of simulations, leaderless group discussion, in-basket exercises, analysis and presentation problems, decision-making exercises, and interviews to appraise the potential for advancement in management. Two thousand women employed by the Bell System were evaluated for third-level management positions using the assessment center method after litigation for discrimination in personnel practices was charged by EEOC.

447. Clutterbuck, David. "Dow Makes the Most of Womanpower." *International Management* 31 (November 1976): 27–28.
After a 5-year program to provide equal opportunity for women at Dow Chemical Co., the percentage of women in management increased from 3 to 10. Women have moved into management positions in inside sales and technical areas.

448. Diamond, Helen. "Wanted: More Women in Management." *Educational Horizons* 53 (Spring 1975): 125–28.
Founder and adviser to Women in Management suggests 4 steps to help companies promote women into management positions. She claims that, even with the Equal Employment Opportunity Act of 1972 and Revised Order 4, top management must be committed to eliminating sex discrimination in employment. Includes references.

449. Ekberg-Jordan, Sandra. "Preparing for the Future: Commitment and Action." *Atlanta Economic Review* 26 (March/April 1976): 47–49.
Offers 16 suggestions for businesses wishing to improve their affirmative action programs. Suggestions include recruitment and hiring of qualified women, career counseling for women, public posting of all open positions, establishment of flexible hours and part-time positions where possible, reevaluation of maternity leave policies, review of relocation policies, and funding of day-care centers.

450. Eklund, Coy G. "Women in Business: What Business Must Do." *Vital Speeches* 42 (June 15, 1976): 539–42.
Outlines a 9-point women's program for business to follow in recruiting and advancing women, including educational and training programs, companywide job postings, flexible work hours, and role models. Gives 6 rules for ambitious career women.

451. Feilke, M. F. "Women, Women Everywhere, but Not a Manager in Sight." *Iron Age* 206 (August 27, 1970): 63–65.

Author describes the middle management gap that will occur in the mid-70s and predicts that companies will seek women to fill some management posts. Describes Honeywell's Manpower Development and Training Program and efforts to include women in management.

452. Flanagan, William. "Employers are Insisting on Women Managers and Supervisors." *Vogue* 167 (March 1977): 222.

Ruby Letsch, president of National Personnel Associates, says employers, aware of discrimination legislation, demand women managers and supervisors. Letsch advises women to take a job in a large corporation where chances for promotion are greater and cites banking, government, the news media, the medical field, and data processing as open career fields for women. The president of a large executive recruiting firm adds retailing, leisure industries, consulting, accounting, and law to the list.

453. Foster, Lillian F. "Bandwagon . . . What Bandwagon? The Doleful Tale of One Company's Tribulations in Marketing Women to Corporate Recruiters." *MBA: Master in Business Administration* 7 (March 1973): 6+.

A job conference sponsored by the Lockwood Group, Ltd., brought together corporate recruiters and 260 women applicants, but only 11 women were hired, all but 3 into entry-level positions at around $10,000. The second conference was equally disappointing when companies didn't even bother to interview the women.

454. Foxley, Cecilia H. *Locating, Recruiting and Employing Women: An Equal Opportunity Approach*. Garrett Park, MD: Garrett Press, 1976.

A comprehensive look at women in today's labor force, the educational background and employment preparation of women, affirmative action programs, and laws and regulations affecting women employees. Discusses myths about women workers including the one that women do not want to be promoted into management positions.

455. Fulweiler, John H. "Help Wanted: More Women Mall Managers." *Chain Store Age* (Exec Ed) 50 (September 1974): 24.

There are only 7 women in the International Council of Shopping Center's roster of 328 Certified Shopping Center Managers (CSMs). Author gives 4 reasons why qualified women are ideal for the position of mall manager.

456. Hart, Lois B. "Steps to Successful Synergy." *Personnel Administrator* 25 (April 1980): 45–48.

Describes how the process of synergy—adding an unknown quantity to a known quantity to create a new composition—can be useful in bringing women into management. Author suggests synergy can be achieved by a review of organizational procedures and policy, an evaluation of the selection process and follow-up, the assessment and development of personnel, training, a review of job descriptions, standards and performance reviews, counseling, and modeling behaviors and attitudes. Includes references.

457. Hedges, Janice Neipert. "Women Workers and Manpower Demands in the 1970s." *U.S. Department of Labor. Monthly Labor Review* 93 (June 1970): 19–29.

Reviews the current employment pattern of women (half of all women workers are employed in only 21 of 250 occupations), describes the professional and technical positions most frequently held by women, lists professions not typically thought of as "woman's sphere," and lists opportunities for women in the professions and the skilled trades. Predicts that women will move into occupations that fit human resource needs in the 1970s, including the move of recent women graduates into entry-level executive jobs.

458. "The Job-Hunting Female." *MBA: Master in Business Administration* 10 (February 1976): 8.

More women are entering upper-level management jobs through placement by executive women search firms. The demand for women in the $20,000-30,000 range and for women MBAs increases, and a New York-Los Angeles executive search firm advises women to branch out into industries that are traditionally all-male, to have higher salary expectations, and to pursue contacts.

459. Johnson, Richard P. "Having Women in Management Makes Good Business Sense." *Food Service Marketing* 38 (November 1976): 12.

President of a food service company argues that it's profitable to increase the number of women in food service management because the food service industry employs a high percentage of women and the turnover rate for women managers in the industry is half that of men. He offers advice on recruiting women to management positions in the industry.

460. Kay, M. Jane. "A Positive Approach to Women in Management." *Personnel Journal* 51 (January 1972): 38–41.

Author suggests positive ways to include women in management. Plan includes open promotion policies, a review of the capabilities of present women employees, providing developmental opportunities for women, and actively recruiting women for professional level positions.

461. Kleinschrod, Walter R. "Management Neglects to Plan for Cutbacks or Hiring under Affirmative Action." *Administrative Management* 36 (August 1975): 23.

An editorial discussing the need to develop a plan for maintaining an affirmative action program for women and minorities when reduction in force is necessary. Reports on a recent study of 12 major corporations that had no specific plans for this situation, although they all had affirmative action programs and full or part-time EEO officers.

462. Levi, Maurice D. "Stimulating Recruitment of Female Managers." *Industrial Relations* (Quebec) 31 (1976): 72–82.

Suggests a way to eliminate the hiring preference for males due to the expected lower turnover rate of male employees. Author believes a contract requiring repayment of training costs if an employee leaves before productivity repays training costs would ensure greater job commitment and eliminate employer preference for males. Summary in French.

463. Levy, Robert. "The Woman Who Wasn't There." *Dun's Review* 99 (June 1972): 63–64.

Federal legislation and the women's liberation movement have forced corporations to seek executive women. Many management jobs are now open to women, but companies complain they can't find qualified, dedicated women to fill them. There are more women in middle management in the federal government than in private industry.

464. Martin, Richard. "Interviewing Women." *Wall Street Journal*, 5 May 1980, p. 24.

A review of Helen J. McLane's *Selecting, Developing and Retaining Women Executives* focuses on problems male personnel managers have interviewing women for management and line positions. Based on discussions with 40 personnel people in top U.S. corporations, McLane advises interviewers to determine if the woman's personality matches the company's.

465. Mathis, Marilyn, and Jones, David H. "Finding More Women and Minorities for Management-Level Jobs." *Banking* 66 (March 1974): 94–100.

A study of national Equal Employment Opportunity Commission data indicates that the supply of potential women and minority managers may be sufficient, but the actual number of women and minorities qualified for bank management is not sufficient at this time. Advises banks to expand their recruitment and training programs for women and minorities.

466. McKenzie, Madora. "A Service that Lofts Women to Top Sales Careers." *Christian Science Monitor,* 23 August 1979, p. 17.

David King founded Careers for Women in 1973 to put women into high-paying executive positions. Careers for Women has offices in New York and Los Angeles, offers seminars in sales, management, and career selection and has placed 30,000 women so far.

467. McLane, Helen J. *Selecting, Developing and Retaining Women Executives: A Corporate Strategy for the Eighties.* New York: Van Nostrand Reinhold, 1980.

Discusses affirmative action and awareness training for management and women and includes chapters on attracting, selecting, developing, and retaining women executives. Gives 10 major reasons for the increasing number of women available for executive positions: greater opportunity, higher motivation, greater educational attainment, more useful curriculum, later marriage, pregnancy by choice, rising divorce rates, rising acceptance of the working woman, desire for higher living standard, and the increase in household technology. Includes index, extensive bibliography, and appendices which list federal legislation dealing with sex discrimination in employment, professional organizations offering assistance to employers (arranged by field), and seminars for and about women in management.

468. Morgenthaler, Eric. "Women of the World: More U.S. Firms Put Females in Key Posts in Foreign Countries." *Wall Street Journal,* 16 March 1978, p. 1+.

Describes the trend of companies to move more women into international business. Most of the women are in lower- to middle-level management positions, frequently in banking, where women have already made progress in this country. Several women in international management relate their experiences, good and bad, and narrate their working relationships with companies in western and eastern Europe and Africa.

469. Orth, Charles D. III, and Jacobs, Frederic. "Women in Management: Pattern for Change." *Harvard Business Review* 49 (July 1971): 139–47.

President and vice-president of Career Development International, Inc. outline obstacles to opportunities for women in management and describe a 4-step program to help corporations bring more women into management: occupational census, exit interviews with former women employees, recruiting procedures, and training opportunities. Concludes with discussion of need for mentors for women.

470. Paddison, Lorraine. "Why So Few?" *Accountant* 180 (January 25, 1979): 98–99.

A study conducted by a research team at Ashridge Management College found 3 main reasons why there are still so few women executives: career paths and personnel systems, attitudes of senior executives, and women's own attitudes. Author calls on British companies to utilize the managerial talents and abilities of women who comprise 40 percent of the work force.

471. "Post-Mortem on Lockwood." *MBA: Master in Business Administration* 7 (May 1973): 40.

A follow-up on the March 1973 *MBA* article on Lockwood's job conferences for women notes that, of 400 women attending the 3 conferences, only 13 were hired by corporate recruiters. President Curtis Lockwood has disbanded the Women in Management Division of Lockwood Group, Ltd.

472. "Room at the Top?" *Newsweek* 80 (December 4, 1972): 96+.

In response to the Labor Department's Revised Order No. 4 which mandates that over 250,000 government contractors file affirmative action programs for women, corporations vie each other for female managers. IBM increased its number of women managers by 18 percent in the first half of 1972. College placement offices note an increase in recruiting women into management, but some companies' job requirements exclude women who have not had enough experience to be qualified.

473. Rosenthal, Beth. "Headhunters (Women's Division)." *Across the Board* 14 (August 1977): 19–23.

A profile of Management Woman, Inc., the New York-based female executive search firm begun in 1974 by Anne Hyde and Janet Jones. Management Woman has 7,000 women in its active resume files, and the average salary placement in 1977 was $41,500.

474. Salpukas, Agis. "Recruiter Is Acquired." *New York Times,* 4 September 1980, sec. 4, p. 2.

Anne Hyde and Janet Jones-Parker, with $3,000, formed an executive woman recruitment firm, Management Woman, Inc., in 1973. The firm was recently sold to Boyden Associates, Inc., adding international clients and greater profits.

475. Schneider, Stephen A. *The Availability of Minorities and Women for Professional and Managerial Positions, 1970–1985.* (Manpower and Human Resources Studies, No. 7) Philadelphia, PA: University of Pennsylvania, Wharton Industrial Research Unit, 1977.

Studies past and present participation by minorities and women in engineering, law, accounting, business and management, chemistry, physics, medicine, and dentistry. Chapters on each profession include data on Blacks, other minorities, and women; describe current programs; and make predictions for the future. Concludes with a summary of changes, 1970–1985, and predicts that by 1985 there will be an improvement in minority and female participation in most of the professions studied. Includes numerous statistical tables, bibliographical references, and index.

476. Sheppard, I. Thomas. "Rite of Passage . . . Women for the Inner Circle." *Management Review* 70 (July 1981): 8–14.

Author argues that the original survival need to exclude women from the hunt and to develop rites of passage for men only have long since become anachronisms. Lists determination, energy, confidence, competence, and work relationships as major factors in scouting for female managerial talent and invites mentors to coach women managers in decision making, risk taking, and leadership style.

477. Stead, Bette Ann. "Real Equal Opportunity for Women Executives." *Business Horizons* 17 (August 1974): 87–92.

Discusses need for companies to develop equal opportunities in management for women and details methods available to provide equal opportunity: developing a companywide systems approach, making commitments, identifying candidates, and including management development programs for women.

478. Stevens, Mark. "Helping Businesswomen Succeed." *Christian Science Monitor,* 6 March 1978, p. 2.

Describes Women's, Inc., an executive search firm for management women, founded by Marge Rossman. Also gives information on 3 other organizations that are addressing the problems of women in business: the National Association of Women Business Owners, the Interagency Task Force on Women Business Owners, and the Small Business Association.

479. Tesar, Jenny. "Finding Promotable Women." *Banking* 69 (December 1977): 41–42, 44.

As a result of a survey which revealed that 72 percent of the employees at Virginia National Banking were women but only 25 percent of the officers and managers were women, the holding company developed an in-house rotational program to qualify women for senior management positions. Lending experience, management skills, and outdated attitudes toward women were the 3 areas stressed in the program.

480. Warren, Virginia Lee. "Women Are Moving into Management— But How Many? And How Far?" *New York Times,* 31 August 1974, p. 24.

An update on affirmative action in some major U.S. corporations including Bell, AT&T, CBS, Polaroid, and Sears. In a financial settlement resulting from an affirmative action suit, AT&T will offer $15 million in back pay and $23 million annually in salary increases for Blacks, women, and Spanish-speaking employees. To prevent their affirmative action plans from becoming available to the public, some companies, like Sears, have filed suits.

481. "Women and Minorities in Management." *U.S. Bureau of Labor Statistics. Monthly Labor Review.* 95 (March 1972): 55.

Abstract of the Women and Minorities in Management and in Personnel Management (Personnel Policies Forum Survey No. 96, December 1971) survey report. A Bureau of National Affairs survey of 163 companies reveals these statistics: companies have more women and members of minority groups in management than 5 years ago, but three-fourths still have no women and two-thirds have no minorities in top management positions; one-half have no Black or Chicano middle managers.

482. "Women in Management: What Needs to Be Done?" *DuPont Context* No. 1 (1974): 13–16.

In an interview with *Context* staff, Drs. Anne Jardim and Margaret Hennig discuss the problems and promises of women moving into management. The two Simmons College professors, authors of *The Managerial Woman,* comment on the lack of women in management, how male managers can help move women into management, and what changes women managers will bring to the business world.

483. ''Women Recruiters Mushroom At Search Firms along the 'Old-Boy' Network.'' *Wall Street Journal,* 7 October 1980, p. 1.

More than 200 executive search firms now have women recruiters. Long hours and 50-percent travel time are factors that still discourage many women from entering the field, claims Helen McLane of Heidrick and Struggles.

Obstacles

484. Baron, Alma S. "Do Managers Clone Themselves?" *The Executive Female* 4 (July/August 1981): 26.

Eight thousand male managers answered a questionnaire on the status of women in management. Author suggests ways to change behavior and attitudes of male managers toward female managers. Followed by a questionnaire for National Association of Female Executives (NAFE) members on their working situation and a second questionnaire to give to a male counterpart. (Reprinted from March 1981 *Personnel Administrator*.)

485. ———. "Women in Business: Are They Still Fighting Shadows?" *Training and Development Journal* 30 (May 1976): 11–12.

Identifies and rebuts 8 myths regarding working women. Author gives examples of women's changing self-image and reasons for the change.

486. Bender, Marilyn. "Women Eye Executive Suite; but Booby Traps Line Road to the Top." *New York Times,* 15 November 1970, sec. 3, p. 2.

Comments on the first conference on women in management held in New York City. Conference concluded with an effort to get more women into Harvard's prestigious training programs, the Advanced Management Program (AMP), and the Program for Management Development (PMD). Participants believe that women are on their way and are moving toward fairer opportunities.

487. Bralove, Mary. "Where the Boys Are: Despite Much Hoopla, Few Women Capture Companies' Top Jobs." *Wall Street Journal,* 18 April 1974, p. 1+.

In spite of the AT&T $38 million sex discrimination settlement and the hiring of more women in management positions, few women advance beyond middle management. A survey shows that, of 2 million employees in 20 large corporations, women constitute less than one percent of the professionals and managers.

488. Chambers, Peter. "No Easy Path for Women Managers." *International Management* 29 (May 1974): 46–48.

Although more nations are legislating for equal pay and equal opportunity, women still comprise only 4 percent of the total management group, and pay is usually below that of men in similar positions. The U.S. is seen as one of the few countries with significant progress in this area.

489. Chan, Janet. "What's Wrong with the 'Success' Books?" *Working Woman* 5 (August 1980): 38+.

A 2-year study by professors in the Wellesley College Center for Research in Women contradicts the advice in some women's "success" books. Identifies some obstacles women managers face: feeling different, discrimination, unequal evaluations, tokenism, and occupational segregation.

490. Crittenden, Ann. "In the Corporate World More Talk than Progress." *New York Times,* 1 May 1977, sec. 3, p. 1+.

In spite of national legislation requiring equal employment opportunities, women have not made real progress in the executive suite. In fact some women managers discern greater male resistance to women in business and management. Women make most progress in banking, insurance, and in more traditionally female industries like food, consumer products, personnel, cosmetics, advertising, and consumer affairs.

491. Day, Charles R., Jr. "Race Women Haven't Won." *Industry Week* 201 (April 2, 1979): 60–61+.

Although women managers in greater numbers are found in retailing, communications, and cosmetics, they have made little progress in manufacturing and other industries. Most women managers are seen as confident and dedicated, not "movement activists," and still fill middle management or staff positions. Younger women fresh out of graduate business schools, however, have done more career planning and expect to get to the top. Lists corporate support, mentors, equal pay, career planning, and supportive spouses as essential to a management woman's success.

492. Ekberg-Jordan, Sandra. "The Woman Manager: Opportunities and Obstacles." *AAUW Journal* 69 (April 1976): 9–12.

Reviews 3 categories of obstacles to women managers' advancement and describes opportunities for women in management.

493. "Fire Women Executives." *Administrative Management* 40 (March 1979): 14.

A partner in an executive recruiting firm notes that women executives are being fired not for lack of skill but for lack of political seasoning. The women lack mentors to help them up the corporate ladder.

494. Hackamack, Lawrence C., and Solid, Alan B. "The Woman Executive: There Is Still Ample Room for Progress." *Business Horizons* 15 (April 1972): 89–93.

Review of the role of the woman executive past and present; characteristics desirable in executives; and obstacles to executive careers for women. Authors draw optimistic conclusion on attitudinal changes.

495. Harlan, Anne, and Weiss, Carol. "Barriers to Mobility for Men and Women in Middle Management." Paper presented at the 28th Annual Meeting of the Society for the Study of Social Problems, Boston, Massachusetts, 24–27 August 1979.

Abstracted in *Sociological Abstracts,* August 1979, Supplement 94, #S10990.

496. ———. "Career Opportunities for Women Managers." In *Work, Family and the Career: New Frontiers in Theory and Research,* edited by Derr Brooklyn. New York: Praeger, 1980.

Reports the findings of research on barriers to women's advancement in management. Sex bias, sex stereotyping, and level of aspiration were found to be barriers, and the authors suggest that managerial training programs, career ladders, and job postings would help. Includes bibliography.

497. Hay, Christine D. "Women in Management: the Obstacles and Opportunities They Face." *Personnel Administrator* 25 (April 1980): 31–39.

Reviews statistics on the status of women in management, how women managers view themselves, and how they resolve conflict. Looks at management training programs currently available for women, the strengths and weaknesses in such programs, and what training is still needed. Includes bibliography. The author's description and analysis of 121 management training programs is available by sending a 30-cent self-addressed stamped envelope to: The Editor/Personnel Administrator, Re: C. Hay Analysis, 30 Park Drive, Berea, OH 44017.

498. Herbert, Theodore T., and Yost, Edward B. "Women as Effective Managers . . . A Strategic Model for Overcoming the Barriers." *Human Resource Management* 17 (Spring 1978): 18–25.

Identifies the shortage of executives and recent legislation as catalysts for the entry of women into management and reviews the current utilization of women in management and research on sex-role stereotypes and role models. Authors outline a strategy for developing women's management potential. Includes bibliographical references and a model for developing women into effective managers.

499. "Job Opportunities for Women Still Sparse at the Top." *Industry Week* 167 (October 12, 1970): 18+.

Cites several companies where the percentage of women in top management positions is still very low in spite of affirmative action programs for women and minorities. One corporation actively recruits women into management but claims it will take time for women to make it to top management positions. Ninety-four percent of this company's first-level managers are women, over 22 percent of their second-level managers are women, but only one female is found at the third level.

500. Kanter, Rosabeth Moss. "The Role of Women in the Corporation." *New York Times*, 21 August 1977, sec. 3, p. 14.

In an excerpt from *Men and Women of the Corporation* the author argues against using the individual model of behavior to increase the number of women in management and suggests an alternative model that would require corporations, not individuals, to change. Kanter, an associate professor of sociology at Yale, believes that trying to change the organizational structure rather than trying to "improve" individuals is the answer to change in the occupational distribution of men and women.

501. Kreps, Juanita. "Beyond the Statistics: Beyond the Rationales." *MBA: Master in Business Administration* 7 (March 1973): 12+.

This article on attitudinal barriers to women in business appeared as a chapter in *Corporate Lib* by Eli Ginzberg and Alice M. Yohalem (1973). Kreps discusses "fear of sameness," executive wives, and immobility and lists the society, the family, and the woman herself as obstacles to women's advancement in management.

502. Machlowitz, Marilyn. "Still Room at the Top." *Working Woman* 6 (July 1981): 75.

Although more women are moving into the ranks of management, few reach the top. Author suggests low salary expectations, limited mobility, avoidance of computers and technology, and specialization as deterrents to women's advancement.

503. Mirides, Ellyn, and Cote, Andre. "Women in Management: Strategies for Removing the Barriers." *Personnel Administrator* 25 (April 1980): 25–28.

Tells how sex-role stereotyping, hiring biases, organizational barriers, self-limitation, and leadership styles are obstacles to women's progress in management. Changes in women's attitudes and organizational awareness are necessary to improve their situation. Includes references.

504. Missirian, Agnes K. "Female Manager as a Shelf-Sitter." *Human Resources Management* 17 (Winter 1978): 29–32.

Discusses the results of research monitoring the career progress of 21 female managers in Boston corporations from 1963–73. Examines possible explanations for the fact that the women's careers were at an impasse. Includes figures and bibliographical references.

505. Norgaard, Corine T. "Problems and Perspectives of Female Managers." *MSU Business Topics* 28 (Winter 1980): 23–28.

Women in lower and middle management positions participated in a 1978 study to determine the most common obstacles to women's management progress. Most frequently cited problems included: lack of opportunity, employer discrimination, child care problems, and lack of ambition.

506. O'Leary, Virginia E. "Barriers to Professional Advancement among Female Managers." Paper presented at the 9th International Congress of Applied Psychology, Munich, Germany, August 1978.

Abstracted in *Resources in Education,* ED 173 549.

507. ———. "Women: Managers Stuck in the Middle?" Paper presented at the Annual Convention of the American Psychological Association, Toronto, Canada, August 1978.

Abstracted in *Resources in Education,* Ed 172 108.

508. Pospisil, Vivian C. "Problems of the Woman Manager." *Industry Week* 181 (April 1, 1974): 33–36.

Examines the unique problems of newly promoted women managers— acceptance, self-image, relationship with former co-workers, personal conflicts, tokenism, supervision of other women and of men, and travel with male peers. Recommendations for companies include counseling and career guidance for women, discussion sessions with top management, supportive superiors who encourage open communications, avoiding paternalism, and on-the-job training.

509. Price, Margaret. "An Uphill Battle for Female Managers." *Industry Week* 205 (June 23, 1980): 33+.

In a forthcoming book *Wising Up: The Mistakes Women Make in Business and How to Avoid Them* Jo Foxworth says only 2.3 percent of executives earning over $25,000 are women. White male managers 40 and over have the most difficulty accepting women in management, according to a survey of female managers by Heidrick and Struggles.

510. Robinson, Joseph Arnold. "Women Managers: Aids and Barriers in Their Career Paths, Performance and Advancement." PhD dissertation, University of California, Berkeley, 1974.

Abstracted in *Dissertation Abstracts International,* April 1975, v. 35, no. 10, #6310-A.

511. Rule, Sheila. "Women Still Knocking on the Door." *New York Times,* 12 October 1980, sec. 12, p. 43.

Recession affects affirmative action programs, and women managers are most often found in "corporate ghettos" of public relations and personnel. Gives statistics on percentages of women at the management level in certain fields and lists mathematics and engineering, computer programming, business, skilled crafts, financial fields, sales, insurance, information processing, and hotel and restaurant management as promising areas.

512. "Sexual Tension: Some Men Find Office Is a Little Too Exciting with Women as Peers." *Wall Street Journal,* 14 April 1981, p. 1+.

Interviews with management-level men and women about how they get along together on the job show that work relationships can be difficult when there's sexual attraction. Many women managers have to parry unwelcome advances from male peers and superiors.

513. Staszak. F. James, and Mathys, Nicholas J. "Women in Management: No Room in the Middle?" *Supervisory Management* 20 (March 1975): 10–13.

Authors list discrimination, lack of formal business education, and the traditional view of women's role as reasons why there are few middle-level women managers. Studies show that marital status, lack of development programs, and lack of awareness of promotional routes hinder women's management progress.

514. "Still More Room at the Top." *Newsweek* 83 (April 29, 1974): 74+.
In spite of federal affirmative action legislation and the women's movement, the 1970 census shows that only 4.8 percent of managers and administrators earning $10,000 or more a year are women. Special problems of women managers include lack of self-confidence, lack of informal contact with male peers, difficulty supervising others, and put-downs from male clients.

515. Swain, Robert L. "Special Dangers for Women Execs." *Industrial Marketing* 65 (June 1980): 84.
Cites 10 reasons why women executives are being fired, claiming that most of the problems deal with "style" of management. The greatest difficulty for women managers is lack of tenure or lack of a mentor within the organization.

516. Templeton, Jane F., and Marrow, Naomi S. "Women as Managers: Still a Long Way to Go." *Personnel* 49 (September/October 1972): 30–37.
In spite of some progress, few women are appointed to managerial positions or receive authority to match their titles. Authors advise women on dealing with "newness panic," role-modeling without a model, and "equal" competence.

517. Veiga, John F. "Women in Management: An Endangered Species?" *MSU Business Topics* 25 (Summer 1977): 31–35.
Results of a survey of 500 management women who attended career development workshops show that women are not socialized to be assertive about their own career advancement, experience "choice anxiety," or have more difficulty making career choices than men do. Includes tables and bibliographical references.

518. "The Woman Executive: She's Not Rising as Quickly as Hoped." *Christian Science Monitor,* 29 June 1973, p. 8.
The president of an executive search firm predicts only 5 out of 100 women will make it to middle management. He believes toiletries, food companies, entertainment, accounting, law, public relations, and education will be areas favorable for women.

519. "Women Managers Experience Special Power Failures." *Harvard Business Review* 57 (July 1979): 69.

In an article on "Power Failure in Management Circuits," Rosabeth Moss Kanter cites several reasons for women managers' "powerlessness": women in management are typically found in first-line supervisory positions or in staff positions; women are often given "safe" jobs to "protect" them from the dangers of risk taking; women often lack managerial support; women are seen as uninformed and are frequently not included in informal socializing; women are more frequently seen as proteges rather than as mentors.

520. Wood, Marion M. "Women in Management: How Is It Working Out?" *SAM Advanced Management Journal* 41 (Winter 1976): 22–30.

Results of a survey of almost 100 male and female managers indicate that, although women managers encounter some unique problems, the problems are less than both men and women expected. Adjustment problems, or role-status problems, cause the most difficulty for female executives.

Comparisons of Men and Women Managers

521. "Are Women Managers Different from Men?" *Management Review* 69 (December 1980): 52.

A study of 2,000 male and female managers reveals that, in 3 out of 5 aspects of management behavior, women do not differ significantly from men. In the other 2 areas, managerial work motivation and interpersonal competence, female managers are seen as more achieving and male managers as more open and candid with colleagues.

522. Baird, John E., Jr., and Bradley, Patricia Hayes. "Styles of Management and Communication: A Comparative Study of Men and Women." *Communication Monographs* 46 (June 1979): 101–11.

An 18-item questionnaire on managerial communicative behavior and employee morale was answered by 150 employees. Results indicate that female managers communicate in ways significantly different from male managers, and the authors conclude that female managers may be more effective supervisors. Includes tables and bibliographical references.

523. Bartol, Kathryn M. "The Effect of Male versus Female Leaders on Follower Satisfaction and Performance." *Journal of Business Research* 3 (January 1975): 33–42.

Instead of relying on the opinion offered by other research that women prefer to work for male bosses, the author compared member satisfaction and group performance in groups led by male or female leaders. Using a simulated business game, *The Executive Game*, the author concluded that satisfaction level was not greatly affected by sex of the leader. Includes table and references.

524. Birdsall, Paige. "A Comparative Analysis of Male and Female Managerial Communication Style in Two Organizations." *Journal of Vocational Behavior* 16 (April 1980): 183–96.

A study to determine if male and female managers demonstrate a significantly different communication style with subordinates in staff meetings. Results show that they use similar communication styles and both selected typical "masculine" attributes in describing themselves as managers. Includes tables and references.

525. Brown, Stephen M. "Male versus Female Leaders: A Comparison of Empirical Studies." *Sex Roles: A Journal of Research* 5 (October 1979): 595–611.

Reviews 32 female leadership studies and divides them into 3 categories of leadership theories: trait, style, and contingency. Research indicates that the sex stereotyping of women as ineffective leaders doesn't hold true in actual work situations. Includes extensive tables and references.

526. Cecil, Earl A.; Paul, Robert J.; and Olins, Robert A. "Perceived Importance of Selected Variables Used to Evaluate Male and Female Job Applicants." *Personnel Psychology* 26 (1973): 397–404.

Gives the results of a study to determine important qualities of male and female applicants for the same job. Indicates job applicants are evaluated differently depending on whether they are male or female, with females perceived as a typical clerical employee and males as an administrative management employee. Includes tables and references.

527. Champion, Donald Lee. "A Comparison of Men and Women Managers on Preferences for Organizational Conflict Management." DBA, Florida State University, 1979.

Abstracted in *Dissertation Abstracts International,* v. 33, no. 5, December 1979, #3399–A.

528. Chapman, J. Brad. "Comparison of Male and Female Leadership Styles." *Academy of Management Journal* 18 (September 1975): 645–50.

Male (195) and female (88) managers responded to the Least Preferred Co-Worker (LPC) questionnaire to test 2 hypotheses regarding differences between male and female leadership styles. Results indicate that, while female managers may exhibit a different leadership behavior than their male colleagues, there are no significant differences in leadership style. Includes tables and references.

529. "The Corporate Woman: Stress Has No Gender." *Business Week* (November 15, 1976): 73+.

Ulcers, heart disease, and cancer become more common among women as more women become executives. Many doctors believe it is "trying" rather than "succeeding" that causes stress—especially if trying is unsuccessful.

530. Davidson, Marilyn, and Cooper, Cary. "The Extra Pressures on Women Executives." *Personnel Management* (London) 12 (June 1980): 48–51.

Researchers conducted a survey of 180 women managers to determine the sources and levels of stress of British women managers. Results indicated that women managers experience higher levels of work-related stress than their male colleagues, a factor which may prevent other women from entering management or limit their desire for promotion. Includes tables and references.

531. Day, David R., and Stogdill, Ralph M. "Leader Behavior of Male and Female Supervisors: A Comparative Study." *Personnel Psychology* 25 (Summer 1972): 353–60.

Thirty-seven male and 36 female supervisors participated in a study to determine how women behave in leadership roles, how effective they are, and the relationship between behavior and effectiveness. Female managers were compared with male managers in similar positions, and results show that, while effective males advance rapidly, the females' effectiveness did not affect rate of advancement. Includes tables and references.

532. Donnell, Susan M., and Hall, Jay. "Men and Women as Managers: A Significant Case of No Significant Difference." *Organizational Dynamics* 8 (Spring 1980): 60–77.

Researchers studied 2,000 managers to make evaluative comparisons of male and female managers. The managers were compared for managerial philosophy, motivational dynamics, participative practices, interpersonal competence, and managerial style. Authors conclude that "women, in general, do not differ from men, in general, in the ways in which they administer the management process." Includes figures and bibliography.

533. Fottler, Myron D., and Bain, Trevor. "Managerial Aspirations of High School Seniors: A Comparison of Males and Females." *Journal of Vocational Behavior* 16 (February 1980): 83–95.

Over 2,000 Alabama high school seniors completed a survey to determine their orientation toward management careers. Results show that more young people aspire to professional rather than managerial careers and the model of the "male manager" persists, with few young women seeking careers in management.

534. Gallese, Liz Roman. "Women Trained to Gain Trust of Male Bosses." *Wall Street Journal,* 16 January 1981, p. 21.

Women managers don't advance as quickly as men because companies either assume women will refuse relocation and have more family responsibility or because they "protect" women from difficult assignments. Some businesses offer management development programs for women to help lessen the gap between male and female managers.

535. Garrard, Meg; Oliver, June; and Williams, Martha. *Women and Men—Colleagues in Management?* (Human Services Monograph Series, No. 2) Austin, TX: University of Texas, 1976.

Proceedings of a conference held at the University of Texas at Austin, May 16–17, 1975. Includes keynote address and text of 9 panel presentations divided into 3 sections: the economic perspective, fear of success, and the informal organization. Concludes with descriptions of 6 work sessions on assertion training, managerial and communication styles, role conflicts, legal rights, and superiors and subordinates. Available from the Center for Social Work Research, School of Social Work Research, University of Texas at Austin.

536. Gould, Karolyn, and Anundsen, Kristin. "The Rise of Womanagement." *Innovation* (September 1971): 14–22.

The authors discuss companies' reactions to increasing numbers of women in management positions and suggest that male and female managers are complementary and that business can profit from employing both sexes in management positions. Corporate policies that may need rethinking or revising include: recruitment, salary, promotion of women, child care, and maternity leave. Concludes with discussion questions and a short list of sources.

537. Helmich, Donald L. "Male and Female Presidents: Some Implications of Leadership Style." *Human Resource Management* 13 (1974): 25–26.

A study of 225 male and 225 female corporate presidents explores the differences in their leadership styles. Results indicate that male presidents are more employee-oriented as a group, while female presidents are more demanding of the task at hand. Includes table and footnotes.

538. Humphreys, Luther Wade, and Shrode, William A. "Decision-Making Profiles of Female and Male Managers." *MSU Business Topics* 26 (Autumn 1978): 45–51.

Compares task, personnel, budgetary, information, and conceptual decisions made by male and female managers and concludes that there are more similarities than differences between male and female managers. Includes tables.

539. Josefowitz, Natasha. "Management Men and Women: Closed vs Open Doors." *Harvard Business Review* 58 (September/October 1980): 56+.

A study of 68 male and 102 female managers found females were twice as accessible to their employees. Researcher hypothesizes 3 reasons for women managers' greater accessibility: inability or unwillingness to say "No," need to check on how things are going, and an "open door" policy. Lists the advantages and disadvantages of accessibility.

540. Kinkead, Gwen. "On a Fast Track to the Good Life." *Fortune* 101 (April 7, 1980): 74–78+.

In a survey of 82 25-year-olds, *Fortune* found a group of confident young men and women already in the upper-income bracket. Many describe themselves frankly as materialistic, competitive, ambitious, and committed to their jobs, sometimes to the exclusion of marriage and children.

541. Knudson, Ann Sawyer Dickinson. "An Analysis of Assertiveness, Locus of Control and Causal Attribution of Success in Purdue Management Men and Women." PhD dissertation, Purdue University, 1980.

Abstracted in *Dissertation Abstracts International*, v. 41, December 1980, #2453–A.

542. Lannon, Judith M. "Male vs Female Values in Management." *Management International Review* 17 (1977): 9–12.

The director of J. Walter Thompson in London warns against adopting the myth of the female nurturer/manager. She argues that hiring women simply to comply with legislation or social pressure represents tokenism.

543. Mai-Dalton, Renate R.; Feldman-Summers, Shirley; and Mitchell, Terence R. "Effect of Employee Gender and Behavioral Style on the Evaluations of Male and Female Banking Executives." *Journal of Applied Psychology* 64 (April 1979): 221–26.

Sixty-two male and 60 female banking executives participated in evaluation of a job-related conflict situation. Participants rated men and women behaving in an unemotional manner and in an emotional manner. The author found that participants evaluated performance of others based both on sex-role expectations and expectations of appropriate employee behavior. Both male and females indicated that a person who acts in a calm, unemotional manner has a greater chance of promotion.

544. Marcum, Patricia J. "Men and Women on the Management Team." *University of Michigan Business Review* 28 (November 1976): 8–11.
Examines the meaning of sex roles and the reaction to changing roles with respect to women in management. Argues for keeping women in management programs, using culturally-learned sex roles creatively and productively, and applying social science research to analyze human behavior.

545. Meyer, Pearl. "Women Executives Are Different." *Dun's Review* 105 (January 1975): 46–48.
Although corporations seek more women managers, women (40 percent of the U.S. labor force) still hold only 5 percent of the managerial positions. Author argues that corporate recruiters need to be aware of the fact that compensation packages designed for middle-aged male executives may not be appropriate for women managers. Compensation differentials might include salaries, pensions, insurance, medical benefits, relocation expenses, and club memberships.

546. Muldrow, Tressie W., and Bayton, James A. "Men and Women Executives and Processes Related to Decision Accuracy." *Journal of Applied Psychology* 64 (April 1979): 99–106.
Two hundred male and female federal executives participated in a study using a managerial task (a personnel promotion decision) to determine if there were significant differences between male and female executives on the task variables. Results showed that there were no significant differences on most of the task variables, but the female executives were significantly less likely to take risks.

547. Press, A. K. "Do Women Handle Power Differently from Men?" *Working Woman* 5 (April 1980): 44–46.
In this interview David G. Winter, author of *The Power Motive*, describes his research which destroys the myth that women aren't interested in power. He also answers questions about power-motivated men and women and their marriages, how men and women use power differently, and how women develop the ability to lead through the study of science.

548. Ritchie, Richard J., and Boehm, Virginia R. "Biographical Data as a Predictor of Women's and Men's Management Potential." *Journal of Vocational Behavior* 11 (December 1977): 363–68.

Studies show that biographical data may be a determinant in the potential of men and women for management. Includes tables and references.

549. Rizzo, Ann Marie. "Patterns of Person-Group Relationships for Female and Male Mid-Level Managers in Three Governmental Agencies." PhD dissertation, Syracuse University, 1976.

Abstracted in *Dissertation Abstracts International*, v. 36, April 1976, #6950–A.

550. Rosen, Benson, and Jerdee, Thomas H. "Effects of Applicant's Sex and Difficulty of Job on Evaluations of Candidates for Managerial Positions." *Journal of Applied Psychology* 59 (August 1974): 511–12.

A study using 235 male undergraduate business students corroborates the author's hypothesis that female applicants for managerial jobs are evaluated as less acceptable than male applicants with identical qualifications. Data also indicates the tendency of rejecting females for more demanding jobs.

551. Schreier, James W. "Is the Female Entrepreneur Different?" *MBA: Master in Business Administration* 10 (March 1976): 40–43.

The Center for Venture Management in Milwaukee conducted a survey of entrepreneurial women and found that 72 percent had an entrepreneurial father. Data from the study show that female entrepreneurs are different from women managers in large corporations but not significantly different from male entrepreneurs.

552. Schuler, Randall S. "Male and Female Routes to Managerial Success." *Ohio State University. Center for Business and Economic Research. Bulletin of Business Research.* 52 (August 1977): 1–4.

Author claims that 3 issues—performance evaluation, job typing, and power—affect the success of male and female managers differently, independent of their actual performance. Suggests methods to reduce the possibility of differential success of managers based on gender.

553. Seidman, Anne, ed. *Working Women: A Study of Women in Paid Jobs.* Boulder, CO: Westview Press, 1978.

Results of data from 8 weekend workshops in the following categories: clerical workers, service workers, blue-collar workers, the professions, managers and administrators, women reentering the paid labor force, Black and other minority women, and education. The chapter on managers and administrators includes tables on the percentage of men and women in managerial and administrative positions and employment statistics for male and female managers in New England, 1960–70. Includes tables, figures, annotated bibliography, and index.

554. Stanek, Lou Willet. ''Women in Management: Can It Be a Renaissance for Everybody?'' *Management Review* 69 (November 1980): 44–48.

The real renaissance in today's organization world is not for women to emulate the traditional male model, but for men and women to learn organization (male) and family (female) norms from each other. Men's fear of losing power and authority and women's fear of success still prevent their working together as a team.

555. Stanley, Betty M. ''A Comparative Analysis of the Work of the Male and Female First-Line Office Supervisor.'' PhD dissertation, Arizona State University, 1972.

Abstracted in *Dissertation Abstracts International*, v. 33, November 1972, #1915–A.

556. Stead, Bette, and Mullins, Terry Wayne. ''The Professional Status of Male and Female Academy of Management Members: A Comparison of Perceptions.'' Paper presented at the 37th Annual Meeting of the Academy of Management, August 1977.

Abstracted in *Resources in Education*, ED 155 995.

557. Van Wagner, Karen, and Swanson, Cheryl. ''From Machiavelli to Ms.: Differences in the Male-Female Power Styles.'' *Public Administration Review* 39 (1979): 66–72.

Results of research conducted to determine if there are differences in the power-related behavior of male and female administrators. Research findings do not seem to show differences by sex on the level of power needs, but men and women may express their power needs differently. Includes references.

558. Veiga, John F., and Yanouzas, John N. ''What Women in Management Want: The Ideal vs the Real.'' *Academy of Management Journal* 19 (March 1976): 137–43.

Gives data on disillusionment of women managers as compared with their male counterparts. Researchers use the Disillusionment Index (DI) to indicate the difference between women's present management position and their ideal management position. Findings show that younger management women generally have a higher level of disillusionment than older management women.

559. "Women Managers Who Perform Poorly Are More Likely to Think They're Performing Well than Men with Similar Performance Ratings." *Wall Street Journal,* 16 October 1979, p. 1.

Researchers in a Cleveland University study say that, even when female managers aren't performing up to standard, male executives may make exceptions for them, leading the women to believe that they're performing better than they actually are.

Advice Literature

560. Antwerp, Dacia Van. "Women in Management." *Journal of College Placement* 39 (February 1979): 45–46.

Cites the importance of counseling and the GET formula for women who are interested in management—Goals, Expertise, Teamwork.

561. Baldridge, Letitia. "When Women Move Up to Executive Jobs." *U.S. News and World Report* 88 (March 24, 1980): 67.

A business consultant interviewed by *U.S. News* discusses the new woman executive, how to compete with men, how to use the lunch network, and how to fight discrimination. She predicts women will be chairs of major corporations within 20 years; their progress will be based on ability and competence.

562. Cannie, Joan K. *The Woman's Guide to Management Success: How to Win Power in the Real Organizational World*. Englewood Clifs, NJ: Prentice-Hall, 1979.

Advice on learning management skills and behavior. Includes information on leadership style, communication, negotiating, management by objectives, conflicts, decision making, and time management. The author is a high school graduate who started her own company at age 24.

563. Comer, Nancy Axelrad. "How to Be a Good Boss . . . and How Not to Be." *Mademoiselle* 85 (January 1979): 97–98+.

Advice from bosses and employees on crying at the office, the Cinderella syndrome, who gets the coffee, tyrants, delegating responsibility, and mentors. A former personnel consultant says detachment is necessary to be a good boss.

564. "Commandments for Women Execs." *Advertising Age* 49 (June 5, 1978): 66.

A book review of Jo Foxworth's *Boss Lady* lists her "Nine Commandments for Women in Business." Foxworth, advertising executive and columnist for *Advertising Age,* offers 6 additional suggestions for women who want to make it in business.

565. ''The Corporate Woman: How to Get Along—and Ahead—In the Office.'' *Business Week* (March 22, 1976): 107–08+.

Do's and *don'ts* for corporate women and male associates fall into 3 categories: women's status, competence, and behavior as managers. Gives advice on taking risks, speaking at least once in every 10-minute meeting, being assertive, easing social tensions, and planning careers.

566. Crain, Sharie, and Drotning, Philip T. *Taking Stock: A Woman's Guide to Corporate Success.* Chicago, IL: Henry Regnery, 1977.

Advice on understanding and winning in a male environment, how to choose a career, how to get the job you want, how to gain self-confidence, how to get a promotion, how to get a raise, and how to handle difficult situations. Separate chapters give ''Advice for the Recent College Graduate'' and ''Tips for Older Women Returning to Work.'' Stresses career planning in ''Strategy for the Corporate Woman'' and concludes with the author's predictions for women's participation in management.

567. Cummings, Judith. ''How Career Women Can Get Ahead by Really Trying.'' *New York Times,* 10 February 1976, p. 33.

Over 250 women attended a conference on ''Women in Management'' at New York University. The women, most of them aiming at assistant vice-presidencies, were told that mentors, professionalism, assertiveness, and training are necessary for success. The conference, sponsored by the Women's Career Forum of the New York University Graduate School, included consciousness raising and technical sessions.

568. Donnelly, Caroline. ''Keys to the Executive Powder Room.'' *Money* 5 (August 1976): 28–32.

Advice to women in management from management consultants, executive recruiters, and women executives: get rid of old attitudes that hamper your progress, do long-range career planning, choose your job carefully, choose your employer with an eye to opportunity for advancement, dress the part, act the part, use networks and mentors to further your career, use femininity—not sex, and take legal action only as a last resort.

569. Downs, Linda B. ''Manager's Credo: Delegate, Delegate, Delegate, Delegate.'' *Working Woman* 5 (August 1980): 18.

Gives paper exercises to determine how well you delegate and tips on being a good delegator. Lists *Moving Up! Women and Leadership* by

Lois Borland Hart and *The Effective Woman Manager* by Nathaniel
Stewart as additional reading.

570. Driscoll, Jeanne Bosson, and Bova, Rosemary A. "The Sexual Side
of Enterprise." *Management Review* 69 (July 1980): 51–54.
Discusses the policy, resources, and team building and cost implications for corporations that must deal with questions of sexual relationships as more women move into management. Offers 6 guidelines for
managers who confront changing work ethics and values.

571. Dunlap, Jan. *Personal and Professional Success for Women.* Englewood Cliffs, NJ: Prentice-Hall, 1972.
Written by a top management woman for women entering management
or those changing careers, this book includes information on career
planning and aptitude-testing, decision making, time management,
professionalism, education, productivity, promotability of secretaries,
changing jobs, selling yourself to superiors and subordinates, and
travel. Includes bibliographical references.

572. Fader, Shirley Sloan. "5 Strategies after a Promotion." *Glamour* 77
(December 1979): 42.
A career and job specialist gives 5 tips for success after a promotion:
don't make sweeping changes immediately; keep your authority; learn
to speak up and take risks; delegate; and help other women up the
ladder.

573. Forbes, Rosalind. *Corporate Stress.* Garden City, NY: Doubleday,
1979.
The chapter on "Stresses and Strains of Working Women" tells what
creates stress for many businesswomen and includes a 29-point quiz to
help women identify those areas that cause them stress. Author offers
"Twelve Rules to Reduce the Strain for Women at the Top," and "Ten
Tips for Moms Who Work" and concludes the chapter with the
"Female Stress Defense Guide."

574. Foxworth, Jo. *Boss Lady: An Executive Woman Talks about Making
It.* New York: Crowell, 1978.
Practical advice on packaging yourself, hiring and firing, working for a
woman, traveling, listening, business clubs, dual careers, and the
Equal Rights Amendment. Specific *do's* and *don'ts* are listed at the end
of each chapter. Includes index.

575. Galvin, Ruth Mehrtens. "Goal Consciousness: You Have to Have a Strategy." *New York* (April 4, 1977): 55–58.

Gives a preview of Margaret Hennig and Anne Jardim's forthcoming book, *The Managerial Woman*. Authors say commitment and specific goals are necessities and encourage women to draw up a 5-year plan for advancing their careers.

576. Harmon, Mary. "After the Promotion, or, How to Survive Once You've Arrived." *Mademoiselle* 86 (November 1980): 226–27+.

Discusses jealousy of old friends and peers, acceptance by new peers, asserting yourself in your new position, breaking old job habits, learning time management, and how to delegate. Secretaries moving up to executive rank may have to rethink attitudes, dress and office decor, and etiquette.

577. ———. "Do You Think Like a Boss Even If You're Not?" *Mademoiselle* 87 (February 1981): 158–59+.

A 6-question, multiple-choice quiz to determine your executive mentality. Hints on how to tell if you're a "boss" or a "plodder."

578. Head, Margaret. "Female Chauvinism: Male Error Repeated." *New York Times,* 3 August 1980, sec. 23, p. 18.

A free-lance writer deplores the chauvinism of young female executives who believe every woman should be employed in the business world. She argues that women should exhibit empathy and tolerance for various life-styles.

579. Hegarty, Edward J. *How to Succeed in Company Politics.* 2d ed. New York: McGraw-Hill, 1976.

A "how-to" of company politics with chapters on playing smart politics with the boss, good communication, taking the knocks, self-improvement, building a team, keeping an eye on the next promotion, and working for a woman boss. Lists at the end of some chapters include specific advice to women in corporations.

580. Higginson, Margaret Valliant, and Quick, Thomas L. *The Ambitious Woman's Guide to a Successful Career.* New York: AMACOM, 1975.

Suggestions for career planning, job-hunting, management skills, and relationships with superiors and peers. Includes resource list, bibliography, and index.

581. Houston, Liz. ''Businesswomanly Wiles: A Few Rules on Disarming the Skeptics.'' *MBA: Master in Business Administration* 11 (September 1977): 30–31.

A Chicago-based management consultant suggests that businesswomen should dress to kill, organize their personal lives, learn to budget time carefully, and stay in good physical shape. She also wishes she could practice what she preaches.

582. ———. ''Taking Off the Kid Gloves: A Handbook for Business Women.'' *MBA: Master in Business Administration* 12 (May 1978): 30+.

Advice to the new business school graduate on job hunting, interview problems/questions, salary negotiations, cooperation with other women, and sex stereotypes.

583. ''How to Get What You Want on the Job.'' *Working Woman* 5 (January 1980): 15.

The co-director of Options for Women, a Philadelphia career advisory and business-consulting service for women, gives advice to middle management women on negotiating a raise and provides strategies for getting the recognition they deserve.

584. Irwin, Victoria. ''Guidance for Women on How to Succeed in Business—By Really Trying.'' *Christian Science Monitor,* 20 October 1980, p. 14.

What to Do With the Rest of Your Life is the title of a new book by Catalyst, the New York-based, nonprofit organization for women's career advancement. According to the book, business, government, law, science, engineering, and health and trade skills will offer the best opportunities for women in the 80s.

585. Jessup, Claudia, and Chipps, Genie. *The Woman's Guide to Starting a Business.* Rev ed. New York: Holt, Rinehart, and Winston, 1979.

Part I reviews the basics of starting a business from conceiving the idea and checking the legal technicalities to financing, marketing, and advertising. Part II is a collection of interviews with successful women entrepreneurs in retailing, services, food, manufacturing, seasonal businesses, and franchising. Part III, ''Business Reading and Informational Sources,'' includes a bibliography; lists of periodicals, additional information sources, women's directories, women's business associations, and organizations; and an index.

586. Kanter, Rosabeth Moss. "Corporate Success: You Don't Have to Play by Their Rules." *Ms* 8 (October 1979): 63–64+.

In an interview, Rosabeth Moss Kanter, author of *Men and Women of the Corporation* and *Life in Organizations* and visiting professor in the Sloan School of Management, Massachusetts Institute of Technology, talks about the "management skills" women have to master, company management training programs for women, the differences women and minorities make in business and industry, structural changes that "humanize" the workplace, and flex-time. Kanter believes that political pressure, productivity concerns, new leadership, and a more educated work force will make the corporate world more humanistic.

587. ———. "How to Stop Being Stuck and Use Your Power." *Working Woman* 5 (October 1980): 6, 70+.

Special problems of women managers contribute to their powerlessness in organizations, says the author of *Men and Women of the Corporation*. The problems include: patronizing, overprotection, tokenism, the assumption that women are uninformed, and lack of a power base in the organization. Kanter offers advice on how women can increase their power in organizations and draws some conclusions about female managers and power. Includes a checklist for evaluating power in your job.

588. Laughridge, Jamie. "Working Woman's Guide to Perks." *Working Woman* 4 (November 1979): 85–86+.

Information for women executives on who gets perks, the financial value of perks, and a list of available perks including: interview and relocation costs, expense accounts, club memberships, company cars, travel-related luxuries, discounts on goods or services, medical examinations, extra insurance, vacation benefits, educational assistance, financial and legal counseling, stock options, savings plans, deferred compensation plans, and reduced-interest loans. Advises women to consider the entire compensation package when evaluating a job offer.

589. Lee, Amy. "A Smorgasbord of Ideas for Her Own Business." *Christian Science Monitor,* 16 March 1978, p. 23.

A book review of *New Businesses Women Can Start and Successfully Operate* by Mary Leslie and David D. Seltz. Each of the 102 leads is given in a 3-step formula: the idea, getting started, and the cash flow. Includes case histories of 5 successful businesswomen and a 16-page appendix on business information sources.

590. Lee, Nancy. "Time Is Money." *Working Woman* 5 (October 1980): 59–60+.

Advice on using the 4 fundamental tools of management—planning, organizing, controlling, and evaluating. Gives information on time studies, making lists, long-range planning, setting up a schedule, and avoiding distractions.

591. ———. "What's It Really Like to Be a Boss?" *Glamour* 78 (October 1980): 250–51+.

The president of a management and marketing consultant firm lists 3 basic skills for effective managers: the ability to analyze situations, to communicate information, and to motivate people. She says you should also know your energy level and whether or not you want power.

592. "Let's Huddle, Women." *Time* 109 (May 2, 1972): 63.

Advice to women executives from Margaret Hennig and Anne Jardim: define goals, acquire technical competence, find a mentor, and take risks. Includes a cartoon.

593. Levine, JoAnn. "Women Managers in Unfamiliar Ballpark." *Christian Science Monitor,* 3 August 1977, p. 18.

Comments from Simmons College professors Anne Jardim and Margaret Hennig, authors of *The Managerial Woman* and graduates of the Harvard Business School. They advise women that a career is a series of jobs and to learn the informal system.

594. Moorhead, John D. "Women in Management." *Christian Science Monitor,* 9 May 1975, p. 2.

DeAnne Rosenberg, a consultant specializing in women managers' problems, gives nationwide seminars for women executives. She advises women to avoid "stand-out" behavior and trains them to compete, not cooperate.

595. Murphy, Marcia Ruth. "Women as Entrepreneurs—The New American Way." *Christian Science Monitor,* 29 March 1979, p. 19.

A review of *The Entrepreneurial Woman,* by Sandra Winston, which covers management information on partnerships, franchises, contacts, and money. Winston says a woman entrepreneur should be adventurous, self-confident, and able to handle stress.

596. Newton, Derek A. *Think Like a Man, Act Like a Lady, Work Like a Dog.* New York: Doubleday, 1979.

Divided into the 3 sections in the title, each section offers a paragraph of advice to women managers. Topics are arranged in alphabetical order and cover Aristotle to Worry, Amusement to Zoo, Airports to Zest.

597. Perry, Ellen, and Krown, Lynn. "How to Get Fired—into a Good New Job: Outplacement Services." *Working Woman* 4 (November 1977): 53–56.

A women's career counselor discusses the growth of outplacement firms, designed to help the fired employee locate a suitable new job in another company. Services are usually available to managers and executives and include counseling, vocational testing, networking, and job searches. Women outplacement counselors and clients are still a minority.

598. Pogrebin, Letty Cottin. *How To Make It In A Man's World*. Garden City, NY: Doubleday, 1970.

Advice to women who want everything—marriage, motherhood, and career. Tells "How to Succeed in Business without Really Typing" and how to "Work and Play the Executive Way."

599. Reif, Rita, "Women Find Specializing Eases Way to Top." *New York Times,* 4 January 1976, sec. 3, p. 52.

In an interview 5 middle management women in banking, finance, and business credit the 1964 federal law banning sexual discrimination in employment for increasing the number of women in the executive suite. A 31-year-old marketing consultant with an MBA from Harvard discusses her motivation to work.

600. Robertson, Nan. "For Ambitious Women, a Survival Guide to the Land of Bosses." *New York Times,* 28 June 1977, p. 36.

The Managerial Woman by Hennig and Jardim, based on interviews with 3,000 female and 1,000 male executives, gives 5 descriptions of women executives, and responses to each of these descriptions. Over-specialization in a particular area limits women's opportunities, say Hennig and Jardim, the first 2 women to receive their doctorates from the Harvard Business School.

601. Rogalin, Wilma C., and Pell, Arthur R. *Women's Guide to Management Positions*. New York: Simon & Schuster, 1975.

Starts with a Managerial Aptitude Analysis Form and forms for evaluating your industry, your company, your job, and your present situation for career growth. Includes information on affirmative action legislation and legal steps to take if you believe you've been discriminated against. Chapters on changing jobs, advice to new college graduates, and women returning to the work force are followed by appendices which include case histories, a list of career counseling services, and information on careers for women in the 1970s.

602. Rosenberg, DeAnne. "The Invisible Manager." *SAM Advanced Management Journal* 42 (Spring 1977): 51–62.
The president of a management consulting firm says visibility is important to promotion. New managers should establish their visibility around the organization and the environment in which it operates, within the organization itself, and within the area of your assigned job.

603. Schaeffer, Dorothy. "Suggestions for the New Woman Supervisor." *Supervision* 40 (November 1978): 3.
Ten suggestions for the new woman supervisor: don't panic, recognize you will make mistakes, expect criticism, face resentment, know there can be spite activities, appraise your performance, keep healthy, prepare for pressure, be patient with yourself, and learn your job.

604. Schwartz, Eleanor Brantley, and MacKenzie, R. Alec. "Time Management Strategy for Dual-Career Women." *Business Quarterly* 42 (Autumn 1977): 32–41.
Identifies 12 paradoxes of time and tells how dual-career women must use the basic management principles of planning, organizing, controlling, and delegating in order to sucessfully manage home and work. Lists common problem areas in the home and office and 12 time savers in the home.

605. ———. "Time Management Strategy for Women." *Management Review* 66 (September 1977): 19–25.
Because many professional women also have responsibility for home and family concerns, time management is critical. Identifies 12 paradoxes in time management and tells how to block interruptions and how to delegate.

606. Stead, Bette Ann. "Women and Men in Management: Getting Along." *Vital Speeches* 46 (October 15, 1979): 10–16.
Speech delivered to National Management Association National Conference, Management University, Houston, Texas, September 22, 1979. Includes suggestions to help women perform in management

positions and to help men recruit and train women managers. Gives advice to women on dealing with the informal system and suggestions for men on commitment to the concept of women in management.

607. Stewart, Nathaniel. *The Effective Woman Manager: Seven Vital Skills for Upward Mobility*. New York: Wiley, 1978.

Advice to the woman manager on planning, coordinating, delegating, evaluating, decision making, time allocating, and developing human resources. Includes appendix and bibliography.

608. Trahey, Jane. *Jane Trahey on Women and Power: Who's Got It? How to Get It?* New York: Rawson Associates, 1977.

Practical advice to women on interviewing, salary negotiations, office location, image, and establishing your own business, from the founder and president of an advertising agency. Appendices include data on the top 50 companies in the *Fortune* 500, a list of the top 50 highest-paid marketing executives, and other "Startling Statistics."

609. Van Gedder, Lawrence. "Women Get Ahead Using His Advice." *New York Times*, 26 October 1980, sec. 21, p. 2.

Nathaniel Stewart, founder of the nonprofit institute for Women in Management and author of *The Effective Woman Manager,* gives his observations about women in management. His next book will be about male and female management peers.

610. Williams, Marcille Gray. *The New Executive Woman*. Radnor, PA: Chilton Book Co., 1977.

In the author's words, " . . . a practical guidebook and survival manual for the striving executive woman." Based on personal experiences and research and interviews with women executives and includes information on dealing with male chauvinism, business entertaining, traveling on business, dressing for success, and dual careers. Concludes with a "Dozen Do's for Executive Success." Includes index.

611. Winston, Sandra. *The Entrepreneurial Woman*. New York: Newsweek Books, 1979.

Six traits are essential for the potential woman entrepreneur: a feeling of displacement, control, independence, role models, resources, and a willingness to take risks. Advice on starting your own business covers everything from assertiveness and the first sale to bankruptcy. Includes bibliography.

612. Wood, Marion M. "What Does It Take for a Woman to Make It in Management?" *Personnel Journal* 54 (January 1975): 38–41+.

Interviews with 100 women managers in the Los Angeles area identify characteristics of the successful woman manager: competence, education, realism, aggressiveness, self-confidence, career-mindedness, femininity, strategy, and support of an influential male.

613. Yorks, Lyle. "What Mother Never Told You about Life in the Corporation." *Management Review* 65 (April 1976): 13–19.

Discusses 7 general guidelines for women (and men) managers on behavior, style, and sensitivity.

614. "You and Your Job: *Bazaar*'s Guide to the Executive Suite." *Harper's Bazaar* 111 (August 1978): 80–83+.

A 4-part article including (1) "Requirements for Success: Three Views" by Denise Fortino. Three career women, Charlotte Curtis of the *New York Times*, Lynn Salvage of New York's First Women's Bank, and Carol Bellamy, New York City Council president, tell how their early backgrounds and personal goals led them to success. They consider teamwork, self-confidence, challenge, and career planning as aids to achieving career goals. (2) "How to Take Risks and Make More $" by Bette Lehan Harragan. Author cites "risk taking" as a skill most women lack, particularly when it comes to asking for a raise or changing jobs. By contrast men view risk taking as long-range business strategy and consider failures just part of the game. (3) "Test Your Management Skills" by Lyn Toetzsch. A 14-point quiz tests women's ability to manage assertively. The multiple-choice questions involve business-related "people" problems. (4) "Loneliness: An Occupational Hazard" by Diana Lea. Competitive individualism can cause loneliness for the executive, particularly for the female executive in a predominantly male company. The president of a women's career development firm says that to combat loneliness middle management women should make themselves visible in the corporate structure and establish friendships with male colleagues.

Psychology of Women in Management

615. Adams, Edward F. "A Multivariate Study of Subordinate Perceptions of, and Attitudes toward, Minority and Majority Managers." *Journal of Applied Psychology* 63 (June 1978): 277–88.

Subordinates rated Black male, White female and White male managers using the Job Descriptive Index, the Leader Behavior Description Questionnaire Form XII and Perceptions of Supervisor, and the Role Tension Index and Job Problems. Subordinates saw Black male and White female managers as more considerate than White male counterparts.

616. Adams, Jean Mason. "Outstanding Successful Women—An In-Depth Study Regarding the Attitudes of Successful Executive Women in Achieving Their Status." PhD dissertation, University of Colorado, 1976.

Abstracted in *Dissertation Abstracts International,* v. 36, February 1976, #4867–A.

617. Alban, Billie T., and Seashore, Edith W. "Women in Authority: An Experienced View." *Journal of Applied Behavioral Sciences* 14 (January/February/March 1978): 21.

Comments on the article "Women in Authority: A Socio-psychological Analysis" on pp. 7–20 in the same issue. Authors call Bayes and Newton to task for "inadequate research and unsound generalization."

618. Athanassiades, John C. "An Investigation of Some Communication Patterns of Female Subordinates in Hierarchical Organizations." *Human Relations* 27 (1974): 195–209.

A study of the distortion of upward communication by female subordinates and its relation to their achievement and security needs. Findings show that both male and female subordinates are aware of job discrimination against women, and women managers feel less independent than male managers. Includes tables and diagrams.

619. Badawy, M.K. "How Women Managers View Their Role in the Organization." *Personnel Administrator* 23 (February 1978): 60–68.

One hundred female managers answered a 9-item questionnaire about perceptions and orientations of women managers. Author calls for training programs, role models, counseling, and changes in attitude toward female managers.

620. Barnes, Josephine. "Health Aspects of the Woman Executive." *Accountant* 180 (January 25, 1979): 99–100.

A look at professional and executive women shows they have better health records and make better use of health services than other women. Women executives complain more frequently of fatigue than their male counterparts, perhaps due to combining career with the demands of home and family, but their general health is frequently better than that of their male colleagues.

621. Bartol, Kathryn M. "Male versus Female Leaders: The Effect of Leader Need for Dominance on Follower Satisfaction." *Academy of Management Journal* 17 (July 1974): 225–33.

Research on issues of female leadership, leader need for dominance, and follower satisfaction used a simulated business game. Results corroborated the hypothesis that there was a significant relationship between the sex of the leader, the sex of subordinates, leader need for dominance, and follower satisfaction, but they do not indicate that followers were dissatisfied with high need for dominance female leaders. Includes tables and references.

622. ———, and Butterfield, D. Anthony. "Sex Effects in Evaluating Leaders." *Jounal of Applied Psychology* 61 (August 1976): 446–54.

Over 300 management students answered questions about leadership style from stories depicting 4 leadership dimensions: consideration, production emphasis, tolerance for freedom, and initiating structure. Results of study show that identical leadership behavior was evaluated differently depending upon whether the leader was male or female. Females were generally thought to be more considerate, while males were thought to be more effective in structuring behavior.

623. Bartusis, Mary Ann. "What Price Success?" *Working Woman* 5 (December 1980): 62.

A clinical associate professor of psychiatry discusses the side effects that come with "overnight success." The reactions of others is one of the most difficult problems, and Bartusis says it takes time to get used to the changes and to allow others to adjust.

624. Bayes, Marjorie, and Newton, Peter M. "Women in Authority: A Sociopsychological Analysis." *Journal of Applied Behavioral Sciences* 14 (January/February/March 1978): 7–20.

Analyzes a case history of a woman manager and her staff in a mental health center to illustrate how basic problems of change are gender-related as more women assume organizational authority. Discussion topics include the generation and use of power, the female leader's relationship to a subordinate, and dependency in the staff group. Includes references.

625. Bedeian, Arthur G.; Armenakis, Achilles A.; and Kemp, B. Wayne. "Relationship of Sex to Perceived Legitimacy of Organizational Influence." *The Journal of Psychology* 94 (September 1976): 93–99.

Male and female managers answered the Schein-Ott Legitimacy of Organizational Influence Questionnaire to test the hypothesis that female managers have job difficulty because they don't accept male-determined organizational behavior patterns. Includes references. Table I shows the 55 items in the Legitimacy of Organizational Influence Questionnaire.

626. Bowin, Robert Bruce. "Motivation to Manage: A Study of Change with Positive Implications for Women Managers." *Psychological Reports* 43 (October 1978): 355–63.

Study of male and female college students indicates that there are no sex differences in the ability of students to change negative attitudes to positive attitudes in regard to motivation to manage. Includes tables and references.

627. Brenner, Otto C., and Greenhaus, Jefrey H. "Managerial Status, Sex, and Selected Personality Characteristics." *Journal of Management* 5 (Spring 1979): 107–13.

Discusses the methodology and results of a study of 66 sets of 4 employees to determine if sex differences in aggression, dominance, achievement orientation, and nurturance were greater among non-managers than among managers. Results indicate that female managers are more similar to male managers than to female nonmanagers. Includes tables and bibliographical references.

628. Brief, Arthur P., and Oliver, Richard L. "Male-Female Differences in Work Attitudes among Retail Sales Managers." *Journal of Applied Psychology* 61 (August 1976): 526–28.

Fifty-two male and 53 female retail sales managers were surveyed to determine if there were male-female differences in work attitudes and motivation. Results of the study show that when occupation and organizational levels are controlled, there are no significant differences in male-female work attitudes.

629. Chernik, Doris A., and Phelan, Joseph G. "Attitudes of Women in Management. I. Job Satisfaction: A Study of Perceived Need Satisfaction as a Function of Job Level." *International Journal of Social Psychiatry* 20 (Spring/Summer 1974): 94–98.

Reports on a study of male and female employees of banks and savings and loan institutions in southern California to determine the relationship between job level and sex as it relates to need satisfaction. Both males and females indicated a greater degree of satisfaction with each higher managerial level. Includes table and bibliography.

630. Chow, Esther, and Grusky, Oscar. "Worker Compliance and Supervisory Style: An Experimental Study of Female Superior-Subordinate Relationships." Paper presented to the American Sociological Association, New York, August 1973.

Abstracted in *Sociological Abstracts*, December 1973, Supplement 37, #S00629.

631. Clifton-Mogg, Caroline. "Ashley Montagu on the Superiority of Women." *Business and Society Review* 25 (Spring 1978): 35–42.

An interview with famed anthropologist Ashley Montagu on his views of women and the corporate world. He comments on why men in business resent women around them, the outlook for women in business, how government can help women, and why powerful women are a challenge to men's masculinity.

632. Davidson, Marilyn J.; Cooper, Cary L.; and Chamberlain, Deborah. "Type-A Coronary-Prone Behavior and Stress in Senior Female Managers and Administrators." *Journal of Occupational Medicine* 22 (December 1980): 801–05.

British senior female managers and administrators were measured for Type-A coronary-prone behavior, stress levels, coping ability, and psychological stress-related symptoms. Over 68 percent of the women reported fatigue as a psychological symptom.

633. Deaux, Kay. "Authority, Gender, Power, and Tokenism." *Journal of Applied Behavioral Science* 14 (January/February/March 1978): 22–25.

Discusses authority, gender, power, and tokenism in the Bayes and Newton case history of a woman mental health manager. Author warns against focusing on these factors to the exclusion of situational realities. Includes references.

634. ———. "Women in Management: Casual Explanations of Performance." Paper presented at the 82nd Annual Meeting of the American Psychological Association, New Orleans, Louisiana, August 1974.
Abstracted in *Research in Education*, ED 098 476.

635. Dubno, Peter; Costas, John; Cannon, Hugh; Wankel, Charles; and Emin, Hussein. "An Empirically Keyed Scale for Measuring Managerial Attitudes toward Women Executives." *Psychology of Women Quarterly* 3 (Summer 1979): 357–64.
Discusses the reliability and validity of the Managerial Attitudes toward Women Executives Scale (MATWES) as a measure of managerial attitudes toward women executives. Researchers propose the MATWES as a means of reducing experimenter and research bias. Includes references and Table I which lists the 38 items on the MATWES scale.

636. Forbes, Rosalind. "Stress and the Executive Woman." *New York Times,* 20 May 1979, sec. 3, p. 16.
An excerpt from the book *Corporate Stress* includes advice to executive women such as: don't criticize a man in public; don't be defensive about being a female manager; work against the conditioning of wanting to be liked by males; keep relations with males on a professional and business level; establish friendships with other top-level women in your company; find a mentor; and make your work visible to the right people. Author suggests techniques to help working mothers avoid stress.

637. Forgionne, Guiseppi A., and Nwacukwu, Celestine C. "Acceptance of Authority in Female-Managed Organizational Positions." *University of Michigan Business Review* 29 (May 1977): 23–28.
While women's lack of qualifications and the insecurity of male managers can be corrected in time, the full utilization of women managers depends on the acceptance of their authority. Results of a study of government, industrial, service, and educational organizations in southern California indicate males are more likely to accept females in management positions than are other females.

638. Garland, Howard, and Price, Kenneth H. "Attitudes toward Women in Management and Attributions for Their Success and Failure in a Managerial Position." *Journal of Applied Psychology* 62 (February 1977): 29–33.

Researchers used the Women as Manager Scale (WAMS) to test their hypotheses about the relation between an individual's generalized attitude toward women in management and the casual attributions he would make for the success or failure of a female manager. The subjects were undergraduate males in a sophomore-level course on human behavior in business at a large state university. Data indicate the bias against women in management operates not only at the beginning of her career, but also after a woman is established in her career and has a superior performance record. Includes bibliography.

639. Gavin, James F. "Self-Esteem as a Moderator of the Relationship between Expectations and Job Performance." *Journal of Applied Psychology* 58 (1973): 83–88.

Male and female employees, classified as "managerial candidates" of a large insurance company, were the subjects of a study using Korman's consistency hypothesis for predictions of work behavior to make correlations between expectancies and job performance. Measures included expectancy, self-esteem, and job performance. The data were analyzed by sex and indicated a slight tendency for males to have higher performance ratings and expectancy scores.

640. Gealy, Jennifer; Larwood, Laurie; and Elliott, Marsha Palitz. "Where Sex Counts: Effects of Consultant and Client Gender in Management Consulting." *Group and Organization Studies* 4 (June 1979): 201–11.

Owners of management consulting firms in Los Angeles and male and female consultants in the L.A. areas answered the Claremont Consulting Survey to determine the importance of consultant and client gender. Results indicate that, in spite of similar training, interests, and strategies, women have more difficulty than men establishing their own firms, advancing in already established firms, and making contact with male clients.

641. Granger, Marylyn Wilkes. "A Descriptive Study of Selected Female Graduate Students Compared with a Model of Managerial Women." PhD dissertation, Georgia State University, College of Education, 1980.

Abstracted in *Dissertation Abstracts International,* v. 41, March 1981, #3801–A.

642. Haccoun, Dorothy M.; Sallay, George; and Haccoun, Robert R. "Sex Differences in the Appropriateness of Supervisory Styles: A Non-management View." *Journal of Applied Psychology* 63 (February 1979): 124–27.

Sixty blue-collar workers (30 male, 30 female) participated in a study rating the effectiveness of 3 supervisory styles: the directive, authoritarian approach; the analytical, rational approach; and the friendly, emotional approach. Results of the study corroborated the view that male supervisors are perceived more favorably than female supervisors, regardless of rater's sex.

643. Helmich, Donald L., and Erzen, Paul E. "Leadership Style and Leader Needs." *Academy of Management Journal* 18 (June 1975): 397–402.

Male and female corporate presidents responded to questionnaires testing the hypothesis that there is a positive relationship between a task-oriented leadership style and a lack of fulfillment of the leader's personal needs. The first questionnaire measured leadership style; the second measured the amount of need satisfaction a manager receives from his/her job. Results for both males and females strongly support the hypothesis and its corollary—that employee-oriented style corresponds to a higher degree of need fulfillment.

644. Herbert, Theodore T., and Yost, Edward B. "Faking Study of Scores on the Woman as Managers Scale." *Psychological Reports* 42 (April 1978): 677–78.

Researchers administered the Woman As Managers Scale (WAMS) to 57 business administration undergraduates to test the ability to fake the 21-item scale. Results indicate that respondents can fake attitudes and that the usefulness of the scale is "severely diminished."

645. Herrick, John S. "Work Motives of Female Executives." *Public Personnel Management* (September/October 1973): 380–87.

Studies of the self-actualization, autonomy, esteem, social, and security needs of federal and state employees show that, for women executives, the greatest lack of satisfaction was in autonomy needs. Male and female executives perceived only a slight difference in the importance of their needs; they encountered few difficulties in the satisfactions provided for their needs. Includes tables and references.

646. Horner, Matina. "Learning to Lead: Beyond Fear of Success." *Working Woman* 5 (April 1980): 47–48+.

Matina Horner, the psychologist who first identified women's fear of success and, at 32, the youngest president of Radcliffe College, defines power and authority and says the hardest thing about being president is making the right personnel decisions. She lists the special problems women have and offers advice on power to young women managers.

647. Horner, S. J. "Women Advised on Stress." *New York Times,* 1 June 1980, sec. 11, p. 18.
Reports on a symposium attended by 80 women on "The Managerial Female and Self-Care Practices for Managing Stress and Anxiety." A superintendent of schools challenged the women to "Change what the schools are doing to inhibit women from managing their rights."

648. Huck, James R., and Bray, Douglas W. "Management Assessment Center Evaluations and Subsequent Job Performance of White and Black Females." *Personnel Psychology* 29 (Spring 1976): 13–30.
Research substantiates the viewpoint that assessment centers are valuable for predicting later management performance. Results indicate that White subjects were better at assessment than Black subjects. Includes tables and references.

649. Jacobson, Marsha B., and Koch, Walter. "Women as Leaders: Performance Evaluation as a Function of Method of Leader Selection." *Organizational Behavior and Human Performance* 20 (October 1977): 149–57.
Male subjects and female leaders were paired on a task with the female leader chosen arbitrarily (by virtue of sex), by chance, or by superior performance on a pretest. The study showed that male subjects regarded the female leader's performance most favorably when she appeared to be chosen equitably. Includes tables and references.

650. Kanter, Rosabeth Moss. "Women and the Structure of Organizations: Explorations in Theory and Behavior." *Sociological Inquiry* 45 (1975): 34–74.
This behaviorial approach to the study of the barriers to women in organizational leadership reviews data on women in management in the section titled "Management: A Male Category." Discusses the implications for female leadership in organizations in the section on "Women and Leadership." Includes notes and bibliography.

651. Kaufman, Debra Renee, and Fetters, Michael. "The Executive Suite: Are Women Perceived as Ready for the Managerial Climb?" Paper presented at the 1980 Annual Meeting of the Eastern Sociological Society, March 14–19, 1980.

Abstracted in *Sociological Abstracts,* April 1980, Supplement 99, #S11691.

652. Koehn, Hank E. "Attitude—The Success Element for Women in Business." *Journal of Systems Management* 27 (March 1976): 12–15.

An assistant bank vice-president says attitudes—men's and women's—are the only things keeping women from management positions. He offers a 7-point management development program designed to assist in changing men's and women's attitudes toward managerial women. Includes bibliography.

653. Koff, Lois Ann, and Handlon, Joseph H. "Women in Management: Keys to Success or Failure." *Personnel Administrator* 20 (April 1975): 24–28.

A 6-year study of 1,775 women designed to find out why certain women were motivated to manage. The researchers assigned women to 3 groups: the upward-mobile prone group, the stay-put prone group, and the overcompensators.

654. Kowalski, Adam, and Kowalski, Edith. "Stress Sandwich: Are You Caught in the Squeeze?" *Glamour* 77 (June 1979): 23–35+.

Directors of the Canadian Stress Institute explain executive stress or the Stress Sandwich Syndrome and identify sources of stress and teach stress-coping skills. Some companies offer stress syndrome reduction programs for their women managers. Includes a 10-point quiz on coping with stress.

655. Lee, Dennis M.,and Alvares, Kenneth M. "Effects of Sex on Descriptions and Evaluations of Supervisory Behavior in a Simulated Industrial Setting." *Journal of Applied Psychology* 62 (August 1977): 405–10.

A study of male and female undergraduate psychology students attempted to answer the question "Are male and female supervisors evaluated and described in a similar manner when exhibiting identical supervisory behaviors?" The study used a laboratory simulation of an industrial task and a questionnaire including a revised version of the Leader Behavior Description Questionnaire (LBDQ), and findings corroborate predictions that there are no sex differences in the descriptions and evaluations of supervisory behavior. Includes bibliography.

656. Maccoby, Michael. "Leadership Crisis: New Room at the Top for Women." *Working Woman* 5 (April 1980): 40–43.

The author of *The Gamesman* and *The Leader* (1981) discusses leadership traits and styles necessary for management. He suggests that women are well-fit for management because of their responsiveness and concern for people.

657. Matteson, Michael T. "Attitudes toward Women as Managers: Sex or Role Differences?" *Psychological Reports* 39 (August 1976): 166.

Author poses several questions relating to attitudes toward women in management and suggests that differences in attitudes toward women as managers reflect role differences rather than actual sex differences.

658. McCuen, Barbara Anne. "Psychological Attributes of Male and Female Students in a Collegiate Business School Potentially Affecting Their Relative Advancement to Managerial Positions." PhD dissertation, Iowa State University, 1977.

Abstracted in *Dissertation Abstracts International,* v. 38, August 1977, #894–A.

659. Miner, John B. "Motivation to Manage among Women: Studies of Business Managers and Educational Administrators." *Journal of Vocational Behavior* 5 (October 1974): 197–208.

Study conducted to determine whether female managers have less managerial motivation than males uses the Miner Sentence Completion Scale (MSCS). Results show that managerial motivation is not significantly different for males and females. Includes references.

660. ———. "Motivation to Manage among Women: Studies of College Students." *Journal of Vocational Behavior* 5 (October 1974): 241–50.

Study uses the Miner Sentence Completion Scale (MSCS), a 40-item instrument, to determine if there are differences in male-female motivation to manage. The subjects are undergraduate and graduate business and education students, and the author concludes there is a large amount of unused managerial potential in the female population. Includes references.

661. ———. "Motivational Potential for Upgrading among Minority and Female Managers." *Journal of Applied Psychology* 62 (December 1977): 691–97.

Managers in a large automobile manufacturing firm completed the Miner Sentence Completion Scale (MSCS) to test the hypothesis that minority managers have a higher level of motivation to manage than White managers and that female managers have a lower level of motivation to manage than males. Results of the study supported the first hypothesis, but not the second. The study found levels of managerial talent among males and females were practically identical. Includes bibliography.

662. Moore, Loretta M., and Rickel, Annette U. "Characteristics of Women in Traditional and Non-Traditional Managerial Roles." *Personnel Psychology* 33 (Summer 1980): 317–32.

A study of nurses and women in business and industry determined that women in nontraditional roles were more achieving and believed they had more characteristics ascribed to men and managers. Businesswomen had fewer children and placed less emphasis on domestic roles. Includes tables and references.

663. Moses, Joseph L., and Boehm, Virginia R. "Relationship of Assessment-Center Performance to Management Progress of Women." *Journal of Applied Psychology* 60 (August 1975): 527–29.

The assessment-center method has been used in the Bell System since the early 1960s for identifying women with managerial talent. The purpose of this study was to determine the relationship between assessment and subsequent progress in management of 4,846 women evaluated by Bell from 1963–1971. Based on final assessment ratings and subsequent promotions, the authors conclude that the assessment process is as accurate a measure of the future performance of women as that of men. Includes references.

664. Moulliet, Deidre Kathryn. "Women Employed in Managerial and Clerical Occupations: Differences in Personality Characteristics and Role Orientations." EdD dissertation, University of Cincinnati, 1979.

Abstracted in *Dissertation Abstracts International,* v. 41, January 1981, #2941–A.

665. Nieva, Veronica F. "Women in Leadership Positions: Research to Date." Paper presented at the Annual Convention of the American Psychological Association, Ontario, Canada, August 1978.

Abstracted in *Resources in Education,* ED 172 125.

666. Norton, Steven D.; Gustafson, David P.; and Foster, Charles E. "Assessment for Management Potential: Scales Design and Development, Training Effects and Rater/Ratee Sex Effects." *Academy of Management Journal* 20 (1977): 117–31.

Southwestern Bell developed 6 rating scales for managers' use in rating subordinates, and 3,261 managers at Southwestern were trained in the use of the scales. Results indicated that raters were more consistent and less lenient after training, with female raters less lenient than male raters. Includes tables and bibliography.

667. Pereira, Berard F. "Organizational and Personal Correlates of Attitudes toward Women as Managers." *Indian Journal of Social Work* 39 (October 1978): 287–96.

Discusses the validity of the Women as Managers Scale (WAMS). A study of male and female employees indicates that women with formal education have the most favorable attitude toward women managers.

668. Putnam, Linda L. "Women in Management: Leadership Theories, Research Results, and Future Directions." Paper presented at the Annual Meeting of the Central States Speech Association, St. Louis, Missouri, 5–7 April 1979.

Abstracted in *Resources in Education,* ED 170 825.

669. ————, and Heinen, J. Stephen. "Women in Management: The Fallacy of the Trait Approach." *MSU Business Topics* 24 (Summer 1976): 47–53.

Describes the trait theory model of leadership and points out the dangers to women managers of following this model. Instead, the authors propose the situational approach to management.

670. Renwick, Patricia Ann. "The Effects of Sex Differences on the Perception and Management of Superior-Subordinate Conflict: An Exploratory Study." *Organizational Behavior and Human Performance* 19 (August 1977): 403–15.

A study of management males and females in a large insurance company examined the effect of an employee's sex on superior-subordinate conflict. Results do not indicate that women will be less assertive or less cooperative in conflict management. Includes tables and references.

671. Riger, Stephanie, and Galligan, Pat. "Women in Management: An Exploration of Competing Paradigms." *American Psychologist* 35 (October 1980): 902–10.

Reviews the psychological research on women's lack of job mobility and their scarcity in managerial positions. Divides research into "person-centered," which argues that women's socialization is re-

sponsible for developing personality traits and behavior patterns that
are not conducive to success in management, and "situation-cen-
tered," research which blames the work environment and organizational situation for the small number of women in management. Includes extensive bibliography.

672. Rose, Sonya Orleans. "Betwixt and Between: Women and the Exercise of Power in Middle Management Positions." Paper presented at the
1980 Annual Meeting of the Eastern Sociological Society, March 14–19,
1980, Boston.
  Abstracted in *Sociological Abstracts,* April 1980, Supplement 99,
#S11806.

673. Rosen, Benson, and Mericle, Mary F. "Influence of Strong versus
Weak Fair Employment Policies and Applicant's Sex on Selection Decisions and Salary Recommendations in a Management Simulation." *Journal of Applied Psychology* 64 (August 1979): 435–39.
  Male and female municipal administrators participated in a study made
to determine how fair employment policies affect selection and salary.
Findings show that neither strong nor weak fair employment policy
statements affect hiring decisions. However reaction by managers to a
strong affirmative action policy results in lower starting salaries for
females. Includes references.

674. Salkowski, Charlotte. "Tenderness in the Boardroom?" *Christian
Science Monitor,* 20 October 1978, p. 16.
  Sociologists and leaders of the women's movement question whether
women have to adopt the male values of strength, aggressiveness, and
power in order to be successful. One sociologist warns this could be
harmful to both sexes and encourages men to focus more on the values
of home, family, children, and quality of life.

675. Schumer, Janet. "To Stay Put or Pioneer: Are You Capable of
Becoming a Manager?" *National Business Woman* 57 (April 1976): 5+.
  A study divided 1,775 businesswomen into 4 categories: the stay-puts,
the pioneers, the climate sensitives, and the support seekers. The
pioneers, only 10 percent of women in business, are the ones who reach
top management.

676. Schwartz, Eleanor Brantley. "Entrepreneurship: A New Female
Frontier." *Journal of Contemporary Business* 5 (Winter 1976): 47–76.

The results of a study to learn the characteristics, motivation, and attitudes of female entrepreneurs. Reviews literature on male entrepreneurs from 1958–1975 and the results of interviews with 20 female entrepreneurs. Includes tables and extensive bibliography.

677. ———, and Waetjen, Walter B. "Improving the Self-Concept of Women Managers." *Business Quarterly* 41 (Winter 1976): 20–27.
Discusses aspects of female self-concept as it relates to management and notes implications for management. Concludes with strategies for improving the work environment and strategies to help the woman manager improve her self-concept. Includes bibliographical references and photograph of the authors.

678. Shafer, Susanne M. "Factors Affecting the Utilization of Women in Professional and Managerial Roles." *Comparative Education* 10 (March 1974): 1–11.
Suggests the following issues society must confront in order to encourage women into professional and managerial positions: women in the labor force, the sex of decision makers, models in elementary readers, household management, the aggressive woman, the reluctant husband, attitudes of the employer, single sex schooling, and legal barriers. Offers 5 specifications for change: coeducation, equal access to education and training, nonsexist textbooks and curricula, determination of the extent of female unemployment, and elimination of anachronistic mores and folkways. Includes bibliographical references.

679. Stevens, George E., and DeNisi, Angelo S. "Women as Managers: Attitudes and Attributions for Performance by Men and Women." *Academy of Management Journal* 23 (June 1980): 355–61.
Male and female undergraduate business students participated in a study to test 3 hypotheses about attitudes toward women in management. Results indicated males and females attribute their successes and failures to the same causes. Includes tables and references.

680. Strauss, Judi, and Sorenson, Peter F., Jr. "The Management Internship and Student Attitudes toward Work." Paper presented at the Annual Meeting of the Illinois Sociological Society, 1977.
Abstracted in *Sociological Abstracts,* October 1977, Supplement 74, #77S07279.

681. "Stress Has No Gender: Women Court the Same Achievers' Diseases as Men on the Corporate Ladder," *Business Week* (November 15, 1976): 73+.

Although it cannot yet be proven statistically, evidence indicates that, as more women become executives, they are more prone to the diseases generally associated with male executives—heart attack, ulcers, cancer, high blood pressure, and other stress-related diseases. Alcoholism is on the rise among managerial women. The director of executive mental health seminars in Topeka, Kansas believes that, once more women have attained management positions, there will be less stress on women in management, and the incidence of executive diseases will decrease.

682. Terborg, James R.; Peters, Lawrence H.; Ilgren, Daniel R.; and Smith, Frank. "Organizational and Personal Correlates of Attitudes toward Women as Managers." *Academy of Management Journal* 20 (March 1977): 89–100.

Researchers conducted a survey of male and female employees of an international company to determine the validity of the Women As Managers Scale (WAMS). Results show the scale is valid for determining attitudes toward women as managers, and females with more education view women as managers most favorably. Table I gives the text of the Women as Managers Scale (WAMS). Includes bibliographical references.

683. Tewari, Harish Chander. "A Study of Women Managers' Need for Achievement, Affiliation, and Power." PhD dissertation, University of Cincinnati, 1977.

Abstracted in *Dissertation Abstracts International*, 39, November 1978, #3040–A.

684. ———. *Understanding Personality and Motives of Women Managers*. (Research for Business Decisions, No. 16) Ann Arbor, MI: UMI Research Press, 1980.

Originally presented as the author's thesis (University of Cincinnati, 1977), the objective of this study is "to determine how strongly women managers are motivated to seek achievement, affiliation, and power, and to what extent these motives are related to their preference for male or female superiors, subordinates, and co-workers." Author makes implications for the selection, training, and placement of women managers. Includes tables, appendices, bibliographies, and indexes.

685. Uehling, Barbara S. "Women and the Psychology of Management." Paper presented at a conference on Women and the Management of Postsecondary Institutions, Syracuse, New York, December 1973.

Abstracted in *Research in Education*, ED 089 562.

686. Vaughan, Margaret Miller. "Social Forms and Sex-Linked Reference Groups in Determinants of Women's Alienation in the Workplace." *University of Michigan Papers in Women's Studies* 1 (June 1974): 149–62.

Identifies status as sex objects, part-time job splits, price differentiation on part-time work, women's high-risk factor, and the myth of women's managerial inadequacies as 5 factors in women's alienation from the workplace. Takes a detailed look at the special problems of women supervisors. Includes bibliography.

687. Webber, Ross A. "Perceptions and Behaviors in Mixed Sex Work Teams." *Industrial Relations* 15 (May 1976): 121–29.

Graduate management students were divided into 83 4-person groups—in 62 groups there were 3 males and one female; in 21 groups there were 3 females and one male. Researchers studied the groups to compare claimed and attributed behavior of males and females in majority and minority situations, and they found that women management students need more experience in female majority groups in order to develop leadership qualities. Includes tables and bibliographical references.

688. "When It Comes to Management Ability, Women May Be *More* than Equal." *Training* 13 (September 1976): 7.

Cites the reasons why growing numbers of human resources development experts believe that women are better equipped than men for management: independence, manipulative proficiency, and verbal communication. Studies also show that women excel in 8 out of 22 basic aptitudes, while men excel in only 2.

689. Williams, Charlotte Allen. "An Experimental Study of the Effects of Assertiveness in the Interpersonal Communication Style of a Woman Manager on Perceptions of Managerial Effectiveness, Credibility Ratings, and Attitudes towards Women as Managers." PhD dissertation, Florida State University, 1979.

Abstracted in *Dissertation Abstracts International*, v. 40, March 1980, #4804-A.

690. Wood, Marion M., and Greenfeld, Susan T. "Women Managers and Fear of Success: A Study in the Field." *Sex Roles* 2 (December 1976): 375–87.

Results of a study to test the fear of success (FOS) hypothesis. The study involved a matched sample of 18 male and female executives. Includes tables and references.

Women Managers in Various Fields

691. Abel, John D., and Rogowski, Phyllis L. "Women in Television Station Management: The Top Fifty Markets." Paper presented at the Annual Meeting of the Broadcast Education Association, Chicago, March 1976.

Abstracted in *Resources in Education,* ED 120 878.

692. Bocher, Rita Bonaccorsi. "A Study into the Representation of Women at the Middle Management Levels of the Pennsylvania State Government Civil Service." PhD dissertation, Temple University, 1980.

Abstracted in *Dissertation Abstracts International,* v. 41, November 1980, #2281-2282-A.

693. "Bringing Women into Computing Management." *EDP Analyzer* 14 (August 1976): 1–14.

Discusses, at length, the myths that women lack career orientation, supervisory potential, dependability, and emotional stability. Presents evidence for discrimination against women in data processing and argues that corporations must create a positive corporate environment, resocialize men's attitudes, and train women for management in order to eliminate sex discrimination.

694. Bryant, Florence V. "Church-Employed Women: Economy Class Citizens." *A.D.* 2 (November 1973): 19–23.

Reviews the status of women in executive positions in the United Church of Christ and United Presbyterian Church. A new UPC organization, Church Employed Women (CEW), works with the Equal Employment Opportunity Office to develop affirmative action programs in the church's national agencies.

695. Byrum, Marcia. "Women in Management." In *Every Librarian a Manager: Proceedings of a Conference by the Indiana Chapter of the Special Library Association and Purdue University Libraries/AVC.* West Lafayette, IN: Purdue University, 1974.

The director of personnel for Jefferson National Life Insurance Company gives an update on the status of women in management at a conference sponsored by Indiana Chapter, Special Libraries Association, and the Purdue University Libraries/Audio Visual Center. She cites statistics, talks about women's management positions in the library profession, and discusses the 10 most prominent myths about women who work.

696. "Calm View of Management." *Datamation* 22 (August 1976): 13.
Describes F International, one of Britain's largest software companies, whose employees are mostly married women with children. Many of the women are project managers who live near their clients and take complete responsibility for finance, personnel, and technical quality for the project.

697. "Conference on Women in Newspaper Management Offers Suggestions in Report." *Media Report to Women* 6 (February 1978): 12–13.
Sixty-eight men and women attended a Conference on Women in Newspaper Management sponsored by the Indiana University School of Journalism, May 25–28, 1977. Participants felt that journalism school was the place to begin discussing women in newspaper management. For a copy of the report, which includes summaries of discussion sessions, comments by guest speakers, a list of the 68 participants, and a selected bibliography, write: Mary Benedict, School of Journalism, Center for New Communications, Indiana University, Bloomington, IN 47401.

698. "The Corporate Woman: Doing Well in Consumer Affairs." *Business Week* (August 16, 1976): 120+.
Profiles Mary Gardiner Jones, who at 55 became vice-president of Western Union Telegraph Co. Women make up 40 percent of the 600 members of the Society of Consumer Affairs Professionals in Business.

699. Crittenden, Ann. "Carter Aides Find Jobs Scarce." *New York Times,* 20 January 1981, sec. 4, p. 1.
Six hundred women political appointees during the Carter administration are experiencing difficulty finding jobs despite their credentials. Two former Carter aides are establishing a clearinghouse to help find jobs for the women who held 22 percent of Carter's presidential appointments.

700. DeFichy, Wendy. "Affirmative Action: Equal Opportunity for Women in Library Management." *College and Research Libraries* 34 (May 1973): 195–201.

A library school student offers suggestions for the development of women in library management: determine the current status of women in the library; initiate affirmative action programs in the library; endorse local and national groups which support equal opportunity for women; review the library's hiring and promotion policies; and publicize the library's affirmative action policy. Concludes with advice to library schools on how to encourage women to take a more active role in librarianship. Includes references.

701. "Donna Pillar: First Woman CMB (Certified Mortgage Banker)." *Mortgage Banker* 40 (February 1980): 27.
A profile of the first woman to gain the title of Certified Mortgage Banker. Her career goal is to be president of a mortgage company. Includes photograph.

702. Dunetz, Mary Chichester. "The Next Decade—Womanpower." *Best's Review* 77 (March 1977): 82–84.
Reviews the status of women in the insurance industry and in the health care professions. Cites statistics on the increasing numbers of young women with professional degrees and calls on insurance executives to erase the stereotype of woman as secretary and promote qualified young women to management positions.

703. French, Phyllis V. "Women in Management: Success at the First Level." *Supervisory Management* 20 (March 1975): 14–17.
An engineering technician at the Arizona Division of Motorola describes Motorola's positive attitudes toward women supervisors and managers. Forewomen are closer to the people they work with and believe in promoting from within.

704. Hanes, Phyllis. "Women in Hotel Management and Food Service." *Christian Science Monitor* 90 November 1978, p. 20+.
There are few experienced women executives in hotel and food service management, and one educator says opportunity for women in the food industry is excellent. Profiles Cari Wyman, the 24-year-old food director of the salad restaurant chain Health Works.

705. Hayes, Elayne Johnnette. "Women in Management: An Analysis of Attitudes toward Women in Television Management." PhD dissertation, Southern Illinois University at Carbondale, 1980.
Abstracted in *Dissertation Abstracts International,* v. 41, August 1980, #449–A.

706. Holly, Susan. "Women in Management of Weeklies." *Journalism Quarterly* 56 (Winter 1979): 810–15.

A national survey of weekly newspapers showed that one-third of the editors were women. While women's status on weekly newspapers is better than on dailies, they are still paid less, have less financial control of their papers, and occupy fewer management positions than men. Includes tables and bibliographical references.

707. Horn, Zoia. "CLA Conference Revisited: Myths about Women Managers and Libraries as Businesses." *Wilson Library Bulletin* 49 (September 1974): 40–42.

The author is upset about a California Library Association preconference that has no women participants on the program, when all but 18 of the 200 preconference attendees were female. She also challenges the assumption that libraries are businesses.

708. Izraeli, Dafna N.; Banai, Moshe; and Zeira, Yoram. "Women Executives in MNC Subsidiaries." *California Management Review* 23 (Fall 1980): 53–63.

Blames sex characteristic stereotypes, sex-role stereotypes, and sex labeling of occupations for limiting the number of women in management. Examines the role of the expatriate manager and gives findings of a study to determine the attitudes of Host Country Organization (HCO) managers to multinational corporation (MNC) subsidiaries' female executives. Includes table and references.

709. King, David, and Levine, Karen. *The Best Way in the World for a Woman to Make Money*. New York: Rawson, Wade, 1979.

"The Founder of Careers for Women Tells How to Get In and Move Up through Executive Sales." Advice on the sales presentation, the business lunch, appointments, time management, sex, and choosing the best industry. Includes index and glossary.

710. Lacy, Gwynette Precia Ford. "An Evaluation of Attitudes toward Women as Managers in a Government Setting." PhD dissertation, University of Wisconsin-Madison, 1979.

Abstracted in *Dissertation Abstracts International*, v. 41, March 1981, #4116–A.

711. Lowenthal, Helen. "A Healthy Anger." *Library Journal* 96 (September 1971): 2597–99.

A reference librarian believes women choose librarianship as a career because of social expectations and what Melvil Dewey described as women's "housekeeping instinct." The author cites statistics showing that, although two-thirds of the academic library staffs are female, there were no females as heads of the largest academic libraries in 1968. She lists awareness of choices, a healthy anger at inequalities in sex roles, and changes in women's attitudes as necessary for change.

712. Lyman, Kathleen D., and Speizer, Jeanne J. "Advancing in School Administration: A Pilot Project for Women." *Harvard Educational Review* 50 (February 1980): 25–35.

Authors identify 3 reasons for the small number of women in educational administration—the myths that women lack the experience, expertise, and drive to advance. They suggest women must work together and form networks in order to advance more women in administration. Includes tables.

713. Miller, Nancy J. "Unlimited Opportunities for Female Managers with 'Attuned' Attitudes." *Data Management* 15 (September 1977): 14–16.

The executive director of Women's Inc., an executive search firm which specializes in recruiting women, quotes 3 women managers in the field of data processing. Women's Inc. consultants give advice to male and female data processing managers.

714. Murphy, Patrick E., and Laczniak, Gene R. "Women Executives: Their Educational Needs in Marketing." *Akron Business and Economic Review* 8 (1977): 51–55.

A survey of 151 female marketing executives revealed that 55 percent had experienced salary discrimination, but 92 percent believed their educational and training opportunities were equal to those of males. Fifty-seven percent of those surveyed favored the development of a specific "Women in Business" course. Includes tables.

715. *New Library World* 74 (October 1973).

A special feature on women librarians, headed with an editorial by Jean Plaister. Includes articles on women's status in library associations, women's progress in the profession in the last 10 years, marriage and the profession, and attitudes toward women librarians' striving toward the top.

716. "Of Sex and Administration." *Protean: Administration, Systems, Management in Libraries* 1 (December 1971): 20–31.

Text of interviews with 6 women administrators on their views of the changing roles of women in librarianship. They discuss the terms "woman" and "administrator," evidence of sex discrimination in libraries, affirmative action policies in libraries, the value of the PhD to library management, issues of combining career and family, and a married woman's commitment to her job.

717. "Office Automation: What Is It." *Working Woman* 5 (November 1980): 10.

A special report prepared by Information Age, Inc. includes information on the latest office technologies: word processing and data processing, micrographics, and copying. Includes a glossary and profiles of women in the field.

718. Pearce, Carol Ann. "New Career: Meeting Planning." *Working Woman* 5 (July 1980): 57–58+.

Fifty percent of the members of Meeting Planners International are women and most work for corporations or associations. Although the field of conference planning is wide open to women, the median salary for women is $17,444, compared to the median salary of $27,250 for all corporate meeting planners.

719. Pearson, Barbara Ellen. "Women's Entry into Managerial Positions at Human Service Agencies: Effect of Applicant's Locus of Control and Leadership Style on Employer Preference for Applicants." EdD dissertation, University of Maine, 1980.

Abstracted in *Dissertation Abstracts International,* v. 41, November 1980, #1958–A.

720. Phillips, Nancy Iran. "A Woman in the Front Office." *Christian Science Monitor,* 5 November 1971, p. 6.

At the 49th Annual Convention of the National Association of Bank Women, Inc., an organization of 9,000 women bank executives in the U.S. and Canada, a panel discussed "the complete woman executive." One of the panel members was Dr. Margaret Hennig, who studied the career patterns of 35 women executives for her doctorate in business administration at Harvard.

721. "Prescribed for CPI Management: A Woman's Touch." *Chemical Week* 115 (August 7, 1974): 15–16.

Chemical process industries develop programs to identify and promote women into management. Describes the Advancement of Women Employees in Dow (AWED) program and efforts at Union Carbide and Kaiser Aluminum and Chemical.

722. Rowe, Margaret Forcht. "The Position of Administrative Assistant as Held by Women." PhD dissertation, Indiana University, 1974.
Abstracted in *Dissertation Abstracts International,* v. 34, February 1974, no. 8, #4579–4580–A.

723. Scale, Bea. "Word Processing: A Road to Management." *Working Woman* 6 (February 1981): 24+.
Although 95 percent of all word processing (WP) work stations are staffed by women, it's difficult for them to get into management. Profiles 4 women who have earned executive slots in the field of WP.

724. Snyders, Jan, and Miles, Mary. "Women in Management." *Computer Decisions* (August 1980): 90–97.
Results of an interview study of men and women in data processing and word processing show that the number of women managers in the field is growing. Male and female managers discuss mentors and management development programs for women.

725. Stratton, Debra J. "Women in Association Management: How Some Make It to the Top." *Association Management* 29 (March 1977): 26–31.
Although more women are entering the field of association management, progress is slow and there are still few women CAEs—Certified Association Executives. Eleven successful female directors offer women advice on getting ahead.

726. "To Ignore Women for High-Technology Managerial Jobs May Be Risky." *Wall Street Journal,* 15 January 1980, p. 1.
An executive recruiter claims there are at least 400 women who are qualified for line management positions in engineering and manufacturing. The women have 4 to 5 years of management experience and earn about $40,000.

727. Warsaw, Jacqueline. and Kagan, Julia. "Trade Secrets: George Ball." *Working Woman* 5 (November 1980): 94+.
President of E.F. Hutton George Ball talks about ability and work habits, Wall Street, and women executives. He makes predictions for women managers in the securities industry in the 1980s.

728. Welles, Chris. "Ms. Management at the First Women's Bank." *New York* (April 4, 1977): 78–81.

The 18-month-old First Women's Bank of New York, founded to combat banking policies discriminatory to women, has financial and organizational troubles. Lynn Salvage replaces Madeline McWhinney as president.

729. Werner, Laurie. "More than Hiring and Firing: Careers in Personnel." *Working Woman* 5 (April 1980): 23.

Of the 405,000 people employed in personnel, 177,000 are women. Gives personnel job titles, descriptions, and salary information.

730. "What Can Women Contribute to Management?" *Public Management* 57 (July 1975): 15–17.

Essays by 8 women professionals in local government. They explain why they selected this field, what their progress has been, and what impact they have had on local government decisions.

731. Wheeler, Elizabeth. "Jobs in Sports Management." *Working Woman* 6 (March 1981): 14+.

Women are filling more management-level jobs in sports, particularly in women's athletics. Possibilities include sports public relations, corporate administrator of sports promotions, sports marketing, college athletic director, agent, manager or owner of a sports franchise, and tournament director or promoter.

732. "Women in Business." *Administrative Management* 39 (August 1978): 9.

According to a survey by National Personnel Associates, women are most likely to find management jobs in personnel, followed in order by accounting, sales, programs/systems, engineering, marketing, administration, data processing, public relations and systems analysis.

733. "Women in Management a Rule, Not Exception at AMI." *Food Service Marketing* 41 (April 1979): 93–94.

The president of American Motor Inns, Inc. (AMI), the largest U.S. franchisee of Holiday Inns, claims 40 percent of his management staff are women. They work as innkeepers, restaurant managers, general managers, and sales managers.

734. "Women in Mortgage Banking: An Update." *Mortgage Banker* 40 (February 1980): 24–25.

Reviews women's progress in the mortgage banking profession in the last 6 years. In 1979 women constituted 30 percent of enrollment in the MBA School of Mortgage Banking. Includes section on the National Association of Professional Mortgage Women.

735. "Women in Personnel—the Little End of the Stick." *Personnel* 51 (November/December 1974): 7.

A salary survey conducted by the Employment Management Association shows that 225 of the 450 male personnel executives who responded earned a base salary of over $20,000, while only one of the 67 female personnel executives who responded earned that amount. Executive secretary of the association, John D. Erdlen, says women may not know what the going rates are.

736. "Women Only 5% in Top or Middle Management of Newspapers: Video Series Released." *Media Report to Women* 6 (August 1978): 1+.

The Indiana University School of Journalism has developed a 7-part videotape series on Women in Newspaper Management, an outgrowth of the Conference on Women in Newspaper Management held in May 1977. The 7 cassettes are available for $50 each, or for $300 per set from: Women in Newspaper Management, Indiana University, School of Journalism, Ernie Pyle Hall, Bloomington, IN 47401.

737. "Women's Work: Consulting." *Business Week* (August 4, 1973): 54.

Quotes women who act as management consultants for several companies. Lists some advantages and some obstacles to women working in this demanding occupation where 60 hour work weeks and 50 percent travel time are standard.

Women Managers in Other Countries

738. Barrett, Nancy S. "Have Swedish Women Achieved Equality?" *Challenge* 16 (November/December 1973): 14–20.

In spite of a concerted government effort to change attitudes regarding traditional sex roles and ensure women's economic equality, 85 percent of Swedish women are still in low-paying, female-dominated occupations. Contrasts Swedish government policy with official U.S. antidiscrimination policy and discusses the limits of social policy. Includes tables.

739. Bartol, Kathryn M., and Bartol, Robert A. "Women in Managerial and Professional Positions: The United States and the Soviet Union." *Industrial and Labor Relations Review* 29 (July 1975): 524–34.

Compares women in professional and managerial positions in the United States and the Soviet Union. Data indicate that there appear to be more Soviet women in professional and managerial positions. Includes tables.

740. Black, Sheila. "Women at the Top." *Director* 27 (August 1974): 180–83.

Profiles 5 British women entrepreneurs and lists the personal characteristics they have in common.

741. Caulkin, Simon. "Women in Management." *Management Today* (September 1977): 58–63+.

Profiles 6 British women managers and discusses the need for greater pressure in the U.K. for acceptance of women in management.

742. Dahlby, Tracy. "In Japan, Women Don't Climb the Corporate Ladder." *New York Times,* 18 September 1977, sec. 3, p. 11.

Forty-six percent of all Japanese women hold jobs, but only 5 percent are in management, according to a 1975 census. Attitudes of Japanese male executives and of females themselves, who still view marriage as the most socially accepted goal, contribute to the status quo. Profiles 3 managerial women who have achieved success. Includes photographs.

743. Davidson, Marilyn, and Cooper, Cary. "What Women Managers Face." *Management Today* (February 1981): 80–83.

Only 8.5 percent of British managers are female, but, in 1977, 32 percent of the management students in Britain's 3 largest universities were women. A survey conducted as part of a 2-year, in-depth study shows women managers aren't as likely as men to be married, that married women managers are often restricted in terms of mobility, that there are pressures in being the "token" woman, and that nearly every woman manager believes she has encountered some form of discrimination or prejudice.

744. Dyer, Colin. "L'Activite Professionelle de la Femme en France au Vingtieme Siecle." *The French Review* 46 (April 1973): 908–18.

Instead of increasing, the number of professional women in France has actually decreased in the last century. In spite of a 1946 law requiring equal pay, women's salaries are lower than men's for comparable jobs.

745. Ferrari, Sergio. "The Italian Woman Executive." *Management International Review* 17 (1977): 13–21.

Profiles the Italian woman executive who makes up only one percent of the total number of executives in Italy and gives figures that compare Italian men and women executives with respect to social origin, education, and turnover. A survey of Italian women managers yields statistical results on assumptions about women executives, what to do to improve the situation in Italy, what style of management is most effective, and who the ideal employee is. Includes figures and bibliography.

746. Hartmann, Heinz. "The Enterprising Woman: A German Model; Are Societies the World over Equally Reluctant to Entrust Women with Top Management Positions?" *Columbia Journal of World Business* 5 (March/April 1970): 61–66.

Tells the role that negative social expectations play in the movement of women into management positions and enumerates characteristics of 55 women entrepreneurs in Germany. Describes the function of the 1,200 members of the German Federation of Women Executives.

747. "Labor Letter." *Wall Street Journal,* 19 February 1981, p. 1.

A survey of 480,000 Japanese companies showed that only 2 percent had women presidents. With an average age of 52, they earned an average salary of $110,000.

748. "New Women—Only Course to Top Manager Talent." *Personnel Management* 12 (March 1980): 13.

Twenty women managers who want to work in an engineering environment will be able to participate in a 6-week training program sponsored by West Midlands Engineering Employees' Association. The course includes 3 weeks at the Association's development center in Birmingham, 2 weeks on team projects, and one week of tutorial work and counseling.

749. Ross-Skinner, Jean. "European Women: Heading for the Executive Suite." *Dun's Review* 108 (October 1976): 80–82+.

Cites gains made in management in the last 5 or 6 years by European women. Most progress is in France, Sweden, and Britain. The number of women in entry-level and middle management positions at Dow Chemical Europe rose from 3 to 9 percent in 4 years as a result of its Women's Equal Job Opportunity Program.

750. "Rush of Recruits for Overseas Duty." *Business Week* (April 20, 1981): 120+.

Cites the rise in the number of women executives assigned to positions overseas. The women tell of reactions they received from foreign clients and from some U.S. managers and talk of the difficulty they've had establishing credibility.

751. Singh, D. R. "Women Executives in India." *Management International Review* 20 (1980): 53–60.

Gives the results of a study to test 8 hypotheses on the attitudes and potential of women business executives in India. Most women executives did not believe a woman should leave her job after getting married, but over 75 percent said a woman's first responsibility should be to her children. Includes tables.

752. Thal, Nancy L., and Cateora, Philip R. "Opportunities for Women in International Business." *Business Horizons* 22 (December 1979): 21–27.

Seventy-four *Fortune* 500 executives and 26 women executives answered questions about attitudes toward women in international management positions. Most respondents agreed that some international experience is necessary to gain promotion to top management, line positions in international divisions are difficult for women to get, and some biases exist in foreign companies against women in management.

753. van Der Merwe, Sandra. "Women as Managers—The Current Attitudes and Programs of Canadian Businessmen." *Business Quarterly* 44 (Spring 1979): 35–39.

Findings of a study of 100 Canadian businessmen indicate a trend toward positive attitudes regarding women in management. The Women as Managers Scale (WAMS) was used and Exhibit I charts the businessmen's answers to the WAMS' 21 questions. Includes bibliographical references and photo of author.

Dress and Travel

754. "Businesswomen Keep Travel Agents Busy." *Christian Science Monitor,* 26 January 1981, p. 14.

Business trips by women have increased 60 percent, but many travel-related businesses need to make changes in their services to accommodate women travelers.

755. Curtis, C.E. "Tailoring the Corporate Woman." *Forbes* 127 (February 16, 1981): 47–48.

While the men's suit business is having problems, sales of women's suits increased 70 percent last year, and one clothing expert says women executives will pay $500 for a suit. Some women, like Judith Daniels, editor of *Savvy,* think suits can become uniforms and suggest that the fashion trend toward suits for women is already waning.

756. Harris, J. "On the Go on the Job." *Essence* 11 (March 1981): 24+.

Travel advice for the woman executive includes tips on luggage, money, hotels, security, and business expenses.

757. Hennessee, Judith Adler. "Progress: Hotels, Airlines, and Even Bartenders Are Catering to the Businesswoman." *Ms.* 9 (February 1981): 38+.

As more businesswomen travel, hotels, airlines, and other travel services learn what women travelers want. The travel industry is becoming sensitive to women dining alone or their picking up checks and provide amenities such as skirt hangers and shower caps in hotel rooms. Includes 7 tips for women traveling on business.

758. Israel, Elizabeth A. "Men's-Maker-Only Career Shops!" *Stores* 62 (October 1980): 28–29.

IQ shops in Chicago enter the market of women's fashions with clothes for the executive woman. The look is tailored and includes blazers, blouses, skirts, sweaters, pants, and accessories. Article gives information on brand names and prices.

759. Louis, Elaine. "Keeping a Fresh Face at the Office." *New York Times Magazine* (August 10, 1980): 54.

Six women executives—a news correspondent, a movie company vice-president, a designer, a judge, a college president, and the president of a cosmetic corporation—tell their office beauty secrets.

760. Molloy, John T. *The Woman's Dress for Success Book*. Chicago, IL: Follett, 1977.

Advice for women from a consultant on dress who has spent 17 years in wardrobe research. Page 185 gives "Dress for Success Guidelines."

761. "Pampering a New Travel Phenomenon: Women Executives." *Canadian Business* 53 (January 1980): 84–85.

Women now account for 18 percent of all business travel in the U.S. and hotels and motels are beginning to realize that women clients' needs are different from men's. Of primary concern to women are safety, dining, and 24-hour room service.

762. Pattner, Emily. "Executive Secrets for Self-Care on the Road." *Working Woman* 6 (April 1981): 105–07.

The number of women business travelers is increasing at 3 times the rate of the number of men traveling for business. Several executive women tell how they handle diet; jet lag; varying temperature, humidity, water quality; lack of exercise; tension; and poor lighting facilities when traveling.

763. "Right Image." *Working Woman* 5 (October 1980): 43–46+.

A look at "image investment"—dress and life-style to suit your career. Lists the well-balanced wardrobe for the woman executive earning $20,000 and up. Colored photographs show the "Basic Blueprint for a Work Wardrobe" by Judy Hadlock.

764. Ringel, Lance. "Making a Firm Statement about Career Dressing, 'Streets & Company'." *Stores* 63 (February 1981): 30–31+.

An interview with Mary Fiedorek of Streets & Co., a New York boutique catering to the career woman. Suits sell best; half the stock is private label. A new store will open in 1982 in either New York or Washington.

765. "Survival Strategies for the Woman on the Road: Don't Be Ladylike about Your Rights." *Canadian Business* 53 (October 1980): 188–89.

An excerpt from *The Travel Report for Corporate Executives* (Corpcom Services, Inc., 112 E. 31st St., New York, NY 10016). Identifies the most common complaints of women business travelers and offers 12 guidelines to ensure better treatment from service personnel.

766. "10 Musts for the Woman on the Road." *Glamour* 79 (March 1981): 160.

A suggested list of 10 items for women executives who travel: (1) running shoes or jump rope, (2) telephone credit card, (3) aspirin and stomach upset remedy, (4) sewing kit, (5) pocket calculator, (6) microcassette recorder, (7) pocket camera, (8) travel alarm, (9) appointment calendar, and (10) luggage cart.

767. Tonge, Peter. "Women in Business Take to the Air." *Christian Science Monitor,* 9 January 1979, p. 15.

This year women business travelers account for 18 percent of total business. According to a United Airlines survey, 39 percent of women business travelers fly to attend conventions, take 10 round trips a year, are away from home 7 nights, and buy their tickets 15 days in advance.

768. "Treating the Traveling Woman Right." *Nation's Business* 68 (January 1980): 77.

Regina M. Henry, author of the booklet *Tips for the Woman Business Traveler,* traveled 60,000 miles for business last year. She advises hotel and motel managers on how to make women business travelers comfortable.

769. Williams, Marci. "The Women in the Grey Flannel Suit." *Christian Science Monitor,* 1 March 1979, p. 23.

The author of *The New Executive Woman* laments the adoption of the business "uniform" for women, a look she claims she helped create. Though she longs to return to a different look, she admits the business image helped her succeed.

770. "Women Travelers Find Safety and Harassment Can Be Major Problems." *Wall Street Journal,* 5 March 1980, p. 1+.

Businesswomen who travel have unique problems: personal safety in hotels and motels, eating alone, bad restaurant and travel service, and unwanted attention from male colleagues. Airlines estimate that women travelers accounted for 17 to 24 percent of their business in 1979.

General

771. Adams, Jane. "It May Be a Jungle Out There, but Successful Women Enjoy It." *People* 13 (January 1980): 44–46.

The author of *Women on Top* interviewed 60 successful career women in a 6-month tour of the country. The women talked about success, femininity, mentors, office sex, "new girl" networks, children, and stress-related diseases.

772. ———. *Women on Top: Success Patterns and Personal Growth.* New York: Hawthorn Books, 1979.

Analysis of data collected in a survey of 60 successful women in business, education, manufacturing, and the professions. Women in the following categories are profiled: Fast-Track Woman, the Principled Striver, the Corporate Woman, the Entrepreneur, the Inheritor, the Public Success, and the Mentored Success. Lists characteristics of the successful woman and examines single women, single mothers, superwomen, childless women, and 2-career family life-styles. Appendices include the questionnaire and statistical data on the interview subjects. Includes bibliography and index.

773. Basil, Douglas Constantine. *Women in Management.* New York: Dunellen, 1972.

Results of a study of positive and negative company attitudes toward women in management conducted by the University of Southern California under a grant from the Business and Professional Women's Foundation. Purpose of the study was to find barriers to the promotion of women into management positions. Includes bibliography, tables, figures, and "Questionnaire on Women in Management for Male and Female Executives."

774. Brown, Linda Keller. *The Woman Manager in the United States: A Research Analysis and Bibliography.* Washington, DC: Business and Professional Women's Foundation, 1981.

Begins with an historical perspective and the current status of women managers in the U.S., discusses sex-role stereotypes and discrimination, profiles the successful woman manager, and reviews the literature on dual-career couples. Chapter VII, ''Career Development of Women Managers,'' is a bibliographic essay on advice books for women executives. Brown is director of the Cross-National Project on Women as Corporate Managers at the Center for the Social Sciences at Columbia University. Includes tables and extensive bibliography.

775. ———. ''Women and Business Management.'' *Signs* 5 (Winter 1979): 266–88.
A review essay on career choice, career development of women managers, and the availability of women for managerial positions. Gives a profile of the successful woman manager and the current status of women managers.

776. Business and Professional Women's Foundation. *Women in Management: A Survey of Recipients of the BPW/Sears-Roebuck Foundation Loan Fund for Women in Graduate Business Studies*. Washington, DC: The Foundation, 1979.
Reviews the current status and needs of women in management, compares loan recipients with other MBA graduates, and gives recipients' comments and suggestions for the program. Includes tables, questionnaires, and bibliography. Available for $2 from: BPW Supply Service, Inc., 11722 Parklawn Drive, Rockville, MD 20852.

777. Cahn, Ann Foote. ''The Corporate Woman.'' *Working Woman* 3 (March 1978): 59–61.
In a telephone survey executives identify the ''Four M's'' for business success: motivation, mentors, merit, and movement. Career planning is essential for women. Includes photographs and quotes by male and female executives of the same corporation.

778. Crawford, Jacquelyn S. *Women in Middle Management: Selection, Training, Advancement, Performance*. Ridgewood, NJ: Forkner, 1977.
Analyzes the findings of a study of middle management women in Minneapolis and St. Paul, MN. The study was conducted as part of the author's masters program at the University of Minnesota and concludes with ''Implications for Career Development and Training Programs for Women.'' Includes bibliography, more than 75 tables and the following appendices: questionnaire, letters to corporations and women managers, and course description for a class called ''Behavioral Aspects of Women in Management.''

779. deMare, George. *Corporate Lives: A Journey Into the Corporate World*. New York: Van Nostrand Reinhold, 1976.

Chapter 2, pp. 29–44, "On the Day I became an Assistant Vice-President They Gave Me a Corsage . . . ," was written by a 28-year-old woman bank officer. It describes her background, education, and work experience.

780. Fenn, Margaret. *In the Spotlight: Women Executives in a Changing Environment*. Englewood Cliffs, NJ: Prentice-Hall, 1980.

The author cites competence, confidence, and credibility as key words for women in management. Individual chapters deal with mentors, power, communication, negotiation, organizational conflict, conflict management, management of change, and risk taking. Most chapters are followed by a summary of the main points in the chapter. Includes bibliography and index.

781. ———. *Making It in Management: A Behavioral Approach for Women Executives*. Englewood Cliffs, NJ: Prentice-Hall, 1978.

Explores barriers to women in management; relations with subordinates, peers, and supervisors; leadership styles and strategies; and decision making. Concludes with a look at the future. Includes figures and index.

782. Foxworth, Jo. *Wising Up: The Mistakes Women Make in Business and How to Avoid Them*. New York: Delacorte, 1980.

Author starts with the premise that the business world is still male territory and tells women how to function in the system. Each chapter ends with a short list of tips. Includes index and illustrations.

783. Frank, Harold H. *Women in the Organization*. Philadelphia, PA: University of Pennsylvania Press, 1977.

Designed for use as a supplementary text in management courses. Part I contains case studies of women in managerial and professional positions; Part II is a collection of readings on sex discrimination, sex-role stereotypes, and 2-career families. Appendix gives a matrix of associated readings and cases.

784. Ginzberg, Eli, and Yohalem, Alice. *Corporate Lib: Women's Challenge to Management*. Baltimore, MD: Johns Hopkins University Press, 1973.

Papers and presentations from the Conference on Women's Challenge to Management held in 1971. Contributors Juanita Kreps, Elizabeth

Janeway, Eli Ginzberg, and others discuss sex discrimination, sources of inequality, family life and careers, affirmative action and equal employment opportunity, vocational counseling, and sex-role stereotypes. Includes tables, figures, and bibliography.

785. Gordon, Francine, and Strober, Myra H., eds. *Bringing Women into Management*. New York: McGraw-Hill, 1975.

Outgrowth of a conference on Women in Management held April 18, 1974, sponsored by the Stanford Graduate School of Business. Ten contributors write about institutional barriers, sex differences, law, strategies for bringing women into management, affirmative action, problems, and opportunities. Includes bibliographical references.

786. Graeber, Laurel. "Job-Hopping: Change for the Better." *Working Woman* 6 (March 1981): 28–30.

More women are becoming "mobile" executives for the same reasons as men: greater responsibility, challenge, and improved status. It is not unusual for top women managers to have had 3 or more employers.

787. Greiff, Barrie S., and Munter, Preston K. *Tradeoffs: Executive, Family, and Organizational Life*. New York: New American Library, 1980.

Diagrams executive, family, and organizational roles in 3 overlapping circles to illustrate the interdependence of these areas. Discusses dual-career marriages, travel, relocation, pressures, and career ups and downs. Chapter 2 includes a section on women executives.

788. Harragan, Betty Lehan. *Games Mother Never Taught You: Corporate Gamesmanship for Women*. New York: Rawson Associates, 1977.

Advice to women on how to play the "game" of corporate politics. Information on the jargon, the players, the symbols, the uniform, and the sex game. Likens the hierarchies of the corporate world to the army and compares the plays in the corporate world to a ball game.

789. Harris, Betty, ed. *Women in Management*. Muncie, IN: Ball State University, College of Business, 1981.

"A condensation of speeches presented at the Women in Management Seminar cosponsored by the Ball State University College of Business and the Shell Foundation on October 4, 1980 at Ball State University." Speakers' topics included: goal-setting, networking, myths of women in management, motivation, becoming rich, and selling yourself. Niki Scott, author of *Working Woman* and *The Balancing Act*, spoke on "The Woman as Manager."

790. Harris, Marlys. "One-Upmanship; Six Books on Women Executives." *Money* 7 (June 1978): 118+.

Reviews 6 books which attempt to explain why women comprised 4 percent of company executives in 1940 and still comprise less than 6 percent today. Books reviewed include: *Men and Women of the Corporation* by Rosabeth Moss Kanter; *The Managerial Woman* by Margaret Hennig and Anne Jardim; *Games Mother Never Taught You: Corporate Gamesmanship for Women* by Betty Lehan Harragan; *The New Executive Woman* by Marcille Gray Williams; *Success! How Every Man and Woman Can Achieve It* by Michael Korda; and *The Woman's Dress for Success Book* by John T. Molloy.

791. Hart, Lois Borland. *Moving UP! Women and Leadership*. New York: AMACOM, 1980.

Contains the basic information the author uses in her *Athena* program, a leadership program for women, which uses workshops and seminars to teach the 7 dimensions of leadership: communications, human relations, counseling, supervision, management science, decision making, and planning. Each chapter includes charts and worksheets for analyzing your effectiveness as a leader. A list of professional women's groups, references, bibliographies, and an index are included.

792. Hennig, Margaret, and Jardim, Anne. *The Managerial Woman*. Garden City, NY: Anchor Press/Doubleday, 1977.

Analysis of the differences between men and women managers and patterns in the lives and careers of 25 women in top management positions. Part 3 suggests what women and men can do to integrate women into management. Includes bibliographical references and index.

793. Jewell, Donald O., ed. *Women and Management: An Expanding Role*. Atlanta, GA: Georgia State University, School of Business Administration, 1977.

A collection of 25 addresses, essays, and lectures on women in management by educators, executives, and government personnel. The 3 sections cover the changing roles of women in society, the current status of women in management, and suggestions and predictions for the future. Includes footnotes and bibliography.

794. Kanter, Rosabeth Moss. *Men and Women of the Corporation*. New York: Basic Books, 1977.

Study of the roles and images of corporations, managers, secretaries, and wives. Discusses power and opportunity, behavior in organizations, minorities, and affirmative action. Includes appendices, notes, bibliography, and index.

795. Killian, Ray A. *The Working Woman: A Male Manager's View*. New York: American Management Association, 1971.

Written as a guide for male and female managers, this book discusses women's expanding role in business, recruiting and training women, and leadership techniques for managing women. Author draws conclusions about employing and supervising women, special skills for leadership of women, and women's leadership potential. Appendices are "Results of Author's Survey" and "Interview with Female Executives." Includes index.

796. Kreps, Juanita. *Sex in the Marketplace: American Women at Work*. Baltimore, MD: Johns Hopkins University Press, 1971.

Results of research on the status of women in the labor force with emphasis on supply and demand. Chapter on the value of women's work is followed by labor force projections to 1980. Includes figures, tables, and bibliography.

797. Landau, Suzanne, and Bailey, Geoffrey. *The Landau Strategy: How Working Women Win Top Jobs*. New York: Clarkson N. Potter, 1980.

A job-hunting manual for women divided into 3 sections: Planning, Promotion, and Making Your Sale. Authors claim some readers may find "the views and recommendations presented in this book rather brutal and self-regarding." Includes index.

798. Larwood, Laurie, and Wood, Marion M. *Women in Management*. Lexington, MA: D.C. Heath, 1977.

Statistical description of women's employment, salaries, and education. Examines the question of women's suitability for management and suggests ways for women to enter management. Includes tables, bibliographies, appendices, and index.

799. Lee, Nancy. *Targeting the Top: Everything a Woman Needs to Know to Develop a Career in Business, Year After Year*. Garden City, NY: Doubleday, 1980.

This book is divided into 4 parts: The Professional You, Managing Your Career, Executive Resources, and Making Your Moves. Includes chapters on the dual-career couple, the professional mother, mentors and models, time management, education, meetings, resumes, perks, and travel. Based on interviews with 400 successful women and information from women who have attended management and career planning seminars given by the author, who is the owner of a marketing and management consulting firm.

800. Levine, Majorie R. *Women Achievers: A Series of Dialogues from the Womanagement Process*. New York: American Telephone and Telegraph Co., 1977.

Describes the Womanagement Process, designed by McKay and Associates management consultants with American Telephone and Telegraph Company, an on-the-job developmental process for women managers. Based on transcripts of meetings with 8 women achievers. Includes portraits and bibliography.

801. Loercher, Diana. "Women in Business." *Christian Science Monitor,* 7 September 1973, p. 10.

Comments by Dr. Sandra Brown, founder and president of Multimedia Education, Inc., and founder of the newsletter, "The Executive Woman." Elizabeth Janeway and Jane Trahey, authors of *Man's World, Woman's Place* and *Power,* respectively, will write articles for the newsletter.

802. Loring, Rosalind, and Wells, Theodora. *Breakthrough: Women into Management*. New York: Van Nostrand-Reinhold, 1972.

Explores the need for changes in patterns of employment for women, particularly for women moving into management positions, and gives guidelines for action. The appendix, "Tools: Information and Sources," includes detailed information on affirmative action, sample survey questions from a governmental agency's survey of men and women employees, possible sources for management and professional women, consultants for awareness training, and an "Aggressiveness in Women Opinion Survey."

803. Lublin, Joann S. "Executive Women: A Special Report." *Wall Street Journal,* 4 August 1981, p. 1.

The Labor Letter section takes a look at women managers and relocation, job stress, "old girl" networks, the pay gap between men and women, salaries, and mentors. The National Association for Female Executives has increased its membership by 1,700 since 1977, with a total membership now of 50,000.

804. Lyle, Jerolyn R., and Ross, Jane L. *Women in Industry: Employment Patterns of Women in Corporate America.* Lexington, MA: Lexington Books, 1973.

Reviews findings on occupational discrimination and discusses equal employment opportunity legislation. Chapter 4, "Women in the Mangerial Elite," discusses women at several levels of management and lists 4 styles of management used by women. Includes tables, figures, extensive bibliography, and index.

805. Lynch, Edith M. *The Executive Suite: Feminine Style.* New York: AMACOM, 1973.

A review of middle- and upper-level women managers in the 1970s from information collected in a survey of 95 women. Explores myths about women managers, unusual and traditional jobs for women, legislation and the women's movement and gives advice to those on the way up. The appendices are: "Quizzes for Women and Men," "Questionnaire Used in the Study," "Report on NOW's Accomplishments," and "Vignettes on the Women Who Participated in the Study." Includes bibliography.

806. Margolis, Diane Rothbard. *The Managers: Corporate Life in America.* New York: Morrow, 1979.

Based on 81 in-depth interviews with managers and their wives in one *Fortune* 500 company in a suburban town. The interviews cover topics such as careers, communities, transfers, friendships, attitudes toward the corporation, and family backgrounds. Note to Chapter 1 gives rationale for exclusion of women managers from the study. Includes the appendix "Characteristics of the Managers and Their Wives," lengthy bibliography, and index.

807. McLane, Helen J. "Listen to the Women Executives." *Across the Board* 17 (September 1980): 48–54.

In excerpts from the book *Selecting, Developing and Retaining Women Executives,* female senior executives, management consultants, and middle managers comment on the executive woman's self-image, combining career and marriage, resistance to executive women, distinctions between male and female executives, the role of women tomorrow, and the consequences of sexually integrated management. Includes cartoons.

808. "More Transfers of Women Indicated." *Christian Science Monitor,* 6 December 1978, p. 13.

A survey of 40 major corporations indicates that more women employees will be transferred in the next few years.

809. Place, Irene, and Armstrong, Alice. *Management Careers for Women*. Louisville, KY: Vocational Guidance Manuals, 1975.
Basic introduction to management, including management philosophies, practices and skills, problems, terminology, and trends. Chapter 6, on the expanding roles of women, identifies areas of management opportunity for women (civil service, professional occupations, technical, marketing and sales, military service) and suggests areas of future growth. Appendices include a glossary of key management terms, a self-analysis exercise, management self-rating chart, bibliography, and index.

810. ———, and Plummer, Sylvia. *Women in Management*. Skokie, IL: VGM Career Horizons, 1980.
An introductory career book which emphasizes objectives, goal setting, self-knowledge, guidelines for long- and short-range career plans, and educational requirements. Includes checklists for evaluating management qualifications, assertiveness, and management self-rating. Gives a list of resource centers for women's programs and selected schools of business.

811. "Questionnaire." *Working Woman* 6 (July 1981): 91.
The *Corporate Woman* section reproduces a questionnaire designed by *Working Woman* and Linda Keller Brown of the Center for Social Sciences at Columbia University. For employees of profit-making corporations, the questionnaire asks about your corporation, your job, your goals, and your background. The results of the survey will be published in a later issue of *Working Woman*.

812. "The *Savvy* Survey of Executive Behavior." *Savvy* 2 (August 1981): 57–60.
A 42-question survey on the professional and personal demands of an executive woman. Results will be reported in a future issue of *Savvy*.

813. Schwartz, Eleanor Brantley. *The Sex Barrier in Business*. Atlanta, GA: Georgia State University, 1971.
Reviews history of women's role in management (pre- and post-Civil War), background on Title VII of the Civil Rights Act of 1964, and executives' opinions of women in management. Includes questionnaires, bibliographical references, tables, and conclusions and recommendations.

814. Stead, Bette Ann. *Women in Management*. Englewood Cliffs, NJ: Prentice-Hall, 1978.

This textbook includes articles on all aspects of women as managers by leading authorities. Each article is followed with discussion questions. Appendices include cases, annotated bibliography, glossary, research tools, and laws.

815. ———. "Women in Management: Gaining Acceptance on an Equal Basis." *Vital Speeches* 41 (July 15, 1975): 589–91.

In a speech delivered at Johnson Space Center, Houston, the author makes 3 suggestions for using women to their fullest potential: management commitment, the developmental management approach, and management development programs for women. Suggestions for management development programs for women include: a week-long concentrated management development program, an 8-week organization problem-solving session, and a 6-month to one-year internship.

816. Thompson, Ann McKay, and Wood, Marcia Donna. *Management Strategies for Women, or Now that I'm Boss, How Do I Run This Place?* New York: Simon and Schuster, 1981.

This guide for the woman moving into a management job includes chapters on power, why men are afraid to hire a woman, taking men to lunch, planning, economics, performance appraisals, conducting effective meetings, pregnancy, and tokenism. The self-evaluation tests are useful for inventorying career desires, identifying professional fears, assessing management skills, evaluating financial knowledge, and playing the decision-making game ZAP! Includes glossary of communication terms.

817. Wallach, Anne Tolstoi. *Women's Work*. New York: New American Library, 1981.

A novel about a female executive in a sexist advertising agency. Written by a woman with 30 years experience in advertising.

818. *The Woman MBA* 1, No. 1 (1977).

Twenty-one articles on career and life, career planning and development, and career options by executives and educators, including William Goode, professor of sociology at Columbia; Felice N. Schwartz, president of Catalyst; and managers of General Mills, General Motors, Arthur D. Little, Equitable Life Assurance Society, Merrill Lynch and Co., GTE, and Aetna Life and Casualty.

819. "You Still Have a Long Way to Go—Baby.' *Business Week* (September 25, 1971): 74+.

Although a survey by *BW* indicates more women are employed at managerial levels in a greater variety of occupations, much remains unchanged. Legislation, changing attitudes, increased skills and education, and The Pill are given as reasons for women's advancement. Handicaps such as female inflexibility regarding travel, possible transfers in dual-career couples, and negative attitudes of female subordinates still remain.

820. Youdin, Beth Greer. "Test Your Executive Quotient." *Savvy* 2 (January 1981): 31.

An 11-question, multiple-choice quiz to see if you've been reading the *Wall Street Journal*. Followed by a joke about the executive woman.

Appendices

Appendix 1.
Films and Filmstrips

Career Achievers: Women
(Series: Career Achievers Series)
Fairchild Books and Visuals
122 frames   sound
$62.50; $50.00 for schools
Abstracted in *Media Review Digest,* 1975/76, Pt. I, p. 277.

I've Got a Woman Boss
Stephen Bosustow Production, 1977
16 mm   10½ min   sound   color
$170.00; rent $15.00
Abstracted in *Media Review Digest,* 1978, p. 131.

On a Par, Not a Pedestal
(Human Resources and Organizational Behavior Series)
Document Associates, 1977
16 mm   26 min
$395.00; rent $40.00
Abstracted in *Landers Film Reviews,* March/April 1979, p. 191.

Portrait of Paula
Karen Back, 1976
16 mm   14 min   sound

Twelve Like You
Cally Curtis
16mm   sound   color
Abstracted in *Media Review Digest,* 1975/76, Pt. I, p. 240.

Women: Up the Career Ladder
UCLA Media Center, UCLA
Instructional Media Library, 1972
16 mm   30 min   sound   b/w
Producer: Rosalind Loring
Abstracted in *National Union Catalog Films,* 1973–77, v. 5, p. 2528.

Women Business Owners
(Series: Are You Listening)
Martha Stuart Communications, 1977
videocassette   30 min   sound   color
$500.00; rent $100.00
Abstracted in *Media Review Digest,* 1979, p. 273.

Women in Business
LSB Productions, 1980
16mm or video   24 min
$395.00; 16 mm rental
Winner of Red Ribbon Award, American Film Festival, 1980.

Women in Management
Martha Stuart Communications
videocassette   28½ min   color
$500.00
Abstracted in *Media Review Digest,* 1975/76, Pt. I, p. 258.

Women in Management, Part I
Educational Communications,
Mainstream International, 1973
6 audiocassettes   30 min each
$97.50

*Women in Management: Threat or
    Opportunity?*
CSM Films; Training Films Inter-
    national, 1975
16 mm   30 min   sound   color
    Abstracted in *Media Review Di-
    gest*, 1975/76, Pt. I, p. 258.

*Women in Management: Threat or
    Opportunity?*
CSM/McGraw-Hill, McGraw-Hill
    Films, 1975
videocassette   26 min   sound
color ¾ in. U-matic

Women in Middle Management
Martha Stuart Communications
videocassette   28½ min   color
$500.00
    Abstracted in *Media Review Di-
    gest*, 1975/76, Pt. I, p. 258.

Women in the Corporation
Document Association, 1977
16 mm or videotape   26 min
sound   color
    Abstracted in *Media Review Di-
    gest*, 1979, p. 273.

Women's Work: Management
Aetna
16 mm   30 min   sound
rent free
    Abstracted in *Media Review Di-
    gest*, 1975/76, Pt. I, p. 259.

Appendix 2.
Pamphlets

"Career Guide for Tomorrow's Women Executives." 1980. 12 p.
   Send 20¢ stamped No. 10 envelope to: Cutty Sark Career Guide, Box
   1058, FDR Station, New York 10022.

Kahne, Hilda. "Women in Management: Strategy for Increase." 1974. 11 p.
   Available for 50¢ from: The Business and Professional Women's
   Foundation, 2012 Massachusetts Ave., Washington, DC 20036.

Heinen, J. Stephen. "Developing the Woman Manager." 1975. 6 p.
   Single copy free from: University of Minnesota, Graduate School of
   Business, Minneapolis, MN 55455.

Stein, Barry A. "Getting There: Patterns in Managerial Success." Working paper, Center for Research on Women, Wellesley College, 1976.
Xeroxed.
   Available from: Center for Social and Evaluation Research, University
   of Massachusetts, Boston, MA.

Stencel, Sandra. "Woman in the Executive Suite." 1980. 17 p.
   Available for $2.75 from: Editorial Research Reports, 1414 22nd St.,
   NW, Washington, DC 20037.

U.S. General Services Administration. Region 2. Directory of Women
Business Owners. 1980. 24 p. Item 559.
   Stock number 022-001-00089-2 $1.75

"Women in Management." Rev ed. 1978. 2 p.
   Available for 50¢ from: GSM Publications Services, Graduate School
   of Management, University of California, Los Angeles, Los Angeles,
   CA 99024.

Appendix 3.
Other Resources

Bird, Caroline. "Women: Opportunity for Management." New York: The President's Association, 1973.
    Available for $10.00 from: The President's Association, 135 W. 50th St., New York, NY.

Lieberman, Harvey. *Women in Management,* (Simulation Game Series), Didactic Systems, 1975.

Peters, Lawrence H.; Terborg, James R.; and Taynor, J. "Women As Managers Scale (WAMS): A Measure of Attitudes Toward Women in Management Positions." *JSAS Catalog of Selected Documents in Psychology* (1974): Ms. No. 585.

"Stress Kit for Women Managers."
    Available for $14.95 from: Canadian Stress Institute, 43 Victoria St., Suite 2930, Toronto, Canada, M5C 2A2.

Wolf, Wendy C., and Fligstein, Neil D. "Sex and Authority in the Workplace: The Causes of Sexual Inequality." Madison, WI: University of Wisconsin, Institute for Research on Poverty, 1978. 41 p.
    Available free from: Institute for Research on Poverty, University of Wisconsin, Madison, WI.

Appendix 4.
Organizations

American Business Women's
Association
9100 Ward Pkwy. Box 8728
Kansas City, MO 64114

Business and Professional
Women's Foundation
2012 Massachusetts Ave., NW
Washington, DC 20036

Catalyst
Felice N. Schwartz, President
National Headquarters
14 E. 60th St.
New York, NY 10022

Executive Women International
2188 Highland Dr. Suite 203
Salt Lake City, UT 84106

Federation of Organizations for
Professional Women
2000 P St., NW Suite 403
Washington, DC 20036

National Association for Female
Executives
421 Fourth St.
Annapolis, MD 21403

National Association for Women
Deans, Administrators and
Counselors
1028 Connecticut Ave., NW
Washington, DC 20036

National Association of Negro
Business and Professional
Women's Clubs
1806 New Hampshire Ave., NW
Washington, DC 20009

National Association of Women
Business Owners
Suite 410
2000 P. St., NW
Washington, DC 20031

See Jessup, Claudia, and Chipp, Genie. *The Woman's Guide to Starting a Business*. New York: Holt, Rinehart, and Winston. Rev ed. 1979.
 Pages 320–22 list 25 women's business associations and organizations.

See also Encyclopedia of Associations under the subject heading: Trade, Business, and Commercial Organizations for organizations of women in various professional fields (example: Advertising Women of New York); and *National Trade and Professional Associations of the United States and Canada and Labor Unions*. 15th Annual Edition. 1980.

Appendix 5.
Network Directories

"First National Women's Network Directory." *Working Woman* 5 (March 1980).

Kleiman, Carol. "National, State, and Local Networks in the United States." Pages 137–210 in *Women's Networks: The Complete Guide to Getting a Better Job, Advancing Your Career and Feeling Great As a Women Through Networking*. New York: Lippincott & Crowell, 1980.

"Networking 1981." *Working Woman* 6 (March 1981): 95–104.

Welch, Mary Scott. "Network Directory." Pages 256–68 in *Networking: The Great New Way for Women to Get Ahead*. New York: Harcourt, Brace, Jovanovich, 1980.

Appendix 6.
Periodicals

Enterprising Women: A business monthly. 11/year. $28.00. c/o Ava Stern, Ed., Artemis Enterprises, Inc., 525 West End Ave., New York, N.Y. 10024.

For women business owners and entrepreneurs. 8½" × 11" format, 8–10 pages/issue. Includes book reviews.

Executive Female. Bi-monthly. NAFE, PO Box C4003, Huntington Station, NY 11746. Publication of the National Association of Female Executives. NAFE membership dues of $29.00 include $18.00 for subscription to *Executive Female.*

Includes feature articles on topics of interest to women managers such as career change, executive search firms, resumes, and interviews. Regular departments include Across the Desk (editorial), Your Views (letters to the Editor), Books, Management Trends/Career Trends, Career Counselor, Happenings (upcoming seminars and conferences), $$$ and You, Profiles, NAFE Network, For Your Information (news shorts), and Financial Counselor.

Executive Woman. 10/year. $28.00. 134 E. 38th St., New York, NY 10016.

A newsletter in a 6-page folded format. Up-to-date information on job-hunting; profiles of successful women; book reviews; news of conferences, seminars; legislative and legal updates.

Savvy. Monthly. $12.00. Judith Daniel, Ed., 111 Eighth Ave., New York, NY. Subscription address: *Savvy* Magazine, PO Box 2495, Boulder, CO 80322.

"The Magazine for Executive Women." Each issue contains several feature articles and regular columns like Consuming Passions, Executive Ethics, Facts of Life, The Going Rate, and Tools of the Trade. Includes book reviews.

Women at Work: An ILO newsbulletin. 3/year (March, July, November). $7.15. International Labor Office, Geneva, Switzerland.

Purpose is to disseminate information on trends and developments concerning women workers. Information on women managers is frequently found in each issue under the section "Participation in Decision-Making."

Working Woman. Monthly. $14.00. Kate Lloyd Rand, Ed., 1180 Avenue of the Americas, New York, NY 10036. Subscription address: *Working Woman*, PO Box 10132, Des Moines, IA 50340.

Each issue contains several feature articles; movie, book, and music reviews; and regular columns like Travel, Careers, and MBA (Management/Business Advice).

See also Jessup, Claudia, and Chipp, Genie. *The Woman's Guide to Starting a Business.* Rev ed. New York: Holt, Rinehart, and Winston, 1979.

Pages 313–14 list 21 periodicals of interest to women in business.

Appendix 7.
Bibliographies

Business and Professional Women's Foundation. *Women Executives: A Selected Annotated Bibliography*. Washington, DC: Business and Professional Women's Foundation, 1970.

    A 29-page annotated bibliography of books, pamphlets, reports, articles, and microfilm on women in management published in the last 10 years. This updated version of a 1966 publication contains 94 items. ED* 057 286.

Caliguri, Joseph P., and Krueger, Jack P. *Women in Management: Bibliography*. Kansas City, MO: Missouri University, School of Education, 1977.

    A 44-page annotated bibliography with more than 100 journals, bibliographies, dissertations, books, and studies on the topic of women in management since 1971. Citations are from ERIC, ABI Inform, and Social Science Citation Index data-based retrieval systems. ED 148 711.

Cheda, Sherrill. "Women and Management: A Selective Bibliography, 1970–73." *Canadian Library Journal* 31 (January/February 1974): 18–27.

    An annotated bibliography of books, essays, and journal articles. Also lists 2 other bibliographies on the topic of women in management.

Haist, Dianne. *Women in Management: A Selected Bibliography, 1970–75*. Toronto: Ontario Ministry of Labour, Research Library, 1976.

Healy, Barbara R. *Women in Management: A Selected Annotated Bibliography of Current and Cited Books and Articles*. Rochester, NY: University of Rochester, Management Library, 1974.

Kurchner-Hawkins, Ronnie. *Resources for Women in Management: A Guide to the Literature and an Annotated Bibliography*. Austin, TX: Southwest Educational Development Laboratory, 1980.

---

*ERIC document

The first part of this 21-page guide gives information on reviewing and selecting materials. The 23-item annotated bibliography is divided by books and journal and magazine articles. Includes list of academic and popular magazines that frequently contain articles on the topic. ED 190 869.

Leavitt, Judith A. *Women in Management, 1970–79: A Bibliography.* (CPL Bibliographies, No. 35) Chicago: Council of Planning Librarians, 1980.
A 47-page bibliography listing more than 500 books, newspaper and journal articles, papers, and dissertations on women in management published in the 1970s. Arranged in 20 subject categories. Available for $8.00 from: Council of Planning Librarians, 1313 E. 60th St., Merriam Center, Chicago, IL 60637.

Pask, Judith M. *The Emerging Role of Women in Management: A Bibliography.* Lafayette, IN: Purdue University, Krannert Graduate School of Industrial Administration, 1976.
Compiled for a seminar held at Purdue in 1976, this 523-item bibliography is limited to women managers in business. Part I is organized by type of publication: bibliographies, dissertations, women's periodicals and special issues, audiovisual materials, and historical and statistical background. Part II is organized by subject: the changing environment, equal employment opportunity, recruitment and training, the business world, and women managers. Includes author index. ED 132 490.

Silver, Donna, and Magee, Jane. "Women Administrators in Higher Education: A Selected Bibliography." Madison, WI: Instructional Media Center, School of Education, University of Wisconsin—Madison, 1978.
A 27-page annotated bibliography on the current status of women administrators in higher education. Arranged by type of material: books, journals, ERIC documents, dissertations, proceedings and government documents. ED 151 024.

Swanick, M. Lynn Struthers. *Women as Administrators: A Selected Bibliography.* Monticello, IL: Vance Bibliographies, 1978.
Listed as P-86 in the Public Administration Series, this 16-page bibliography is available for $1.50 from: Vance Bibliographies, P.O. Box 229, Monticello, IL 61856.

Williams, Martha; Oliver, June S.; and Garrard, Meg. *Women in Management: A Selected Bibliography*. Austin, TX: University of Texas, Center for Social Work Research, 1977.

Lists over 600 books, articles, and papers arranged in 8 categories: women in the work force, legal issues, internal factors, personal-work roles, women as leaders, organizational factors, and organizational and personal change strategies. Each category is introduced by a short essay on the topic. Available from: The Center for Social Work Research, School of Social Work, University of Texas, Austin, TX 78712.

Yarborough, JoAnne. *Women in Management: Selected Recent References*. Washington, DC: U.S. Department of Labor, 1978.

A 29-page annotated bibliography covering the years 1975–78 with items divided into the following categories: general; women managers—development; women in business; and women in education. The general category is further divided into bibliographies, books, and articles and papers.

Author Index

Abel, John D., 691
Abrahms, Sally, 262
Adams, Edward F., 615
Adams, Jane, 1, 2, 771, 772
Adams, Jean Mason, 616
Adams, Velma A., 102
Ahnen, Pearl, 305
Alban, Billie T., 617
Allen, Frank, 46
Alpander, Guvenc C., 103
Alpert, Dee Estelle, 168
Alvares, Kenneth M., 655
Anderson, Carl R., 215
Anderson, Ellen, 401
Anderson, Peggy Engelhardt, 228
Andiappan, P., 249
Antwerp, Dacia Van, 560
Anundsen, Kristin, 104, 536
Armenakis, Achilles A., 625
Armstrong, Alice, 809
Arneaud, Susan, 148
Arrington, Christine Rigby, 47
Arvis, Paul Frederick, 442
Athanassiades, John C., 169, 618
Auerbach, Stephen M., 177

Badawy, M.K., 619
Bailey, Geoffrey, 797
Bain, Trevor, 533
Baird, John E., Jr., 522
Baldridge, Letitia, 561
Banai, Moshe, 708
Barmash, Isadore, 402
Barnes, Josephine, 620

Baron, Alma S., 3, 4, 105, 106,
    170, 214, 263, 444, 484, 485
Barrett, Nancy S., 738
Bartol, Kathryn M., 215, 523, 621,
    622, 739
Bartol, Robert A., 739
Bartusis, Mary Ann, 623
Basil, Douglas Constantine, 773
Bates, Mercedes, 5
Bayes, Marjorie, 624
Bayton, James A., 546
Beckman, Gail McKnight, 216
Bedeian, Arthur G., 625
Bekey, Michele, 306
Bender, Marilyn, 107, 108, 109,
    217, 374, 375, 425, 486
Bennett, Amanda, 62
Bennetts, Leslie, 307
Bernstein, Peter W., 308
Bethany, Marilyn, 309
Biles, George, 171
Bird, Caroline, 48
Birdsall, Paige, 524
Black, Sheila, 740
Blackmore, John, 240
Blaxall, Martha, 220
Bocher, Rita Bonaccorsi, 692
Boehm, Virginia R., 548, 663
Bolton, Elizabeth B., 63, 110
Botto, Louis, 376
Bova, Rosemary A., 570
Bowin, Robert Bruce, 626
Bradley, Patricia Hayes, 522
Bradley, Tess, 310

Bralove, Mary, 487
Bray, Douglas W., 445, 446, 648
Bremer, Roslyn, 426
Brenner, Marshall, 111
Brenner, Otto C., 627
Brief, Arthur P., 628
Brown, Linda Keller, 774, 775
Brown, Stephen M., 525
Bryant, Florence V., 694
Budd, Elaine, 64
Burgen, Michele, 427
Burke, Marian, 177
Burke, Ronald J., 264
Burkhead, Marie, 112
Burns, Cherie, 6
Burrow, Martha G., 113, 114, 221
Business and Professional
    Women's Foundation, 776
Butterfield, D. Anthony, 193, 622
Byrum, Marcia, 695

Cahn, Ann Foote, 777
Campbell, Bebe Moore, 311
Candela, Cristine, 372
Cannie, Joan K., 562
Cannon, Hugh, 635
Carlson, Elliot, 404
Cateora, Philip R., 752
Caulkin, Simon, 741
Cecil, Earl A., 526
Chamberlain, Deborah, 632
Chambers, Peter, 488
Champion, Donald Lee, 527
Chan, Janet, 489
Chapman, J. Brad, 528
Chastain, Sherry, 49
Chernik, Doris A., 629
Chipps, Genie, 585
Chow, Esther, 630
Clarke, Richard V., 222
Clifton-Mogg, Caroline, 631
Clutterbuck, David, 447

Cohen, Stephen, L., 172
Comer, Nancy Axelrad, 265, 428,
    563
Cook, Joan, 223, 313
Cook, Judith A., 66
Cook, Mary F., 67
Cook, Suzanne Mary Halbrook,
    314
Cooper, Cary L., 174, 267, 530,
    632, 743
Copeland, Jeff, 281
Costas, John, 635
Costello, John, 173
Cote, Andre, 503
Coumbe, John W., 379
Craine, Sharie, 566
Crawford, Jacquelyn, 778
Crittenden, Ann, 490, 699
Cummings, Judith, 315, 567
Cunningham, Mary E., 316
Cunningham, Sheila, 317
Curtis, C. E., 755

Dahlby, Tracy, 742
Daniels, Arlene Kaplan, 68
D'Aprix, Roger M., 224
Davidson, Marilyn J., 174, 530,
    632, 743
Day, Charles R., Jr., 491
Day, David R., 531
Deaux, Kay, 633, 634
DeFichy, Wendy, 700
deMare, George, 779
DeNisi, Angelo S., 679
Dentzer, Susan, 281, 362
DeWitt, Karen, 225
Diamond, Helen, 115, 268, 448
Donnell, Susan M., 532
Donnelly, Caroline, 568
Dorling, Jenny, 116
Doudna, Christine, 7
Downs, Linda B., 569

Driscoll, Jeanne Bosson, 570
Drotning, Philip T., 566
Dubin, Samuel Sanford, 117
Dubno, Peter, 635
Dullea, Georgia, 69
Dunetz, Mary Chichester, 702
Dunlap, Jan, 571
Durie, Elspeth, 318
Dyer, Colin, 744

Eby, Sheila Mary, 226
Edmiston, Susan, 380
Edmonds, Mim Randolph, 51
Eiseman, Alberta, 405
Ekberg-Jordan, Sandra, 8, 449, 492
Eklund, Coy G., 450
Elliott, Marsha Palitz, 640
Emin, Hussein, 635
Erzen, Paul E., 643

Fader, Shirley Sloan, 572
Faier, Joan, 320
Fanning, Patricia, 118
Feilke, M. F., 451
Feldman-Summers, Shirley, 543
Fenn, Margaret, 70, 780, 781
Ferber, Marianne, 429
Fernandez, John P., 227
Ferrari, Sergio, 745
Fetters, Michael, 651
Field, Anne, 119
Fischer, Mary A., 71, 321
Fitt, Lawton Wehle, 72
Flanagan, William, 52, 322, 452
Flanders, Dwight P., 228
Fogarty, Michael Patrick, 381
Foote, Donna, 281, 362
Forbes, Rosalind, 573, 636
Forgionne, Guiseppi A., 637
Fortino, Denise, 614
Foster, Charles E., 666
Foster, Lillian F., 453

Fottler, Myron D., 533
Fowler, Elizabeth M., 11
Fox, Eugene H., 270
Foxley, Cecilia H., 454
Foxworth, Jo, 574, 782
Frank, Harold H., 783
Freeman, Jean, 125
French, Phyllis V., 12, 703
Fretz, C. F., 229
Friedman, Dick, 382
Fulweiler, John H., 455
Fury, Kathleen, 73

Gackenbach, Jayne I., 177
Gallese, Liz Roman, 230, 231, 383, 534
Galligan, Pat, 671
Galvin, Ruth Mertens, 575
Garland, Howard, 638
Garrard, Meg, 535
Gavin, James F., 639
Geach, Lillian, 178
Gealy, Jennifer, 640
Gehret, Kenneth G., 13
Ginzberg, Eli, 784
Goldstein, Paul J., 120
Gordon, Francine E., 271, 785
Gould, Karolyn, 536
Graeber, Laurel, 786
Graham, Ellen, 121
Granger, Marylyn Wilkes, 641
Graves, Earl G., 232
Greenfeld, Susan T., 690
Greenhaus, Jeffrey H., 627
Greiff, Barrie S., 384, 787
Greisman, Harvey C., 179
Griffin, William, 180
Grina, Aldona Aida Malcanas, 122
Grusky, Oscar, 630
Guidry, Frederick H., 272
Gustafson, David P., 666
Gutmann, Jean E., 103

Haccoun, Dorothy M., 642
Haccoun, Robert R., 642
Hackamack, Lawrence C., 494
Halcomb, Ruth, 53, 74, 325
Hall, Jay, 532
Hammel, Lisa, 273
Hammer, Signe, 430
Hancock, Wilma Loraine Bergman, 233
Handlon, Joseph H., 653
Hanes, Phyllis, 704
Harkinson, Daniel J., 385
Harlan, Anne, 495, 496
Harley, Jan, 123
Harmon, Mary, 576, 577
Harragan, Betty Lehan, 431, 432, 614, 788
Harris, Betty, 789
Harris, J., 756
Harris, Marlys, 790
Harris, Sharon L., 188
Harris, T. George, 75
Hart, Lois B., 456, 791
Hartmann, Heinz, 746
Hartnett, Oonagh, 124
Haseltine, Florence P., 90
Hawkins, Brian L., 192
Hay, Christine D., 497
Hayes, Elayne Johnette, 705
Hayes, Thomas C., 326, 327
Hayman, Joanne, 229
Head, Margaret, 578
Hechinger, Grace, 234
Hedges, Janice Neipert, 457
Hegarty, Edward J., 579
Heinen, J. Stephen, 125, 669
Helmich, Donald L., 537, 643
Hennig, Margaret, 76, 126, 181, 235, 328, 792
Hennessee, Judith Adler, 757
Herbert, Theodore T., 498, 644
Herrick, John S., 645

Herrick, Snowden T., 407
Higginson, Margaret Valliant, 580
Hoffman, Marilyn, 127
Holly, Susan, 706
Horn, Jack, 236
Horn, Zoia, 707
Horner, Matina, 646
Horner, S. J., 647
Houston, Liz, 581, 582
Huber, Joan, 429
Huck, James R., 648
Huffmire, Donald, 237
Humpreys, Luther Wade, 110, 538
Hymowitz, Carol, 77

Ilgren, Daniel R., 682
Inderlied, Sheila Davis, 135
Iowa Commission on the Status of Women, 129
Irwin, Victoria, 584
Israel, Elizabeth A., 758
Izaeli, Dafna N., 708

Jacobs, Frederic, 469
Jacobs, Rita, 78, 434
Jacobson, Marsha B., 649
Jacoby, Susan, 330
Jardim, Anne, 76, 235, 328, 792
Jelinek, Mariann, 131
Jensen, Beverly, 238
Jensen, Michael C., 275
Jerdee, Thomas H., 197, 251, 550
Jessup, Claudia, 585
Jewell, Donald O., 331, 332, 793
Johnson, Mary C., 79
Johnson, Michael L., 182
Johnson, Richard P., 459
Johnston, Mary Jean, 276, 277
Jones, David H., 465
Jones-Parker, Janet, 183
Josefowitz, Natasha, 539

Kagan, Julia, 184, 727
Kanter, Rosabeth Moss, 435, 500,
    586, 587, 650, 794
Kaufman, Debra Renee, 651
Kay, M. Jane, 460
Kemp, B. Wayne, 625
Kihss, Peter, 54
Killian, Ray A., 795
King, David, 709
Kinkead, Gwen, 540
Kirmser, Earl, 278
Klebanoff, Susan, 55
Kleiman, Carol, 80
Kleinschrod, Walter R., 461
Klemesrud, Judy, 333, 334, 386,
    387
Knudson, Ann Sawyer Dickinson,
    541
Koch, Walter, 649
Koehn, Hank E., 652
Koff, Lois Ann, 123, 132, 335, 653
Kowalski, Adam, 654
Kowalski, Edith, 654
Kozoll, Charles E., 133
Krane, John Charles, 134
Krasny, Robin, 279
Krebs, Alvin, 315
Kreps, Juanita, 501, 796
Krown, Lynn, 597

Lacy, Gywnette Precia Ford, 710
Laczniak, Gene R., 714
Lambert, Marge, 239
Landau, Suzanne, 797
Langway, Lynn, 281
Lannon, Judith M., 542
Larkin, Kathy, 336
Larue, Robert, 388
Larwood, Laurie, 135, 240, 640,
    798
Laughridge, Jamie, 588
Lea, Diane, 614

Leader, Gerald C., 293
Lear, Frances, 241
Leavengood, Sally, 172
Lee, Amy, 589
Lee, Dennis M., 655
Lee, Nancy, 590, 591, 799
Legeros, Constance, 125
Lemmon, Melody Kay, 15
Levi, Maurice D., 462
Levin, Sharon G., 254
Levine, JoAnn, 593
Levine, Karen, 709
Levine, Marjorie R., 800
Levy, Robert, 463
Lewis, Barbara, 267
Lipson, Eden Ross, 337
Loercher, Diana, 801
Lohr, Steve, 338
Loring, Rosalind, 802
Louis, Elaine 339, 759
Lowenthal, Helen, 711
Lublin, Joan S., 243, 803
Lyle, Jerolyn R., 804
Lyman, Kathleen D., 712
Lyman, Ralph, 340
Lynch, Edith M., 805
Lynton, Edith F., 253

Maccoby, Michael, 656
Machlowitz, Marilyn, 502
MacKenzie, R. Alec, 604, 605
Maeroff, Gene I., 282
Mai-Dalton, Renate R., 543
Malamud, Phyllis, 281
Marbach, William D., 362
Marcum, Patricia J., 544
Margolis, Diane Rothbard, 806
Marrow, Naomi S., 516
Martin, Claude R., Jr., 244
Martin, Richard, 464
Martin, Virginia H., 389
Masters, Robert J., II, 137

Mathis, Marilyn, 465
Mathys, Nicholas J., 513
Matteson, Michael T., 657
McCord, Bird, 138
McCuen, Barbara Ann, 658
McGlauchlin, Dorothy, 125
McKenzie, Madora, 466
McLane, Helen J., 467, 807
Meisner, Dwayne, 56
Mericle, Mary F., 673
Meyer, Pearl, 545
Meyer, Priscilla S., 187
Michinsky, Paul M., 188
Miles, Mary, 724
Miller, Nancy J., 713
Miner, John B., 659, 660, 661
Miranda (L.) and Associates, 139
Mirides, Ellyn, 503
Missirian, Agnes K., 504
Mitchell, Terence R., 543
Mitnick, Margery Manesberg, 246
Molloy, John T., 760
Monczka, Robert M., 196
Moneyhun, George, 18
Moore, Loretta M., 662
Moore, Ronald E., 140
Moorhead, John D., 284, 341, 594
Morgenthaler, Eric, 468
Morris, Roger, 22
Morrison, Robert F., 189
Moses, Joseph L., 141, 663
Mouckley, Florence, 23
Moulliet, Deidre Kathryn, 664
Muldrow, Tressie W., 546
Mullins, Terry Wayne, 556
Munson, Mary Lou, 142
Munter, Preston K., 384, 787
Murphy, Marcia Ruth, 595
Murphy, Patrick E., 714
Murray-Hicks, Margo, 143

Neal, Patricia, 342
Nemec, Margaret M., 83
Nemy, Enid, 410, 411
Newstrom, John W., 196
Newton, Derek A., 72, 596
Newton, Peter M., 624
Nicholson, Delaine R., 144
Nieva, Veronica F., 665
Norgaard, Corine T., 505
Norton, Stephen D., 666
Novarra, Virginia, 124
Nwacukwu, Celestine C., 637

Olds, Sally Wendkos, 145
O'Leary, Virginia E., 190, 506, 507
Olins, Robert A., 526
Oliver, June, 535
Oliver, Richard L., 628
O'Mara, Julia, 143
Organt, G. J., 59
Orr, Leonard H., 412
Orth, Charles D., III, 469
Osborn, Richard N., 191
O'Toole, Patricia, 285
Overton, Elizabeth, 413

Paddison, Lorraine, 470
Patrick, Patricia Ann, 25
Pattner, Emily, 762
Paul, Robert J., 526
Pearce, Carol Ann, 718
Pearson, Barbara Ellen, 719
Pell, Arthur, R., 601
Penley, Larry E., 192
Pereira, Berard F., 667
Perry, Ellen, 597
Peters, Lawrence H., 682
Phelan, Joseph G., 629
Phillips, Linda Lee, 87
Phillips, Nancy Iran, 720
Pilla, Barbara A., 147

Piot, Debra K., 349
Pitts, Elaine R., 350
Place, Helen, 351
Place, Irene, 809, 810
Plummer, Sylvia, 810
Pogrebin, Letty Cottin, 437, 598
Pollard, Carolyn R., 332
Pospisil, Vivian C., 508
Powell, Gary N., 193
Press, A. K., 547
Price, Kenneth H., 638
Price, Margaret, 509
Price, Martha, 148
Priestland, Sue, 58
Pryatel, Holly A., 171
Putnam, Linda L., 668, 669

Quick, Thomas L., 580
Quinn, Jane Bryant, 194
Quint, Barbara Gilder, 149

Rader, Martha H., 150
Raffel, Dawn, 195
Rago, James J., Jr., 252
Rankin, Deborah, 286
Raphael, Bette-Hane, 438
Rapoport, Rhona, 381
Rapoport, Robert N., 381
Rayburn, Leticia Gayle, 248
Reagan, Barbara, 220
Reeves, Elton T., 214
Reha, Rose K., 287, 288
Reif, Rita, 599
Reif, William E., 196
Reilly, Theresa M., 353
Renwick, Patricia Ann, 670
Reynolds, Sydney, 289
Rhea, Jeanine N., 151
Riccardi, Toni, 152
Rich, Les, 354
Rich-McCoy, Lois, 355, 356
Rickel, Annette U., 662

Riger, Stephanie, 671
Ringel, Lance, 764
Ritchie, Richard J., 548
Rizzo, Ann Marie, 549
Robertson, Nan, 153, 600
Robertson, Wyndham, 290, 357, 358
Robinson, Joseph Arnold, 510
Roche, Gerard R., 88
Roe, Anne, 26
Rogalin, Wilma C., 601
Rogowski, Phyllis L., 691
Rolfes, Rebecca, 291
Ronan, W. W., 59
Rose, Gerald L., 249, 250
Rose, Sonya Orleans, 672
Rosen, Benson, 197, 251, 550, 673
Rosenberg, DeAnne, 602
Rosenthal, Beth, 473
Rosenthal, Glenn, 27
Ross, Jane L., 804
Ross-Skinner, Jean, 749
Rowberry, Stewart H., 208
Rowe, Margaret Forcht, 722
Rowe, Mary P., 90
Rule, Sheila, 511
Rupp, Carla Marie, 359

Safran, Claire, 360
Salamon, Julie, 28
Salkowski, Charlotte, 674
Sallay, George, 642
Salpukas, Agis, 474
Sandler, Bernice, 292
Scala, Bea, 723
Schaeffer, Dorothy, 603
Schein, Virginia Ellen, 198, 199, 200, 201
Schermerhorn, John R., 293
Schneider, Stephen A., 475
Schneier, Craig Eric, 215
Schockley, Pamela S., 154

Schoonover, Jean Way, 202
Schreier, James W., 551
Schuler, Randall S., 552
Schumer, Janet, 675
Schwartz, Eleanor Brantley, 252,
    294, 604, 605, 676, 677, 813
Schwartz, Felice N., 416
Seashore, Edith W., 617
Sebald, Maria-Luise, 189
Seidman, Anne, 553
Shaeffer, Ruth Gilbert, 253
Shafer, Susanne M., 678
Shah, Diane, 89
Shapiro, Mildred B., 361
Shapiro, Eileen C., 90
Shapiro, Ruth, 439
Shatto, Gloria, 29
Sheehy, Gail, 91
Sheils, Merrill, 362
Sheperd, William G., 254
Sheppard, I. Thomas, 476
Shifren, Carole, 363
Shrode, William A., 538
Silber, M., 204
Simmons, Judy, 255
Simpson, Janice C., 256
Singh, D. R., 751
Slappey, Sterling G., 364
Smith, Frank, 682
Smith, Lee, 30
Smith, Ralph E., 393
Smolowe, Constance, 257
Smudski, Martha Dardarian, 205
Snelson, Ann L., 293
Snyders, Jan, 724
Solid, Alan B., 494
Sorensen, Jane, 120
Sorenson, Peter F., Jr., 680
Spain, Jayne B., 206
Speizer, Jeanne J., 712
Stacy, Donald, 258
Staley, Constance M., 154

Stanek, Lou Willett, 554
Stanley, Betty M., 555
Stashower, Gloria, 365
Staszak, F. James, 513
Stead, Bette Ann, 295, 296, 366,
    477, 556, 606, 814, 815
Steiger, Jo Ann M., 297
Stern, Barbara S., 92
Stevens, George E., 679
Stevens, Mark, 478
Stewart, Nathaniel, 607
Stodgill, Ralph M., 531
Stone, Thomas H., 250
Stratton, Debra J., 725
Strauss, Judi, 680
Strober, Myra H., 271, 785
Stronk, Mary E., 298
Stull, Richard Allen, 156
Stultz, Janice E., 419
Sullivan, Colleen, 367
Swain, Robert L., 515
Swanson, Carol, 557
Szanton, Eleanor S., 297

Templeton, Jane F., 516
Terborg, James R., 158, 682
Tesar, Jenny, 479
Tewari, Harish Chander, 683, 684
Thackray, John, 32
Thal, Nancy L., 752
Thompson, Ann McKay, 816
Thompson, Jacqueline, 93, 259
Tobias, Sheila, 207
Toetzsch, Lyn, 614
Tonge, Peter, 767
Toyne, Marguerite C., 159
Tracy, Eleanor Johnson, 369
Trahey, Jane, 441, 608

Ueling, Barbara S., 685
Ulbrich, Holley H., 60
Underwood, June, 160, 299

Vance, Carmen Lee, 161
van Der Merwe, Sandra, 753
Vandervelde, Maryanne, 394
Van Gedder, Lawrence, 609
Van Wagner, Karen, 557
Vaughan, Margaret Miller, 686
Veiga, John F., 517, 558
Vicars, William M., 191

Waetjen, Walter B., 677
Waling, Ann Marie Britt, 162
Wallach, Anne Tolstoi, 817
Wankel, Charles, 635
Warihay, Philomena D., 94
Warren, Virginia Lee, 480
Warsaw, Jacqueline, 727
Weathers, Diane, 260
Webber, Ross A., 687
Weber, C. Edward, 95
Weber, Elizabeth, 370
Weir, Tamara, 264
Weiss, Carol, 495, 496
Welch, Mary S., 96, 97
Welles, Chris, 728
Wells, Theodora, 163, 802
Werner, Laurie, 300, 729

Wheeler, Elizabeth, 731
Whelan, Elizabeth M., 396
Whitcomb, Helen, 302
White, Kay S., 208
Wilhelm, Marion Bell, 209
Willett, Rosalyn S., 210
Williams, Charlotte Allen, 689
Williams, Marci, 769
Williams, Marcille Gray, 610
Williams, Martha, 535
Wilson, Jane, 98, 99
Winston, Sandra, 611
Witte, Robert L., 170
Wood, Marcia Donnan, 372, 816
Wood, Marion M., 135, 520, 612,
    690, 798

Yanouzas, John N., 558
Yelverton, Sandra, 373
Yohalem, Alice, 784
Yorks, Lyle, 613
Yost, Edward B., 498, 644
Youdin, Beth Greer, 820

Zeira, Yoram, 708

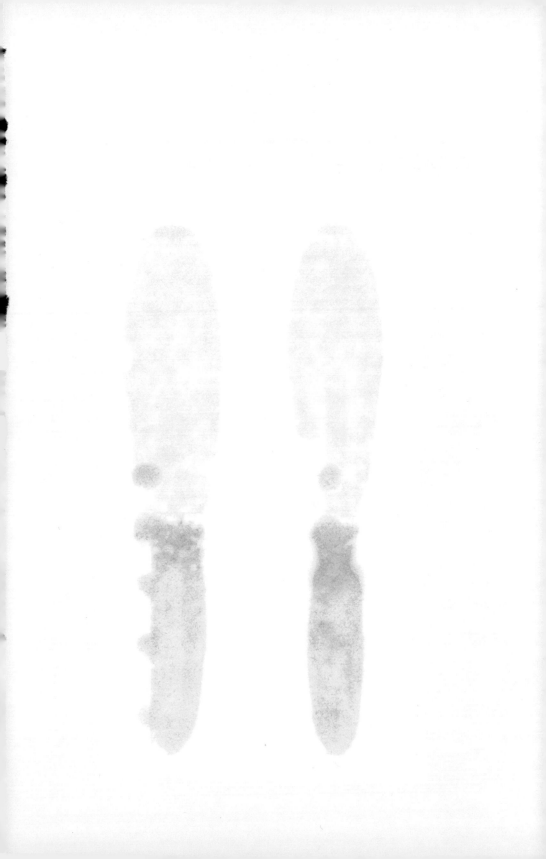

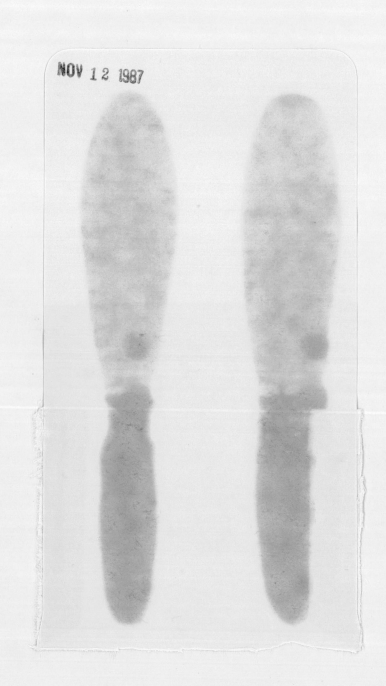